Constitutional Dilemmas

*Conflicts of Fundamental Legal Rights
in Europe and the USA*

Constitutional Dilemmas

Conflicts of Fundamental Legal Rights in Europe and the USA

LORENZO ZUCCA

UNIVERSITY PRESS

OXFORD
UNIVERSITY PRESS

Great Clarendon Street, Oxford OX2 6DP

Oxford University Press is a department of the University of Oxford.
It furthers the University's objective of excellence in research, scholarship,
and education by publishing worldwide in

Oxford New York

Auckland Cape Town Dar es Salaam Hong Kong Karachi
Kuala Lumpur Madrid Melbourne Mexico City Nairobi
New Delhi Shanghai Taipei Toronto

With offices in

Argentina Austria Brazil Chile Czech Republic France Greece
Guatemala Hungary Italy Japan Poland Portugal Singapore
South Korea Switzerland Thailand Turkey Ukraine Vietnam

Oxford is a registered trade mark of Oxford University Press
in the UK and in certain other countries

Published in the United States
by Oxford University Press Inc., New York

© Lorenzo Zucca, 2007

The moral rights of the author have been asserted
Database right Oxford University Press (maker)

Crown copyright material is reproduced under Class Licence
Number C01P0000148 with the permission of OPSI
and the Queen's Printer for Scotland

First published 2007
First published in paperback 2008

All rights reserved. No part of this publication may be reproduced,
stored in a retrieval system, or transmitted, in any form or by any means,
without the prior permission in writing of Oxford University Press,
or as expressly permitted by law, or under terms agreed with the appropriate
reprographics rights organization. Enquiries concerning reproduction
outside the scope of the above should be sent to the Rights Department,
Oxford University Press, at the address above

You must not circulate this book in any other binding or cover
and you must impose the same condition on any acquirer

British Library Cataloguing in Publication Data
Data available

Library of Congress Cataloging in Publication Data

Zucca, Lorenzo.
 Constitutional dilemmas: conflicts of fundamental legal rights in Europe and
the USA/Lorenzo Zucca.
 p. cm.
 Includes bibliographical references and index.
 ISBN–13: 978–0–19–920497–7
 1. Civil rights—Europe—Philosophy. 2. Civil rights—United States—
Philosophy. I. Title
 K3240. Z83 2007
 342.08'5—dc22   2007013085

Typeset by Newgen Imaging Systems (P) Ltd., Chennai, India
Printed in Great Britain
on acid-free paper by
Biddles Ltd., King's Lynn, Norfolk

ISBN 978–0–19–920497–7 (Hbk.)
ISBN 978–0–19–955218–4 (Pbk.)

1 3 5 7 9 10 8 6 4 2

Acknowledgments

This work is a revised version of my PhD, which I defended at the European University Institute, Florence in May 2005. In the course of preparing this study of fundamental legal rights I have become indebted to numerous people who have helped me in many ways. The European University Institute provided an idyllic place for writing my PhD. In short, I think it is the best place to embark on the writing of a dissertation. Professors, researchers, administrators, and librarians have been extraordinarily helpful. In particular I wish to thank Wojciech Sadurski for his supervision and friendliness, and Neil Walker for believing in researchers, and supporting them in all their initiatives. Outside the Institute, my greatest debt is to Otto Pfersmann who was (literally) there wherever I went, be it Paris, Oxford, Florence, or New York. I benefited greatly from the discussions we had. Finally, my thanks go to Stephen Perry who kindly accepted the invitation to be a member of the panel that examined my thesis and provided very thoughtful comments.

While in Florence, I had the opportunity to present my ideas and discuss them with various friends. At the European University Institute I would like to thank all of those who attended the weekly sessions of the legal theory discussion group. It is impossible to mention all of the people who attended, however it is possible to recall how it all began. Euan MacDonald, Georg Sommeregger, Srdjan Cvijic, Raphael Paour and I met in the beautiful countryside of Fiesole to discuss our embryonic ideas. We continued our exchanges up until the delivery of this book.

Since moving to Aberdeen, Scotland, I have had the chance to test my ideas with my students in a seminar on theories of rights. They all responded enthusiastically and provided very interesting insights. I thank them all. Also, I thank Derek Finchman for proofreading the whole manuscript.

I want to express my gratitude to Rebecca Smith and Fiona Stables at OUP for their assistance, and to Caryn Maclean, whose editorial work on the manuscript was impeccable.

My family and friends deserve my special thanks. Bertone, Biagio, Chris, Ellie, Giovanni, Giuseppe, Evelyn, Javier, John, Osla, Paolo, Peter, Silvia, Tobias, and Balazs (with his gulash) have been there all along, and their presence was invaluable. My final thanks go to my parents, Grace and Hercules.

Contents

Introduction   ix

PART I: THE THEORY OF CONFLICTS OF FUNDAMENTAL LEGAL RIGHTS

1. Law, Morality, and Conflicts of Fundamental Legal Rights   3
    1. The Dilemma   3
    2. The Structure of FLRs' Norms: Rules v Principles   7
    3. Weighing Principles in Competition: Harmony or Conflict?   12
    4. Conflicts of FLRs: From Morality to Law   23
    5. Conclusion   25

2. The Concept of Fundamental Legal Rights   27
    1. FLRs and Analysis   27
    2. A Preliminary Problem: Reductionism   27
    3. The Structure and Point of Rights   29
    4. The Scope (or Content) of FLRs   42
    5. The External Dimension or the Function(s) of FLRs   45
    6. FLRs: A Stipulative Definition   47

3. The Anatomy of Conflicts of Fundamental Legal Rights   49
    1. Introduction   49
    2. *Lato Sensu* and Spurious Conflicts of FLRs   49
    3. The Core of Conflicts of FLRs   52
    4. Theories of Rights, Normative Inconsistencies, and Incommensurability   55
    5. Beyond Absolute or Prima Facie FLRs   60
    6. A Typology of Conflicts of FLRs   64

4. A Framework to Deal with Conflicts of Fundamental Legal Rights   67
    1. Why a Framework?   67
    2. Conflicts and the Constitution   68
    3. Interpretation and Conflicts of FLRs   74
    4. Deference and Conflicts of FLRs   79

5. Balancing and Conflicts of FLRs	84
6. The Rule of Conflict as the Ultimate Rule of Law	90

PART II: THE PRACTICE OF CONFLICTS OF FUNDAMENTAL LEGAL RIGHTS

Introduction	97
5. The Fundamental Legal Right to Privacy	99
1. Privacy: An Ambiguous Concept	99
2. The Structure of the FLR to Privacy	101
3. The Legal Protection of the FLR to Privacy	107
4. Conflicts and the FLR to Privacy	112
6. The Fundamental Legal Right to Informational Privacy v The Fundamental Legal Right to Free Press	114
1. Introduction	114
2. Situating the Conflict	115
3. Solving the Conflict?	131
7. Mortal Conflicts of Fundamental Legal Rights—The Fundamental Legal Right to Life v The Fundamental Legal Right to Decisional Privacy	142
1. Introduction	142
2. Physician-assisted Suicide Around the World	145
3. The Anatomy of a FLRs Conflict	148
4. Moral and Legal Conflicts	156
5. Whose Tragedy Is It?	160
6. Present Solutions: How do Courts Solve the Conflict?	162
7. Accepting or Imposing Sacrifices	166
8. Conclusion	168
Bibliography	171
Index	179

Introduction

When Fundamental Legal Rights (FLRs) conflict with one another we are left with no guidance. I call these cases constitutional dilemmas. These are characterized by deep disagreement over who should decide such issues, and in what manner. Moreover, constitutional dilemmas involve a deadlock where a solution cannot be found without sacrificing one or the other FLR at stake.

Constitutional dilemmas are a potential threat to the unity and cohesion of a society and of a legal system. The existence of persistent disagreement, coupled with the existence of a deadlock, may provoke a breakdown in communication between two opposing parties. The opposition between pro-life and pro-choice parties in abortion cases provides one illustration of a failure to successfully deal with a pressing social issue.

In response to such problems, constitutional rights theorists have argued either that dilemmas do not resist closer inspection or that there is a procedure that can maximize the protection of FLRs, while minimizing their sacrifices. Those espousing the former strategy commonly believe in the possibility of 'right answers' for each and every problem; those preferring the latter argue that the results of any such conflict can be optimized through balancing the rights.

The question that underlies this book is the following: is it possible to solve genuine conflicts of FLRs? In order to come up with an answer, I had to define more precisely what such a conflict is, and then analyse how legal systems respond to them. In other words I ask both a conceptual and a practical question. The conceptual question—what is a conflict of FLRs?—examines the conditions under which disagreements over rights claims become genuine conflicts of FLRs. The practical question—how do legal systems deal with genuine conflicts of FLRs?—examines the possibility of setting up institutions and procedures that are tailored to make the issue of such conflict more manageable.

That said, it is surprising to note that this issue has rarely been discussed either at the domestic or international level.[1] Legal scholarship on FLRs has focused on other issues. For instance, in the UK the question of the horizontal effect of rights occupies a great deal of attention. The same applies when we examine the work of international courts, such as the European Convention on Human Rights. One commentator has noted the following: 'Very little has been written on the proper

---

[1] The same point is raised by Helen Fenwick, 'Clashing Rights, the Welfare of the Child and the Human Rights Act', (2004) 67(6) MLR 889–927. Fenwick concludes her piece by noting that: 'the article's concern has been to make a contribution to the current debate just beginning to get under way as to the approach that should be taken under the HRA to certain clashes of Convention right.' See also Shazia Choudry and Helen Fenwick, 'Taking the Rights of Parents and Children Seriously: Confronting the Welfare Principle under the Human Rights Act' (2005) 25 OJLS 453–92.

domestic approach to clashes of Convention rights. Indeed, this topic is also neglected in relation to the Convention itself'.[2]

Rights theorists have written on this issue, albeit as a side issue rather than a central one. Authors engaged in the debate between interest—and will-based theories of rights, for example, have sometimes dealt with the question of rights conflicts.[3] However, such an issue is mainly used by one side of the debate to illustrate the failures of the other. Hence, on the one hand, the interest theory is accused of seeing conflicts everywhere, thereby *de facto* demeaning the importance of clashes of rights. On the other, the will theory is accused of defining away conflicts by shaping the domain of rights in a very rigid way.

The primary goal of this book is to place the problem of conflicts at the centre of the theory, and practice, of Fundamental Legal Rights. This is not merely an abstract question. On the contrary, I believe that some of the most important issues that divide our societies relate to conflicts of FLRs. For instance, the vexed question of physician-assisted suicide could be framed as a conflict between the FLR to life and the FLR to decisional privacy. Therefore, understanding how to deal with such conflicts allows us to delve more deeply into some of the basic problems that we face collectively, and to measure the strengths and weaknesses of rights discourse within constitutional democracies.

In other words, the point of this book is to demonstrate that genuine conflicts of FLRs cannot be avoided or defined away; they are unavoidable. This means that adjudication in these matters necessarily imposes sacrifices and losses on the part of one or both right-holders, or the state as a party to the conflict.[4]

The conflict of FLRs' issue is important because it stands at the crossroad of different enquiries related to theories of rights. Hence, the problems of the source of rights, their limits, their interpretation, and adjudication based thereon are brought together in an effort to understand the relations between them, rather than postulating the overarching importance of one over the others. Many authors argue that the problem of the source of rights—where do rights come from?—is the most important issue from which we can derive all the remaining answers.[5] Such a claim, however, is something that I intend to reject in the course of this book.

From this point of view, the extent to which FLRs conflict obviously depends on the underlying conception of FLRs that one adopts. This, however, does not mean that we can boil down every question to a conceptual/definitional problem as to what is the best conception of rights. If one adopts a dynamic conception of

---

[2] Helen Fenwick (n 1 above) 889.

[3] Matthew Kramer, Nigel Simmonds, and Hillel Steiner, *A Debate about Rights* (Oxford: OUP, 1999).

[4] This, in turn, may suggest that the juridification of moral dilemmas in terms of fundamental legal rights may not be necessarily desirable. This point goes beyond the scope of this book which is primarily concerned with the issue of unavoidability of genuine conflicts of fundamental legal rights.

[5] Alan Dershowitz, *Rights from Wrongs—A Secular Theory of the Origins of Rights* (New York: Basic Books, 2004) see also MJ Perry, *Toward a Theory of Human Rights*, (Cambridge, Mass: CUP, 2007).

FLRs—a conception that regards the demands made by such rights as constantly expanding—then conflict will be omnipresent. If, on the other hand, one adopts a static conception of FLRs—one that regards their function as the protection of discrete types of actions—then the possibility of conflict will be notably reduced, although not eliminated entirely. I will try to move away from both the dynamic and the static conceptions, offering an alternative definition of the concept in chapter 2, which rests on the idea that FLRs determine a constitutional status of individuals. Such a conception is not exclusively dynamic because the constitutional status is determined by a number of fixed properties (eg some basic interests of the individual). Yet it is not purely static either, as the strength of the protection offered by the constitutional status depends on the way each individual decides to use it in order to protect/promote himself.[6]

The discourse of rights hardly acknowledges that there may be a dark side to rights-based adjudication. Generally it is widely argued that the expansion of FLRs is highly desirable, if not a necessary condition of human development. Hence rights are often used to define political affiliations in an extremely caricatured fashion: rights' expansion is associated with liberals, while rights' contraction is typically understood as conservative. A deeper understanding of conflicts illustrates that the previous characterization is simplistic; liberals, for instance, are bound to favour a contraction of at least one FLR in the case of conflict. The problem, therefore, is not so much how to expand/contract FLRs, but instead how to adjudicate conflicting claims.[7]

Some believe that to devote too much energy to the issue of conflict of FLRs is a waste of time; instead, rights activists argue, one should spend time thinking how to expand their reach in Western democracies, and propagate them in countries in which these standards are not met. I think, on the contrary, that to understand the deepest problems related to FLRs could help shape better policies both in countries in which respect of rights is highly developed, and in those in which it is less so. For a genuine questioning of the limits may help us move beyond a type of 'faith' taking for granted that the only progressive direction is that of expansion of FLRs. Our experiences show us that FLRs sometimes expand and sometimes contract depending on a range of circumstances. For a couple of decades (from the beginning of the 1960s until the end of the 1990s) human rights discourse enjoyed considerable success both at the theoretical and practical levels. Some authors referred to it as 'the age of rights'.[8] Nowadays rights are under considerable strain, primarily

---

[6] From this perspective, the constitutional status theory attempts to merge the insights of both interest and will theories of rights. The result, however, is meant to be a distinct theory of fundamental legal rights.

[7] To suggest that dilemmas related to rights should be dealt with by another institution than the judiciary (eg the legislature) does not solve the problem of conflict of rights. Parliaments, like courts, do not have the epistemic resources to deal with dilemmas in a satisfactory way. In fact, parliaments tend to avoid those problems as often as possible.

[8] Norberto Bobbio, *L'eta' dei diritti* (Torino: Einaudi, 1990). Louis Henkin, *The Age of Rights* (New York: Columbia UP, 1990).

due to the international political situation that takes the war on terrorism as an overarching policy objective. That primacy serves as a justification to limit domestic liberties, as the Patriot Act did in the USA.

I submit that a proper grasp of the notion of conflicts between FLRs may also serve to dispel confusion as to the limitations of such rights themselves. To begin with, it is important to draw a basic distinction between conflicts of rights proper, and clashes between utilitarian concerns and such rights. A proper understanding of the issue of conflicts is necessary in order to shed some light on how we limit FLRs, both on the basis of rights-based arguments (internal grounds) and in terms of utilitarian concerns (external grounds). Dworkin's conception of rights as trumps is an illustration of that confusion. Dworkin defines rights as trumps over utility, thereby inescapably tying together rights and utility. Such a conception, however, leaves no room for the possibility of conflicts that postulate the existence of two non-utilitarian arguments opposing each other.

The notion of conflicts of FLRs is very broad; thus some points are in order to set the limits of the study. This book is not about rights in general, and it is not about moral or legal rights in particular. It is about FLRs as a specific type of rights. FLRs are general rights in that they embed valid claims, or liberties, on the part of the individuals. FLRs are legal rights to the extent that they are encapsulated in broad rules that have a legal significance (eg bills of rights). FLRs are fundamental rights as they protect certain fundamental aspects of the life of right holders.

More specifically, this book departs from the majority of other works in this field in the following ways:

First, I do not attempt to provide an explanation of the language of rights in every instance, as many theorists in search of a unitary foundation of rights do. Rights are used in almost every legal and political fora and they generally designate a simple claim or a liberty on the part of the right-holder. FLRs confer upon the right-holder a special constitutional status, which allows him to challenge unfavourable legislation. FLRs are thus important from both substantive and procedural viewpoints. Substantively, they single out a mini-sovereignty for individuals. Procedurally, they guarantee that a proper separation of powers is enforced.

Second, I do not claim to explain what rights we ought to have from a moral point of view. This book does not attempt to give a list of moral rights that we have independent from the fact that we live in a given community. FLRs are considered as special legal devices protecting very important aspects of one's beliefs, thoughts, and actions. However, the list of those FLRs is determined by contingent, local arrangements.

Third, I distinguish between spurious and genuine conflicts of FLRs.[9] In this book I am only interested in the latter. I offer my own explanation of what constitutes a genuine conflict in relation to the concepts of normative inconsistencies, and legal trade-offs. A normative inconsistency arises when a legal system

---

[9] See ch 3.

incorporates norms that may be interpreted as making an action both permissible and impermissible, depending on the point of view adopted. For example, the FLR to free speech may permit a journalist to publish the full details of a rape story while the FLR to informational privacy may make it impermissible to do so. A legal trade-off occurs when a legal system has to adjudicate between conflicting values such as free speech and privacy. Whatever the decision, a loss of value is incurred.

Fourth, in discussing some illustrations of conflicts in the second part of the book, I have concentrated on the FLR to privacy. The reason for this choice is that we live in a world in which threats to privacy have become extremely widespread thanks to technological developments. Hence, gathering information about each and every one of us is extremely easy for any government.[10] Surprisingly, our resistance to that intrusion is not always vigorous and it tends to be lower when the government justifies the intrusion in the name of enhanced security. The content of the FLR to privacy is deeply dependent upon our social norms and habits; if we accept all too easily restrictions of our privacy, we quickly reach the point at which the FLR to privacy is just a fig leaf that merely hides our full nakedness before the governmental gaze.[11]

Privacy is a good illustration of how little one's own liberty is valued when balanced against a public concern (security, for instance). Equally, it weighs little when in conflict with certain other FLRs such as free speech. Following my previous distinction between conflicts of FLRs proper and clashes between FLRs and utilitarian concerns, I focus on conflicts between the FLR to privacy and other FLRs, rather than on its public interest limitations. However, in order to understand the importance of privacy, I'd like to point out that respect for the FLR to privacy enhances our own security vis-à-vis the government. We should not, therefore, accept too easily arguments for the restriction of privacy, based on our interest in enhancing security.[12]

The approach of this book borrows insights from legal philosophy, constitutional theory, and comparative constitutional law. Although the first part is more explicitly philosophical and the second part more explicitly legal-comparative, there are no rigid boundaries between the two. I believe instead in the mutual supportiveness of those points of view. For example, I think that when we talk about the structure of FLRs we have to relate that issue to the architecture of the legal system. In fact, the emergence of FLRs within domestic and international settings modifies the way we conceive of those settings themselves.

Legal theorists often use examples drawn from the legal system they know best. They try to fit their theories to legal practice as much as possible. But their claims,

---

[10] Various authors, 'On NSA spying: A letter to Congress', *New York Review of Books*, Vol 53, No 2, 9 February 2006, 42–44.
[11] Jeffrey Rosen, *Unwanted Glance* (New York: Vintage Press, 2001); see also, by the same author, *The Naked Crowd: Reclaiming Security and Freedom in an Anxious Age* (Random House, 2004).
[12] David Cole, 'Uncle Sam is Watching You', *New York Review of Books*, Vol 51, No 18, 18 November 2004, 56.

by virtue of their abstraction, usually aim to go beyond the borders of a national legal system. If a theory is sound for one legal system then it may apply to any legal system, at least at the level of general principles. To put it bluntly: 'Law's Empire' knows no borders. Dworkin, however, speaks of his 'Law's Empire' in reference only to Anglo-Saxon legal systems. I believe that it is necessary to test theoretical claims in a wider context, one that goes beyond the common law/civil law dichotomy. At the opposite end of the spectrum, Alexy refers to his theory of constitutional rights as being firmly rooted in the German experience. Alexy clearly exaggerates, claiming that his explanation can only be valid in the German context. I defend the idea that if the theoretical insights are accurate, they can claim to be extended to other legal systems. To what extent that is possible depends in turn on the accuracy of the accompanying comparative analysis. Whilst I do not believe that we can ever depict a global empire in which the law rules independently from its context, I believe in the possibility of enriching one's own understanding of different domestic experiences by comparing them and drawing out common patterns and differences. For this reason, comparison sharpens understanding: it points to the role of contingencies and local practices in shaping legal concepts.

By using a comparative analysis as a framework in which to understand and test conceptual arguments, this book is also committed to studying the constant, dynamic interplay between theory and practice. The intuitions that are spelled out at the theoretical level are discussed, articulated, and revised at the level of practice. As a result, the very intuitions that informed the theoretical enquiry are refined and modified, and can contribute to the fleshing out of a fully-fledged theory of FLRs.

To illustrate my position, I take as a background the French, US, and UK constitutional experiences. Those three countries provide the main sources of inspiration but not the only ones. Some examples come from other legal systems, such as Germany, Canada, or Italy. I devote relatively little attention to international or regional jurisdictions such as the European Court of Human Rights because I believe that its use of the doctrine of the margin of appreciation blurs the question of conflicts. That, however, is such a complex issue that it can only be dealt with properly in a separate study. Moreover, I believe that the domestic contexts of well-established democracies provide a more fruitful viewpoint in that we can observe more clearly the tension between FLRs-based adjudication and democratic representation.

The book is divided into two parts that follow the conceptual and the practical questions as presented above. Part I deals with the conceptual question concerning the conditions that make a conflict of FLRs a genuine one. From that point of view, I take it to be a theory of conflicts. Part II deals with the practical question regarding the factual possibility of legal systems managing to cope with such conflicts. Hence, I called Part II 'The Practice of Conflicts'.

In the first part there are four chapters. Chapter 1 deals with the structure, and point, of FLRs. It is argued that the deepest structure of FLRs is that of constitutional norms setting broad permissive rules. That understanding is opposed to the conventional understanding of FLRs as principles. As a consequence of such a conception of FLRs, the role played by morality in shaping the answer to hard cases is narrowed down and made dependent upon the understanding of norms of FLRs. Chapter 2 proposes a stipulative definition of FLRs that attempts to single out the most important features of those rights. Chapter 3 focuses on the anatomy of conflicts of FLRs. Hence, it attempts to grasp the central case of such conflicts, thereby coming up with a distinction between genuine and spurious conflicts. As a conclusion to chapter 3, I present a typology of genuine conflicts of FLRs in order to elucidate the great variety of those conflicts. Chapter 4 tries to bridge the first part—the theory of Conflicts—with the second part—the practice of conflict. In order to do that it deals with some orthodox legal responses to the problem of conflict of FLRs. It deals, for example, with the doctrines of balancing and deference, and criticizes them as tools for the resolution of genuine conflicts. A comparative analysis of France, the UK, and the USA in this chapter attempts to flesh out the theoretical skeleton that provides the framework for the thesis.

The second part is divided into three chapters. Chapter 5 deals with the FLR to privacy; its protean nature is exposed as well as its propensity to conflict with other FLRs. Lacking a common core, the FLR to privacy is broken down into four sub-FLRs: the FLR to informational privacy, the FLR to decisional privacy, the FLR to formational privacy, and the FLR to physical privacy. Here, it is suggested that there is a link between the lack of a narrow definition of privacy and its aptitude to conflict. Therefore, the FLR to privacy is likely to conflict with other FLRs in several contexts, as is shown in chapters 6 and 7.

Chapter 6 presents the conflict between the FLR to informational privacy and the FLR to the free press. Hence, I set out to examine the core case of conflict that can be summarized as follows: permission to disclose the truth v permission to conceal one's private life. Chapter 7 presents the conflict between the FLR to decisional privacy and the FLR to life in physician assisted suicide. This last case is more controversial insofar as people disagree on whether it can be treated as a genuine conflict. After all, they argue, the FLR to life should include the liberty to choose what to do with one's own life. My own definition of the conflict instead focuses on the near-to-absolute obligation not to intentionally kill, set by the FLR to life. This conflict is a vertical one, between the obligation of the state not to intentionally kill and the permission of the individual to decide how to deal with one of the most intimate issue of one's existence.

The difficulty raised by the existence of constitutional dilemmas ought not to shield us from that problem. I think that it is important to confront it in an open manner, seeking a better understanding, rather than ready-made answers. The tensions that underlie conflicts of FLRs cannot be dispelled altogether, although they can be better accepted if explained and justified.

Genuine conflicts of FLRs are unavoidable because of the very texture of our liberty. We are constantly struggling for its expansion, and yet that very expansion may lead to the contraction of someone else's liberty. Moreover, the pluralist outlook of our societies makes the conflict all the more likely in that the interpretation of constitutional permission is consequently extended. Finally, a better understanding of the *structure* of individual freedom contributes also to the elucidation of the Constitution of the society. Dilemmas will always arise. However, the strength of a society can be tested in these adversarial circumstances. Thus, to be able to cope with constitutional dilemmas (without falling into pieces) is the best sign of a healthy democracy.

PART I

THE THEORY OF CONFLICTS OF FUNDAMENTAL LEGAL RIGHTS

1
Law, Morality, and Conflicts of Fundamental Legal Rights

> If, as I believe, the ends of men are many, and not all of them are in principle compatible with each other, then the possibility of conflict—and of tragedy—can never be wholly eliminated from human life, either personal or social.[1]

1. The Dilemma

Law is rooted in conflict. Its aim is to prevent or settle cases where two (or more) parties hold conflicting claims. Legal rights are meant to provide a solution to conflicts. When a party has a right, then her claim must prevail over that of the opponent. In that sense, a right trumps other claims. But what if both parties have a trump card? That is, what happens if, in a given situation, the constitution or legislation confers rights on both parties, such that each has equal status and the rights are simultaneously enforceable? In such a case, the application of either right entails the violation of the other. As a result, we face the dilemma of the conflict of rights. This book will focus exclusively on the conflicts of Fundamental Legal Rights (FLRs),[2] ie those rights entrenched in bills of rights and therefore protected by a specialized institution, against the violation of norms on an inferior level.

Constitutional lawyers and political philosophers have struggled over the interpretation of basic liberties in the last few decades. Not only do bills of rights, charters and declarations[3] outline FLRs in a very broad and sweeping fashion, but it is also very unclear as to how to administer such legal documents in a coherent way. The point of departure in those debates is in the recognition of widespread disagreement on what FLRs require.[4] I am concerned with something possibly

---

[1] Isaiah Berlin, *Liberty* (Oxford: OUP, 2002) 214.
[2] Ch 2 will offer a stipulative definition of the concept of FLRs.
[3] In this book, I will use these terms interchangeably.
[4] Ronald Dworkin, *Taking Rights Seriously* (London: Duckworth, 1977 (1991 reprint)) (hereinafter referred to as *TRS*), 14; Robert Alexy, *Theory of Constitutional Rights* (Oxford: OUP, 2002) (hereinafter referred to as *TCR*), 2; Jeremy Waldron, *Law and Disagreement* (Oxford: OUP, 1999), 1. For a very recent study on the role of disagreement in law, see Samantha Besson, *The Morality of Conflict—Reasonable Disagreement and the Law* (Oxford: Hart, 2005).

even more problematic: the agreement about what rights require. Let me explain. Suppose that we agree on what free speech and privacy imply separately. Imagine now that two famous people are getting married but they want to maintain the privacy of their wedding. However a journalist manages to acquire, from the participants, some pictures of the wedding, and now wants to publish them. The journalist can claim protection under his FLR to free speech, while the famous couple can claim their FLR to privacy. Which claim should prevail?[5]

A second example of a conflict of FLRs is abortion.[6] This is a case of conflict between the FLR to privacy, which protects the mother's decision to abort, and the FLR to the life of the foetus. The FLR to life protects every person from being killed; therefore, it protects the life of every child. Why would it be different for a foetus?[7] The FLR to life for the foetus conflicts with the FLR to privacy of every woman. We know, all too well, the difficulties surrounding the choice to abort or not. If a woman decides to abort, are we justified in encroaching into her private life to ask her reasons for doing it? Or, should it be for her alone to choose? Whichever the answer, one will encounter a clash between pro-life and pro-choice partisans.

It may be argued that the above examples are *spurious* FLRs conflicts. That is, if we closely look at them, we will be able to present the case in a way that dispels the conflict. It will be possible to either reconcile the two parties' claims, or it will be possible to rank them hierarchically, in a way that allows the increased weight of one claim over the other. However, the fact that some conflicts can be viewed as spurious, and can be defined away, does not mean that *genuine* FLRs' conflicts do not exist. Here my point is a conceptual one: I claim that genuine conflicts do exist and that this is explicable due to the very structure, and point, of FLRs. To be more precise, FLRs protect such a wide range of actions that it is unavoidable that two or more of them sometimes overlap in a way that make them mutually incompatible. Consequently, the application of one FLR, in some cases, entails the violation of another.[8]

To put the issue in metaphorical terms, we could describe genuine conflicts of FLRs as constitutional tragedies.[9] I view this as a good metaphor, as it encapsulates the idea of a *choice* between two irreconcilable goods (or evils) and the idea of a *loss* for someone of something valuable, regardless of the outcome. A tragedy

---

[5] For an example in English law, see *Douglas and Zeta Jones & Others v Hello!* [2001] QB 967, CA. For a theoretical discussion, see Frederick Schauer, 'Can Public Figures have Private Lives?' in Paul, Miller and Paul, *The right to privacy* (Cambridge: CUP, 2001).

[6] Laurence H Tribe, *Abortion: The Clash of Absolutes* (New York: WW Norton, 1992).

[7] For the sake of my argument, I assume here that a foetus has the same rights as a child. Of course this is a problem in itself, but this is not the place to deal with this particular question.

[8] Hans Kelsen defines conflict of norms as follows: 'A conflict exists between two norms when that which one of them decrees to be obligatory is incompatible with that which the other decrees to be obligatory, so that the observance or application of one norm necessarily or possibly involve the violation of the other.' *General Theory of Norms* (Oxford: Clarendon Press, 1991) (transl), ch 29, 123.

[9] WN Eskridge and S Levinson (eds), *Constitutional Tragedies and Constitutional Stupidities* (New York: NYUP, 1998).

often discussed in legal fora is that of Sophocle's Antigone.[10] Antigone was condemned to death by Creon, the sovereign of Thebes, for having buried the corpse of her brother and thereby breaching the sovereign's edict not to bury the corpses of traitors. Antigone was claiming that the statute enacted by Creon violated the religious right to bury members of your family. The choice is between the religious edict and that of the sovereign. The loss is either one of authority, or one of morality. The epilogue of the tragedy is in fact a total loss: Antigone dies and Creon is left alone after the death of his son and his wife. The tragedy occurs because neither of the two parties wants to acknowledge that the other has a valid claim that goes in the opposite direction. The loss is great on the two sides because neither Antigone nor Creon see that there is a conflict in each other's claim. Both assert that they stand for the right position and both are victims in their failure to acknowledge the existence of a conflict.

While the claim that genuine conflicts of FLRs exist is hardly surprising, some authors deny this.[11] Ronald Dworkin, for example, famously defended the fantastic claim that there is a right answer for every case.[12] The implication of that position is that there is ultimately no scope for genuine conflicts of FLRs. Similarly, Robert Alexy holds that when FLRs compete, the constitutional court can balance them and therefore reach a maximizing outcome in most cases. I disagree with both of them. First, to talk of 'the right answer' or 'the maximizing answer' obscures the idea of dilemmas and tragedies. More importantly, such positions display a commitment to the assumption of a coherent, harmonious, whole at the level of constitutional essentials. But we are going to see that such an assumption is not consistent with the idea of genuine conflict of FLRs. Some authors, therefore, plainly fail to address the important problem of conflicts. In what follows, I want to address precisely that problem, and its implications for the theory and the practice of rights.

It should be stressed that courts do indeed reach a solution in every case. Yet, this does not mean that that solution is either the right or the best one. The outcome is only one possible solution among many, and courts do exercise a certain amount of discretion in reaching any particular conclusion. Hence, the practical resolution of conflicts within the framework of legal systems begs questions that must be kept separate from the conceptual ones. Commentators favour different ways of solving a conflict of FLRs. We can identify two different strategies that attempt to offer a solution. First, it is often suggested that it suffices to define the scope of FLRs in such a way that makes it possible to avoid the conflict. Thus, we

---

[10] In American jurisprudence, for instance, this tragedy is used to criticize legal positivism for its lack of moral sensitivity. See on this point A Sebok, *Legal Positivism in American Jurisprudence* (Cambridge: CUP, 1998) 7–19. Antigone's tragedy is particularly interesting from the point of view of incommensurability. Both Creon and Antigone's position claim exclusive validity.

[11] I am referring here to *TRS* and *TCR*. The choice of these two theories is justified by their influence and by their nature. Arguably, they are the most important theories of constitutional rights.

[12] Ronald Dworkin, 'No right answers?' in PMS Hacker and Joseph Raz (eds), *Law, Morality, and Society* (Oxford: OUP, 1978) 58–84.

could narrow either the scope of privacy or of free speech in order to facilitate this task. But what if each claim falls within the core of the respective rights? For example, imagine that an affair between a president and a *stagiaire* is exposed to the public; if challenged, the newspaper will argue for its FLR to free speech concerning political actors, while the president will argue for his FLR to privacy. Where do you set the boundary between those two rights? Will the president be left with a fig leaf or will he be completely stripped of his right to privacy?[13]

The second strategy is less concerned with the scope, and more with the strength of rights—this is what some authors call an evaluation of the 'importance' or 'weight' of FLRs. Statements such as 'free speech is more important than privacy', or 'the violation of free speech is more serious than the violation of privacy', and 'the permission of privacy prevails over the prohibition of free speech' amount to evaluative statements that are meant to highlight the strength of each FLR. The implication in expressing such statements undermines the genuine importance of FLRs. Even if it was possible to calculate the strength of each claim, it could be easily argued that when a social goal is of particular weight it therefore has to prevail over FLRs. But this defeats the very purpose of a FLR: to provide a special protection for individuals against the interference of the state.

My hypothesis is that the question of conflicts of FLRs is inescapable. I shall argue that the dominant trend in the literature fails to elucidate the problem of conflicts of FLRs. Instead, they offer their moral evaluations under the guise of objectivity and rationality.[14] In this chapter I attempt to unravel some of the assumptions that underline the position of both commentators and practitioners. As an illustration of the major trends I will discuss selected issues from Alexy's and Dworkin's constitutional theories, and I will endeavour to stress their lack of a proper treatment of conflicts of FLRs.[15] These theories try to minimize conflicts, either by claiming that there is a political morality that provides a right answer to each conflict, or by stating that a judge can solve a 'competition of principles' by balancing them. In section 2, I focus on the structure of FLRs' norms; therein, I examine, and criticize, the theory of principles which treats FLRs as having a dimension of weight as opposed to the dimension of validity of rules. In section 3, I focus on the assumptions of harmony at the level of constitutional essentials, and its implications for the notion of conflicts. Finally, in section 4, I present my standpoint. FLRs should be treated as rules as this can help us understand their conflicts, as distinct from the notion of 'conflict of values' and 'competition of principles'.

---

[13] Some of you may think that the answer to this problem is straightforward. I would disagree. Bill Clinton's loss of political virginity points to a more troublesome lack of privacy culture within the American society. See on this point, Thomas Nagel, *Exposure and Concealment* (Oxford: OUP, 2001).

[14] Ronald Dworkin, 'Objectivity and Truth: You'd Better Believe It', Philosophy and Public Affairs 25 (1996) 87. Robert Alexy, 'Constitutional Rights, Balancing, and Rationality', Ratio Juris 16 (2003) 131–40.

[15] I discuss these two authors because I take them to represent the most articulate theories of constitutional rights in Europe and in the USA.

2. The Structure of FLRs' Norms: Rules v Principles

The point of departure in identifying FLRs is their reference to higher norms, usually of constitutional status. This, however, does not settle the problem of the grounds of rights.[16] To the contrary, it has been argued that the formulation of rights in bills of rights is so broad and sweeping that they should be considered as statements of moral principles rather than statements of constitutional rules.[17]

FLRs, whether understood as rules or principles, require interpretation and instantiation. Therefore, it is only misleading to believe that if we depict them as broad principles, we can avoid inconsistencies with other principles.[18] A superficial overview leads to a belief that rules in conflict lose their validity, while principles are said to be always valid, although susceptible to modulation, and to being overridden. Yet the question faced here is much more complex: it concerns the problem of the reality of rights. Do rights exist only by virtue of the specific interest of the individuals they protect, or can they be embedded in a more general, rule-like, statement?[19]

The question of the reality of rights can be best understood by reference to a very close issue: the generality of rights. A right is general if it exists independently from, and prior to, its concrete application. Hohfeld, who differs on this point along with rights theorists such as Carl Wellman, believe that a right is real only if a court upholds it.[20] That is, a right exists, if and only if, a court favours one claim over another. The recognition of a right is the upshot of a legal process, and not a feature of the reasoning leading to a given result. In other words, to say that Wesley has a right amounts to a description of his actual legal positions and relations, as worked out by the court. From this point of view, the reality of a right coincides with its particularity, in that the right belongs to a given individual. A competing view is that rights are first and foremost general.[21] They exist prior to any actual confrontation, and they shape the way decisions are taken. In this book, I favour the latter approach.

FLRs have been, in recent years, the main battlefield in the dispute between legal positivists and their opponents. The latter have argued that legal positivists

---

[16] For an interesting discussion of the relationship between rights and rules, see Tom Campbell, *Rights: A Critical Introduction* (Oxford: Routledge, 2006) 27–30.

[17] Ronald Dworkin, 'The Moral Reading of the Constitution' in R Dworkin, *Freedom's Law* (Oxford: OUP, 1996).

[18] Robert Alexy, 'Rights, Legal Reasoning, and Rational Discourse', Ratio Juris 12 (1992) 143–51 (rules as definitive, or principles as prima facie rights).

[19] Frederick Schauer, 'The Generality of Rights', Legal Theory, 6 (2000) 323–36. Frederick Schauer, 'Rights as Rules', Law and Philosophy 6 (1987) 115–19. Fredrick Schauer, 'A Comment on the Structure of Rights', 27 Ga L Rev 415 (1992–1993).

[20] See Carl Wellman, *Real Rights* (New York: OUP, 1995). Frederick Schauer explains that Hohfeld's theory is underlined by an American realist concern, 'The Generality of Rights', Legal Theory 6 (2000) 323–28.

[21] Frederick Schauer, 'The Generality of Rights', Legal Theory 6 (2000) 323–36.

cannot account for the structure of FLRs in terms of rules.[22] Instead, they associate FLRs with the language of principles. To do this, they developed a theory of principles, grounded on a logical distinction between rules and principles: rules have a dimension of all-or-nothing validity, whereas principles have a dimension of weight or importance.[23] Such a theory of principles allows them to assert that, whenever FLRs are at stake, a moral evaluation of their weight or importance is required. This assessment can be based, either on a substantive theory of moral principles (eg Dworkin), or on a procedural one (eg Alexy). It goes beyond the scope of this section to present, at length, the constitutional theories of Dworkin and Alexy. Here I would rather focus on the role of conflict of rights within those theories as an illustration of contemporary controversies on the structure of FLRs, and of the norms supporting them. First, I will locate the debate in the broader context, and then I will concentrate on the problems raised by the existence of conflict of rights.

A. An Overview of the Debate

To cut a long story short, the dispute over the structure of FLRs began with the publication of two leading books on rights: Dworkin's *Taking Rights Seriously* and Alexy's *Theory of Constitutional Rights*. Both books can be regarded as critiques of positivism, as espoused by either HLA Hart's or Hans Kelsen's legal theories. Despite some significant differences in approach, the underlying concern of legal positivists was to systematize the study of the concept of law by presenting legal rules as a system of rules. The response of scholars interested in the role of rights aimed at highlighting inaccuracies of the positivist theories: a system of rules—so the argument goes—is not adequate in accounting for the role of legal principles. This is the manner by which rights based theories criticized the very idea of a closed system of rules. First, pointing to the existence of principles that better depict the way FLRs behave; they then added that principles opened up the legal system to morality.

A second question provoked by legal positivists was related to the so-called open texture of norms. This resulted in an acute problem as to the liberty of the interpreter; especially, when dealing with very broad statements of principles, such as FLRs. Kelsen and Hart insisted on the existence of a great liberty of the interpreters that they called discretion. The retort of rights theorists was that both Kelsen, and Hart, had a very rudimentary theory of adjudication. Dworkin's criticism insisted that positivist theories of adjudication made the task of the judge

---

[22] *TRS*, passim. *TCR*, 44–110.
[23] That distinction is illustrated by the way rules and principles conflict. Rules are all-or-nothing: when rules conflict, one is valid and the other is not. This has both immediate and long-term consequences. In the immediate, one rule is preferred over the other and the outcome will be determined accordingly to the rule that applies. In the long run, the rules that have been put aside will be considered invalid and will lose their membership to the legal system.

too dependent on the task of the legislature. This failed to account for the breadth given to the courts in the interpretation of statutes. Dworkin developed an alternative theory of adjudication, based on his theory of principles; in short, he argues that the liberty of the interpreter is far less than that which positivists called for. In fact, judges are directly bound by morality, and therefore the way they establish legal rights and duties is not only dependent on the relevant legislation, but also on what morality requires them to be. This is particularly the situation when judges decide very hard cases where legislation is silent.

Robert Alexy mounted a very similar attack on positivism in his leading book, *Theory of Constitutional Rights*. He summarizes his central thesis very clearly: 'The central thesis of this book is that regardless of their more or less precise formulation, constitutional rights are principles and that principles are optimisation requirements'.[24]

Alexy's critique of positivism is, at the outset, similar to Dworkin's. As Alexy points out, his own thesis is based first on the distinction between principles and rules, and second on the idea that principles are 'optimization requirements'. The first point is similar to Dworkin's, while the second is the core of Alexy's own contribution.

Principles as 'optimization requirements' (OR) suggests that there is an overall advantageous combination of principles, given the legal and factual possibilities.[25] Such malleability of principles, it is argued, allow them to be satisfied at varying degrees. This is what makes them fundamentally different to rules which are either fulfilled or not. The nature of principles as OR sheds light on the particular relationship between principles and proportionality. According to Alexy, FLRs are principles and this commands, on the part of constitutional courts, a *constant exercise of balancing* between competing principles. Since principles are OR, and as such they can be satisfied at different degrees, the burden of the court is to reach a solution that strives to maximize the realization of the principles taken together.

B. Conflicts of Rules and Competition of Principles

My main aim here is to show that both Dworkin's and Alexy's theories of principles heavily depend on [the avoidance of] the problem of FLRs' conflict. Indeed, the very nature of principles depends on their divergent behaviour from rules *when in conflict*. Both insist that some features, other than rules, constitute the legal system. FLRs in particular, they hold, cannot be viewed simply as rules, as they cannot be invalidated in the same way rules can. The theory of principles acquires significance especially in relation to FLRs, as it aims to explain the way FLRs behave when they collide with other norms. Dworkin and Alexy could be interpreted as attempting to provide a solution to the dilemma that I have tried to

[24] TCR, 388.   [25] Ibid, 47.

sketch in the previous section. However, their argument reduces the dilemma to a mere *flatus voci*. For, if their theories were correct, then a solution to every problem would be reached, either by maximization of liberty through the balancing technique, or by way of the right answer thesis.

Dworkin's treatment of the question of conflict of rules is very brief and sketchy. In *Taking Rights Seriously*, he tries to explain the way principles and rules operate; in order to do that, he compares the way rules and principles conflict.

> If two rules conflict, one of them cannot be a valid rule. The decision as to which is valid, and which must be abandoned or recast, must be made by appealing to considerations beyond the rules themselves. A legal system might regulate such conflicts by other rules, which prefer the rule enacted by the higher authority, or the rule enacted later, or the more specific rule, or something of that sort. A legal system *may also prefer the rule supported by the more important principles*. (Our own legal system uses both of these techniques.)[26]

Dworkin distinguishes two types of solutions in resolving the conflict of rules. On the one hand, he reminds us of the classical ways of solving a conflict through *lex posterior* or *lex specialis* or, more generally, by the application of another rule. On the other hand, he states that the rule supported by the more important principles may overrule the competing rule. He takes the latter as a well-established feature of the American legal system. This is problematic because it is exactly what he is trying to prove, namely that there are some principles that behave in a different way to rules, and that they can even determine the outcome in a conflict of rules.

But Dworkin does not provide a test to identify principles. On the contrary, he holds that it is difficult to say when a standard is a rule or a principle. However, if it is a principle, then what is essential is to establish its weight, and to compare it to that of competing principles. This brief discussion is the core of the doctrine. To establish the qualitative difference of principles is crucial for the remaining part of Dworkin's theory, in particular when he deals with hard cases.[27] According to *TRS*, hard cases are those in which it is difficult to establish the legal rights and obligations at stake. Legal positivists—Dworkin says—subscribe to a theory that identifies legal obligations and rights by relying on the discretionary interpretation of properly selected legal sources (source thesis). He suggests that in hard cases rules do not provide any guidance; therefore, we have to rely on the standards that permeate the law: principles and policies. Principles support individual rights. Outside principles, legal sources also embed policies, that is, decisions supporting certain social goals.

The gist of the distinction between principles and policies lies in the reality that the strength of principles is measured by their capability to withstand competition with policies.[28] The 'Rights thesis' assumes that, whenever a principle competes with a policy, the principle—by virtue of its protection of an individual right—prevails over the policy. But, what is really striking is that in the end the distinction

[26] *TRS*, 27.   [27] Ibid, 81 and ff.   [28] Ibid, 92.

between rights and goals depends on the background political theory that 'assigns rough relative weight to each type of rights'.[29] Ultimately, therefore, the way by which a conflict of standards works depends on how a political theory assigns relative weights. How that could work in practice is hard to grasp. To that purpose, Dworkin introduces the idea of Hercules, the mythical judge endowed with superpowers and enabled to work his way from a powerful political theory down to the practical world.

Alexy presents the conflict of rules in much the same way Dworkin does: if two rules conflict, either one of them is invalid or one of them is the exception. *Lex posterior* may apply to the first case, while *lex specialis* can be used for the second one. Alexy states that principles do not compete in the same way that rules do. Conflicts of rules raise a question of validity, while competition of principles is a matter of weight. If the weight is variable a principle may outweigh another in certain circumstances, and be outweighed in others. It should be noted here that the notion of principle suggested by Alexy is wider than Dworkin's: a principle can include both individual rights and collective goals.

Alexy argues that he has discovered a 'law of competing principles'.[30] The law is 'discovered' through the observation of the case law of the *BundesVerfassung Gericht;* the German constitutional court. A case, *Lebach*, is quoted as an example. The court holds that there is 'a tension between the duty of the state to maintain a properly functioning criminal justice system and the interest of the accused in his constitutionally guaranteed rights, which the state is also obliged to protect under the Basic Law (the constitution)'. In continuing, the court holds that the tension is not to be resolved by giving in to one's claim of 'precedence per se but by balancing conflicting interests'. Alexy explains that the use by the court of terms such as tension or conflict can be substituted by the notion of competition. Moreover, the notions of duties and constitutional rights can be swapped by the language of 'principles'.

This semantic shift is puzzling. In the language of the court, there is no clear sign to distinguish a conflict of rules from those of constitutional rights. Alexy concludes that the distinction is one of nature. A conflict of rules ends with a declaration of invalidity. A competition of principles ends with 'a conditional relation of precedence', where precedence is established case by case by the weight or importance of the principle under given legal and factual possibilities. I believe that Alexy's outline is misleading from the outset.

Both Dworkin and Alexy encounter problems in their interpretation of conflict of rules, and competition of principles. According to their sketchy discussions, the manner by which rules conflict can be summarized as a question of validity. But this is *inaccurate* because it is clearly not the case that every time rules conflict, one is valid and the other invalid. Sometimes one rule will be considered as the exception to the other. Moreover, it is not the case that the solution of a conflict of rules

---

[29] Ibid, 93.   [30] Ibid, 50.

depends on the application of another rule, while the solution of a competition of principles depends on the evaluation of their importance. If it were true that a court could evaluate the importance of principles, this in itself would depend on a rule that grants a broad competence to the court. Therefore both situations depend, at varying levels, on the application of rules. Finally, Dworkin and Alexy are the victims of their own distinction between validity and weight. If validity is a relatively easy concept to grasp and apply, the metaphor of weight or importance exposes legal reasoning to a great number of uncertainties and problems.

3. Weighing Principles in Competition: Harmony or Conflict?

How do we resolve a competition of principles then? Can we really measure their weight? Dworkin gave a bold answer: there is no legal way to measure the weight of principles. Hence, judges must develop a moral theory allowing them to evaluate the weight or importance of each principle. At this stage another fundamental problem arises: what if the moral theory itself encounters dilemmas? To this question, Dworkin replies that, for each case there is a right answer. But what if there is a case where two principles are irreconcilable? Would it still be possible to come up with a right answer?

Alexy, in contrast with Dworkin, holds that competition of principles should be resolved by appeal to balancing, which is the way legal reasoning works when applied to principles.[31] He builds on the concept of principles as optimization requirements in order to reach the conclusion that balancing is the optimal form of legal reasoning in dealing with competition of principles. Although Alexy stops short of articulating a fully-fledged substantive moral theory, he nonetheless draws heavily on the idea of principles behaving in the same way values do.

In what follows I will sketch Dworkin's substantive theory of constitutional rights and, subsequently, Alexy's procedural theory. In both sections I shall attempt to unravel some of the fundamental assumptions which both authors make with regard to the existence of conflicts of FLRs. As it will be argued, despite using different methods in solving issues of competition of principles, both Dworkin and Alexy express views that are, as such, incompatible with a full understanding of the problems raised by FLRs' conflict. More precisely they assume a harmonious (coherent or objective) order of values from which any decision can be drawn. But that very assumption is the object of unrelenting controversy and obscures rather than illuminates the central question of conflicts of FLRs.

---

[31] Robert Alexy, 'On Balancing and Subsumption. A Structural Comparison', Ratio Juris 16, (2003) 449.

A. A Substantive Theory of Constitutional Rights

(i) Objectivity and the right answer thesis

What is the point of engaging in moral and political theory when dealing with legal questions? After all, moral evaluations, as such, convey individual preferences and they do not seem to advance the case for better justice in the courtroom. However, Dworkin offers us a fantastic claim that purports to dissolve our concerns over moral evaluations.[32] For, as the American scholar argues, moral evaluations have only one right answer. In other words they are either true or false. That is, as a matter of principle, it is possible to justify on moral grounds every single choice that an adjudicator makes. This argument is central to the correctness of his 'interpretivist' theory of law: judges should follow the legislator, but when the instructions have run out, they should find which moral or political principle best illuminates the practice.

Dworkin's claim has been refined somewhat in recent works on objectivity and truth.[33] The argument has a strong strategic component, since Dworkin suggests that those who hold that a certain moral evaluation is not objective, or that it cannot be true or false, are using those terms in a controversial way. Dworkin argues that to say a moral claim is objective amounts to saying that we believe in it and that we find it persuasive. For example, when we say 'abortion is wrong' we are asserting, in an objective way, a moral claim: namely, that 'it is a true statement to say that abortion is wrong'. The truth of a proposition therefore, depends on the weight of the arguments that support it. If there are good moral arguments to hold that euthanasia is desirable, then euthanasia must be truly and objectively desirable. The same applies to the death penalty, or any other moral issue we can think of.[34] As such, the choice of the right conception of law is morally justifiable by correct moral evaluation. Equally, the resolution of FLRs' conflicts has one, and only one, right answer based on strong moral arguments.

Dworkin's position is deeply contested. For example, many modern moral and political philosophies insist on value pluralism. In the realm of morality, they argue, there are numerous values and these can be combined in various ways without yielding to one correct answer. In fact, a range of valid answers is possible and reasonable. I believe that value pluralism portrays more accurately the actual conditions of deliberation and decision-making in modern Western societies. More

---

[32] Hilary Putnam defines it this way in, 'Are moral values made or discovered?', Legal Theory 1 (1995) 1–15.

[33] Ronald Dworkin, 'Objectivity and Truth: You'd Better Believe It', Philosophy and Public Affairs 25 (1996) 87. More recently he deals with the question in his paper 'Rawls and the Law', republished in his recent book *Justice in Robes* (Cambridge, Mass: HUP, 2006) 241–61.

[34] The inconvenience of such accounts is that often the moral objectivity of a claim does not entail a legal outcome. For instance, although I am sure there is a good moral case to be made against the death penalty, judges do not rely on the objectivity of that claim but on the instructions given by the American legislators.

importantly, in this context, I think that value pluralism helps to elucidate the phenomenon of conflicts of FLRs. Indeed the legal/constitutional sphere partly reflects pluralism at the moral level. After all, bills of rights entrench a set of FLRs that are neither perfectly coherent, nor organized in a harmonious way.

(ii) Coherentist assumptions and 'conflict of values'

Dworkin argues that judges can only evaluate the weight or importance of principles by appealing to moral considerations. Moral theory, he says, permeates the entire constitutional domain through the principled reading of the constitution.[35] Whenever principles conflict it is always possible to evaluate each claim, and to come up with a right answer. But, if this were the case that would mean that no genuine conflicts of FLRs really exist. Here I will argue that Dworkin's theory actually obscures the problem of conflicts of FLRs from its very foundation. The reason is to be found in Dworkin's coherentist theory of values underpinning both law and morality. His position can be summarized in three points. First, Dworkin's theory claims a fusion between morality and law. Second, it suggests that it is possible to single out one coherent set of values. Third, it presupposes that one value, among all others, is supreme (a sovereign virtue of equal concern and respect). Once we understand these assumptions we can better understand why Dworkin denies that genuine conflicts of values (or of rights, since in his theory the two overlap) can arise.

(a) The fusion thesis

Recall that Dworkin opposed the idea of law as a system of rules, by arguing that that characterization overlooked the role played by principles. In *Model of Rules I*,—possibly Dworkin's best contribution to legal theory—the scholar argues that, in virtually every case, practitioners disagree on the legal rights and obligations that are at stake. Thus, in hard cases, it is often held that rules do not provide a definite answer. Legal positivists argue that the law displays a number of gaps which are filled by judges exercising their own discretion. Dworkin disagrees precisely on this point. He claims that where rules are incomplete, principles should be deployed to fill in the gaps. In this way legal rights and obligations are said to be ultimately determined by appealing to morality.

The clearest statement of the fusion thesis is to be found in Dworkin's own words:

Constitutional law can make no genuine advance until it isolates the problem of rights against the state and makes that problem part of its own agenda. That argues for a **fusion** of constitutional law and moral theory, a connection that, incredibly, has yet to take place. It is perfectly understandable that lawyers dread contamination with moral philosophy, and particularly with those philosophers who talk about rights because the spooky overtones of that concept threaten the graveyard of reason.[36]

---

[35] Ronald Dworkin, *Freedom's Law* (Oxford: OUP, 1999) (hereafter referred to as *FL*).
[36] *TRS*, 149.

The fusion thesis argues for a single normative standpoint: that of morality. From that point of view it is impossible to conceive of the possibility of conflict between law and morality because morality and law are one thing. Equally, FLRs are considered to be grounded in morality and require a moral reading.[37] How then can we explain the phenomenon of conflicts of FLRs? The short answer is that Dworkin does not explain it. A longer answer, however, requires us to examine that which allows Dworkin to identify the relevant set of values in forming his notion of morality.

(b) One set of values

Dworkin has a clear monist position at both the level of abstract values, and at a more concrete level. We can separate the two although it is clear, in Dworkin's mind, that one supports the other.

Dworkin's political philosophy, at the more abstract level, is opposed to Isaiah Berlin's pluralism of values. A few words on Berlin's position are required in order to introduce Dworkin's views. In his renowned essay, 'Two concepts of liberty', Berlin defends the distinction made between positive and negative liberty. This distinction corresponds to the formula of freedom to and freedom from. Every individual strives to be his own master and seeks to be as successful as possible in planning his own life. This amounts to the idea of positive freedom. However, an individual may, because of adverse circumstances or bad planning, fail to achieve his plans. Yet, he still has the choice to retreat into his own inner citadel where the state is not allowed and the individual can isolate himself from the others. This is what characterizes negative freedom in a nutshell.

A pluralist theory of values is customarily very respectful of negative freedom. In this, the central idea is that each individual pursues a number of different ends which are not, in themselves, always compatible with each other.[38] Rather naturally this suggests that the possibility of conflict cannot be entirely removed from life, unless we assume that a harmonious society is achievable. But how do we achieve harmony? The metaphysical belief of harmony proves problematic. Berlin suggests that: 'lacking a convincing metaphysical explanation—we must fall back on the ordinary resources of empirical observation and ordinary human knowledge. And this certainly gives us no warrant for supposing that all good things, or all bad things for that matter, are reconcilable with each other'.[39]

In *The legacy of Isaiah Berlin*,[40] Dworkin asks: 'Do liberal values conflict?'. Dworkin's answer is predictably negative. That's his belief, or to be more precise his *hope*.[41] But it is in fact a truism: we all hope, of course, that conflicts of values

---

[37] *FL*, 1–38.
[38] Isaiah Berlin, 'Two concepts of liberty', in Isaiah Berlin (edited by Henry Hardy) *Liberty* (Oxford: OUP, 2002) 214.   [39] Ibid, 213.
[40] Mark Lilla, Ronald Dworkin, and Robert Silvers, *The legacy of Isaiah Berlin* (New York: New York Review Books, 2001). This essay is reproduced in *Justice in Robes* (n 33 above).
[41] This is the very last word of Dworkin's essay in *The legacy of Isaiah Berlin* (n 40 above) at 90.

will not arise. However our experiences and our discourses display tensions and hard choices between two or more mutually exclusive options.

Dworkin argues that value pluralism may entrench certain conflicts and, therefore, justify perennial evils. For instance, he invites us to consider poverty in Western countries. Many people—he says—live in less-than-decent conditions, and the justification for this despicable state of affairs is that equality conflicts with liberty.[42] However, Dworkin does not prove why that is the case. Poverty is not a necessary consequence of the conflict between equality and liberty. Every society experiences poverty and unbearable cleavages between classes. The extent to which disparities exist, and are maintained, depends on the interplay of various factors: economics, politics and historical precedents should be taken into account here.

Berlin's view is overall more appealing, because it points to real hazards, and he attempts to explain the root of the problem. More importantly, he offers a position that not only states that harmony is unobtainable (factually), but that is in fact also incoherent. Dworkin however, attacks another central thesis of Berlin's value pluralism: the notion that when values conflict, any given choice taken entails an irreparable loss endured by some party. Dworkin insists that value pluralism, by claiming that it has reached the bottom of the dilemma, is extremely ambitious and possibly wrong.

Dworkin argues that the previous conclusion depends on how we conceive of the source of our responsibilities. In order to buttress this point, Dworkin uses in a puzzling way the biblical example of Abraham. Abraham is required by God to kill his child. But of course his morality, which Dworkin describes as having an independent source from obedience to God, would require him to refrain from killing his own child. Dworkin explains that the crux of the problem lies in the fact that Abraham is torn between two sovereign commandments. In this sense, whatever he does, he is bound to commit a wrong. But this way of reading Abraham's case is open to debate. Abraham sees a tension in this situation, however, he believes in the superiority of God's command, and therefore in the subordination of morality to God's command. He hesitates as God is asking for a tragic sacrifice; nonetheless, he decides that his son will be sacrificed. This is a supreme example of how religious doctrine claims value monism, in how justice would only prevail by conforming to the will of God. Hence I am not so sure that Abraham's case, as used by Dworkin, does convincingly demonstrate the existence of the evils he attributes to value pluralism. Moreover, Dworkin argues that politics is nothing like Abraham's choice because in politics 'we are drawn to each of the rival positions through arguments'.[43] Again, this is more wishful thinking than an accurate reflection of the way politics work. For example, think about issues like abortion.

---

[42] Ibid, 81.   [43] Ibid, 82.

Value pluralism is a more interesting position as it leaves dilemmas open to scrutiny. A value pluralist is able to examine both sides of the question, and to recognize that each party has a fundamental and irreducible claim. The only truth is that there is a conflict and that any resolution incurs a loss. That conceptual truth is likely to have important implications for the outcome. If each party feels that, regardless of the outcome, something of fundamental value will be lost, then there will be a possibility for compromise. But compromise is not an optimal solution, as it means that each party still forfeits something, and so the loss is shared. On the contrary, if each party firmly believes in the truth of his claim, and fails to acknowledge that of the adversary, then the result is unlikely to involve reconciliation, as value coherentists maintain.

In response to Dworkin, I also want to add that harmony and coherence are potentially dangerous ideals. Why? The answer is that they conflate ideal and reality, and in doing so they compromise the explanatory role of theory: we are unable to understand why some decisions are tragic and feel tragic. A coherentist is not concerned with the meaning of those tragic moments; he simply wants to adjust our understanding of the problem in order to define tragedy away.

Value pluralism maintains the same ideal as coherentism. It would indeed be great to achieve a fully harmonious society. But the truth value pluralism is stating (a truism) is that harmony cannot be achieved in our real world. It is therefore necessary to understand the gap between ideal and reality, and value pluralism is better equipped to do so.

Dworkin's defence of coherentism directly proves one of my points. Dworkin does not conceive of the possibility of genuine conflicts of liberties, but instead argues for reconciling fundamental values that appear to be in conflict. In what way does the fact that values do not conflict bear on the question of FLRs' conflicts? This problem is not self-evident as legal systems single out the very values they wish to protect. This may narrow the scope of certain values too much by defining them in a way that takes into account the existence of competing liberties; similarly, a legal system may decide to limit the number of values it protects. And yet the problem is quite straightforward in Dworkin's mind. In *Freedom's Law*, Dworkin elaborates the idea of 'moral reading' of the constitution, and thereby suggests that most clauses in the Bill of Rights are cast in inescapable moral language. Therefore, they have to be interpreted by appealing to political morality: 'The moral reading therefore brings political morality into the heart of constitutional law'.[44]

The moral reading is a way of stating that conflicts of individual rights are very similar to conflicts of values. But that is an overly simple way of presenting the problem. Dworkin is, of course, aware that the commitment to some abstract values is not the same thing as the commitment to some rights as entrenched in the Constitution. That is why he suggests that the moral reading needs be

---

[44] *FL*, 2.

disciplined in two important ways. First, constitutional history plays a role, although a minor one, in ascertaining what the framers intended to say—and not the different question of what other intentions they had. Second, the moral reading is disciplined by the requirement of integrity. That is, judges should not read, neither their own or others', moral convictions into the constitution. Instead, they must test their convictions against the background of the constitution, taken as a whole.

'They must regard themselves as partners with other officials, past and future, who together elaborate a *coherent constitutional morality*, and they must take care to see that what they contribute fits with the rest'.[45] This is the most explicit statement of coherentism, at the constitutional level, in Dworkin's writing.

(c) Sovereign virtue

It is not the place here to expand on Dworkin's substantive political philosophy; I will limit myself to only a few remarks in order to understand his underlying commitment to value monism. The title of his book leaves no room for doubt. Sovereign virtue refers to the existence of an overarching political virtue under which all others must be reconciled. The sovereign virtue is equality understood as 'equal concern for the fate of all the citizens'.[46] The subject matter of the book is to establish what genuine equal concern requires from government. Examining this is a very important issue from the point of view of this thesis. Dworkin spends a considerable amount of time dispelling any potential conflicts between his conception of equality and other values—liberty being the central case of possible conflict.

It is not surprising to find a sovereign virtue in Dworkin's theory of political morality. But is there room for liberty in this theory? The answer is offered in clear words: 'Any genuine conflict between liberty and equality—any conflict between liberty and the requirements of the best conception of the abstract egalitarian principle—is a contest that liberty must lose'.[47]

Assuming that the best conception of equality is Dworkin's, then where do fundamental freedoms fit within such a framework? Dworkin insists that their place is safe. The conception of equality places certain constraints on fundamental freedoms which may remove some of the advantages brought by fundamental freedoms. But what if these constraints remove all the advantages related to fundamental freedoms? In such a case, the constraint is not a valid one as it is not compatible under any defensible distribution of freedoms.[48] But this hasty conclusion is unsatisfactory as it obscures the problem of conflicts of values. Genuine conflicts arise in situations where a choice, between two mutually excluding liberties, arises. Dworkin provides an incoherent account; he states that genuine conflicts

---

[45] *FL*, 10 (emphasis added).
[46] Ronald Dworkin, *Sovereign Virtue* (Cambridge, Mass: HUP, 2001) 1 (hereafter referred to as *SV*).
[47] *SV*, 130.   [48] *SV*, 180.

never arise, but he acknowledges that if they do arise—in the case where a liberty is threatened to its core—then it means that the conception of equality must be changed.

This section did not aim to provide a comprehensive account of the moral philosophy underpinning Dworkin's theory of constitutional rights. The aim is much narrower, although it is fundamental. It attempted to uncover the philosophical assumptions at the basis of the denial of the existence of genuine conflicts of FLRs. I think that the previous discussion makes Dworkin's position clear on the question of genuine conflicts of values.

> Any genuine conflict is not just a philosophical discovery but an emotional defeat. We have that important reason for striving to show that no genuine conflict exists, that no right to liberty we would otherwise want to recognise would be compromised by the policies our conception of equality demands.[49]

Interestingly, Dworkin does not deny the conceptual possibility to demonstrate the existence of genuine conflicts of values. What he does insist on is that a theory of political morality must *strive* to show that conflicts can be avoided. But this is, as such, an entirely different matter—it is one thing to identify the conceptual possibility of conflict; it is another, to strive to reduce them to a minimum. Dworkin's argument is a curious one and, in the end, it does not appear as convincing in arguing the case of the absence of conflict of values. What he maintains is that conflicts do not exist, simply because it is more desirable if they did not exist. As such, there is a great deal of wishful thinking in this kind of argument.

B. A Procedural Theory of Constitutional Rights?

The key to the success of any theory that considers FLRs' norms as principles is to be able to measure their weight in a way that is predictable and that respects the importance of any FLR in adjudication. Alexy suggests that, in German Constitutional Law,[50] there is a form of practical reasoning that deals with competing principles, and he calls it balancing or proportionality *stricto sensu*. The latter term can be expressed as follows: 'The greater the degree of non-satisfaction of, or detriment to, one right or principle, the greater must be the importance of satisfying the other'.[51]

Balancing is presented as a necessary process when there is a collision of principles. Alexy's theoretical endeavour is to show that balancing is one of the two major forms of legal reasoning, the other being subsumption. Thus, when judges deal with rules they apply a subsumptive type of reasoning that infers certain conclusions, starting from an identifiable set of premises. Balancing, on the other

---

[49] *SV*, 131.
[50] Alexy draws back to the *Lüth*'s Case 7 B Verf GE 198, 1958 the beginning of a modern understanding of constitutional rights' adjudication. See Alexy, 'Constitutional Rights, Balancing, and Rationality', Ratio Juris 16 (2003) 132. [51] *TCR*, 102.

hand, can be broken down into three stages. First, one measures the extent of non-satisfaction of the first principle. Second, one determines the importance of satisfying the second principle. Third, it is asked whether the relationship between (1) and (2) can be justified.

Each stage involves a judgement on the intensity of interference, the degree of importance, and the relationship between the two. Each judgement can be expressed in a 'triadic scale'. This is a scheme we apply in determining the degree of interference with (or satisfaction of) the realization of a principle. The triadic scale includes terminology such as 'light', 'modest' or 'serious'. Alexy argues that in each case we are faced with, we are capable of determining whether the intensity of interference can be described as 'light', 'modest' or 'serious'. Accordingly, the first two stages involve the application of that triadic model. Once this is carried out, the third stage is simply a matter of comparing the first and the second stages and choosing which one is more rational to follow. Of course, if (1) and (2) are equal, then this involves the discretion of the judiciary in relation to what the legislator establishes.

The arithmetical nature of this balancing process should not obscure a major similarity between it and the subsumptive form of reasoning. Both start from the same premise, which is a judgement on the degree of interference. Both are purely formal, and they do not contribute anything directly to the justification of the content of the aforementioned premise.[52] Yet they do differ, so Alexy claims, in how they move from the premise to the outcome. Subsumption reaches a result by using the rules of logic, while balancing interprets the premise through numbers.

In Alexy's theory both subsumption and balancing flow from common premises or judgements. What kind of premises are they? Where do they come from? Dworkin attempted to give a ground to those kind of premises or judgements by claiming that they are 'true' or 'objective' moral propositions. That's the nature of principles. Alexy does not offer such a position. He simply assumes that principles are part of constitutional law. Then he maintains that not only can we assess numerically the importance of, or detriment to, principles, but he also asserts that we can compare these judgements as if those principles were perfectly commensurable.[53] This is hardly uncontroversial and is unlikely to convince those who do not agree with the implicit assumption that there is an objective order of values.

In my opinion, Dworkin is at least consistent all the way up, although his attempt (to claim for objectivity) reminds me more of Icarus' flight rather than Hercules' labours. Alexy, on the other hand, provides us with a thin political theory that can hardly help to strengthen the premises outlined.

Alexy's theory of constitutional rights does not provide a theory of political morality; although some assumptions are developed throughout his book. We know that constitutional rights are principles and that principles are optimization

---

[52] Robert Alexy, 'On Balancing and Subsumption. A Structural Comparison', Ratio Juris 16, (2003) 448. [53] Ibid, 442.

requirements. But, what are we exactly required to optimize? Alexy offers a completely circular definition of what principles are optimizations of. He states that the meaning of optimization actually depends on what the principles themselves mean.[54] And the definition of principles is: 'norms that require the greatest possible realisation [optimisation] of something relative to what is factually and legally possible'.[55] Hence, in short, principles are optimization requirements, and optimization is what principles require.

Alexy knows that providing a substantive definition of optimization could jeopardize his claim for the necessity for balancing in constitutional law cases. That constitutional courts apply the principle of proportionality whenever they face constitutional rights' adjudication is one of the major points stressed by Alexy.[56] However, his carefully crafted procedural position hides its inherent weaknesses behind the circular definition of optimization and principles.

Alexy's view is much more nuanced than Dworkin's, and betrays Alexy's scepticism towards a substantive theory of constitutional rights. However, the solution Alexy offers—namely the suggestion that it is possible to deal with the competition of principles through a balancing exercise—is in many ways more problematic than Dworkin's thesis.

Alexy suggests that there is an overlap between law and morality. This is observed through the comparison, and indeed the equation, between principles and values. He starts by suggesting that principles and values behave in the same way, since we can talk of competition and balance for both values and principles. He also suggests that the German Constitutional Court's discourse on conflict of values could be swapped with the language of competition of principles without any loss of meaning.[57] The primary difference between principles and values concerns their classification under the heading of deontological and axiological concepts respectively (as presented by G Von Wright). Deontological concepts belong to the realm of the ought, whereas axiological concepts belong to the realm of the good. The overlap between principles and values allows Alexy to buttress his point on the metric of principles, since he compares this to different types of value-judgements (such as classificatory comparative and metric).[58]

The important point to notice is that the overlap between values and principles is meant to capture the fundamental unity between the language of law and that of morality. Moreover, this relationship means the determination of legal sources is entangled with moral evaluation and it ultimately boils down to that. Consequently, competition of principles is dealt with by using moral evaluation.[59]

The second important feature of Alexy's own theory is the idea that constitutional courts work with an easily identifiable set of values. The most striking

---

[54] *TCR*, 397.   [55] *TCR*, 42.
[56] He insisted very recently on this point in the postscript of *TCR*.   [57] *TCR*, 86–87.
[58] *TCR*, 88.
[59] Robert Alexy, 'On Balancing and Subsumption. A Structural Comparison', Ratio Juris 16, (2003) 449.

affirmation of that position is known as the 'objective order of values' thesis developed by the German Constitutional Court.⁶⁰ Alexy argues that the articulation of a *complete and closed order of values* is a rather problematic issue, and yet he notes that it is relatively easy to outline it at an abstract level. 'A few ideas such as dignity, liberty, equality, and the protection and welfare of the community cover just about everything that needs considering when balancing constitutional principles'.⁶¹ But is this really uncontroversial? In order to really understand Alexy's position it is necessary to draw a distinction between an abstract, and a more detailed, set of values. Alexy acknowledges that to be able to identify an abstract set of values does not advance the task of adjudication between conflicting claims.

Even if an abstract set of values were easy to spell out, this would not be of much help since we would still have to determine the ranking of those values. Alexy is sceptical as to whether it is possible to work out a theory that can achieve a coherent set of values, and also establish a ranking of values. There are several problems with the idea of ranking. First, Alexy distinguishes between ordinal and cardinal ranking. Ordinal ranking works in a way that attributes a number to each value. Cardinal ranking is concerned with specific relationships between two values in order to identify a preference for one over another. Alexy rightly argues that both types of ranking are fraught with problems. On one hand, when values conflict and they have the same ordinal number (equal rank) their ranking is impossible, but on the other hand, when values conflict and they have a cardinal ranking, a right may prevail over the other without real justification. If freedom of speech always prevails over privacy, then a tyranny of values becomes a potential outcome. So far I am in agreement with Alexy.

Alexy's account is less convincing when he addresses the problem of a concrete set of values. He believes in the possibility of entrenching preferences. In order to do that, he introduces a distinction between a 'soft ordering' and a 'hard one'. A soft ordering is constituted of: (a) a set of prima facie preferences for certain values or principles; (b) a network of concrete preference-decisions. The soft ordering is achieved and justified through an exercise of balancing. But what does this all mean?

Is there a difference between preferences that are prima facie ranked but they can be overweighed if a stronger justification supervenes, and values that are equal prima facie but they have a varying weight according to circumstances? Moreover, what is the relationship between prima facie preferences and concrete preferences established by prior court decisions? For instance, in the USA there is a strong prima facie preference for free speech. In addition the US Supreme Court clearly established a network of concrete preference-decisions. Does this mean that privacy will never be able to outweigh free speech? Again which right is weightier? A prima facie preference or a clear line of preference-decisions? Is there any

---

⁶⁰ Robert Alexy, 'Constitutional Rights, Balancing, and Rationality', above n 50, passim.
⁶¹ *TCR*, 96.

difference? When a court systematically protects one right, does this establish an outright prima facie preference?

Alexy's notion of soft ordering appears to be fully circular: principles are qualitatively different from rules, insofar as they possess a dimension of weight that can only be ascertained through balancing. Balancing clearly differs from subsumption in that balancing attempts to measure the weight, while subsumption works only with hard rules. Alexy takes a controversial position, both at the abstract level and at a more concrete one. He acknowledges that it is difficult to work one's way down from the abstract to the concrete level. But this does not seem to prevent him from establishing a soft ordering at the concrete level.

To conclude, Alexy's theory is monist by default: he does not want to engage in substantive moral arguments but he is quite willing to assume that the system of constitutional rights has a strong monist component. But what is more important to note is that Alexy is compelled to show how any competition of principles can always be equated to an exercise of balancing, thus dispelling any potential dilemma.

The underlying value pluralist thesis that I prefer insists on the importance of the conflict of values. The implication of that position is that FLRs are very likely to conflict in the legal realm. As a corollary to that position, the notion of FLRs as principles can be doubted. For this very reason I put forward, in the second chapter, an alternative understanding of FLRs, which is meant to illuminate the way in which FLRs conflict.

4. Conflicts of FLRs: From Morality to Law

Conflicts of FLRs cannot be defined away or avoided. They are bound to stay with us and haunt theorists and practioners. To believe that we can construe a harmonious realm of constitutional essentials is not only naive, it is deeply problematic as it blurs our understanding of some central constitutional issues as well as human tragedies. In order to achieve harmonious results Dworkin defends what he calls a 'moral reading' of the constitution; but it does not help in achieving better solutions. It simply adds to the confusion we face regarding the proper articulations of some of our basic values. The US Constitution, for example (and especially its Bill of Rights) must be given a 'moral reading'. As it is this provides an already startling proposition. It states something that needs to be proved; namely that lawyers sometimes engage in a legal reading, and sometimes in a moral reading. The moral reading, however, is considered a natural reading of constitutional principles as encapsulating rights. But what is this 'moral reading?' Dworkin never explains it precisely. Roughly, the moral reading requires that the Constitution be read in light of the best moral philosophy available. Needless to say, for Dworkin, the best moral theory is his own theory; thus a moral reading should see equal concern and respect as its overarching goal. To be fair, we can further understand Dworkin's moral reading by focusing on its constraints. When engaging in the moral reading, a judge should bear in mind what the framers intended to say (history) and what other judges said about it before him (integrity). Since Dworkin's moral reading is not given any particular definition, a standard interpretation could be the following: a judge is free to read the constitution as he wishes, provided that he respects the limits set by history and integrity. Admittedly those two constraints alone are quite demanding. And yet, they do not contribute to our understanding of the moral reading itself.

In contrast with the moral reading, I propose a 'constitutional reading' of bills of rights that will be outlined in chapter 4. The constitutional reading I favour plainly accepts the fact of genuine conflicts of FLRs. This means that it does not attempt to dissolve them or define them away. If genuine conflicts exist they can only be adjudicated. By furthering understanding of some legal and social phenomena, it also aims at placating possible social breakdowns that arise from the lack of communication between individuals or groups who hold strong beliefs on certain deeply controversial issues.

The constitutional reading leaves the door open to deeper, non-legal, interpretations of conflicts of FLRs. If we take medical ethics, for example, it is far from clear that legal practitioners should take the lead in the resolution of those cases. Should we allow euthanasia? Should we separate Siamese twins? Should we withdraw life-supporting treatments? These questions may go beyond the normal reach of legal interpretation and practice. They are questions broader than life, quite literally. They therefore deserve close scrutiny and a wider perspective than a strictly judicial one. Medical dilemmas may point to a failure of our communities *qua* ethical communities, and not simply to a failure of our legal system to cope with hard cases.

Genuine conflicts of FLRs may be very few numerically if compared to other cases that are routinely decided.[62] However, to decide a genuine conflict does not amount to providing a case-by-case analysis. It means to prioritize certain values over others under certain circumstances. By so doing, we may reshape the whole identity of our communities. We have to think carefully before suggesting outcomes that are potentially disruptive. Courts are sometimes asked to take decisions that go beyond their responsibility or competence.[63]

If courts are prepared to deal with such issues, however, we should understand what type of guidance bills of rights give. In the USA, for instance, the battle is between a history-based and a philosophy-based reading of the Constitution. My suggestion is that we have to go beyond such a dichotomy and propose a more encompassing reading of the Constitution.[64] This means that instead of being

---

[62] The notion of genuine conflicts of FLRs will be studied in ch 3.
[63] A good example is the case of *Evans v the UK* (Application No 6339/05), 7 March 2006.
[64] For a similar endeavour, see Richard H Fallon Jr, *Implementing the Constitution* (Cambridge, Mass: HUP, 2002).

pulled in one or the other direction, courts should bring together both history and philosophy within their own constitutional umbrella, which is constituted by an institutional and procedural framework.

This does not mean that philosophy or history do not play roles. On the contrary, they can be extremely useful for elucidating certain clauses where their meaning is obscure. In a sense history and philosophy can also be understood as constraints on the reading of the constitution. A judge must respect constitutional history. Thus, if one of his interpretations defies history, this may mean that interpretation is not accurate. Similarly, if an interpretation is completely repugnant to his view of morality, then he may well decide to exercise his FLR to civil disobedience.

5. Conclusion

In this chapter, FLRs were loosely defined as rules entrenched in bills of rights, and judicially enforced over all other rules. That characterization of FLRs in terms of rules was opposed to much more widespread theories of constitutional rights which treat rights as principles. Principles, as possessing a dimension of weight or importance, would either require a substantive constitutional theory that provides a right answer as to the weight of each principle in any given case; or a procedural theory that justifies the rationality of every decision taken by a court. However, the existence of genuine conflicts of FLRs points to the fact that in certain cases neither a right nor a rational answer are readily available; these cases underlie the weaknesses of mainstream theories of constitutional rights such as Ronald Dworkin's or Robert Alexy's.

Some commentators suggest that Dworkin's Rights Thesis cannot be taken seriously because it did not pay enough attention to the nature and structure of rights.[65] Others have argued that Alexy's conception of constitutional rights as principles commanding optimization undermines the *firmness* of rights, by requiring that sometimes rights be outweighed by collective goals.[66] Their firmness can only be guaranteed by a deontological structure, that is, by their having the character of rules.[67] Both lines of criticism (of which there are many more), insist on the lack of analysis or the inaccurate analysis of the nature, and structure of rights. Chapter 2 will offer a stipulative definition of FLRs that singles out the main structural features of constitutional rights.

---

[65] Neil MacCormick, 'Taking the "Rights Thesis" seriously' in *Legal Right and Social Democracy—Essays in Legal and Political Philosophy* (Oxford: Clarendon Press, 1982), esp. 140–45. For a similar critique of lack of analysis, Andrew Halpin, *Rights & Law—Analysis & Theory* (Oxford: Hart Publishing, 2001) 4–8. See also Matthew H Kramer, 'Rights without Trimmings' in Matthew Kramer, Nigel Simmonds, and Hillel Steiner, *A Debate Over Rights* (Oxford: OUP 1999) 36–37.
[66] Jurgen Habermas, *Between Facts and Norms* (trans W Rehg) (Cambridge, Mass: HUP, 1996) 254.
[67] Ibid.

Finally, I would like to point out a last justification in supporting the 'constitutional reading' of bills of rights. Law is rooted in conflicts, as was stated at the outset. From this viewpoint, FLRs are double-edged swords. On one hand, they help solving certain cases by providing strong reasons that support a right holder's claim. On the other, FLRs give rise to constitutional dilemmas, especially when they clash with one another. Sometimes these conflicts are merely spurious, and it is sufficient to define the scope or the strength of the FLRs at stake in order to clarify the quandary. Other times, FLRs give rise to genuine conflicts as the two FLRs are jointly incompatible. A constitutional tragedy lurks behind these types of conflict. However, even in this case, the society is compelled to come up with an answer. What is clear is that no right answer, in those cases, is possible. Nor is there an answer that is inherently more rational than others. In such instances there are a number of reasonable solutions; though in each, a loss for one party remains inevitable.

2
The Concept of Fundamental Legal Rights

1. FLRs and Analysis

Fundamental Legal Rights (FLRs) are complex concepts that have several layers. The very acronym I have selected points to this issue. We are not simply talking about rights. We are concerned with legal rights as opposed to moral. Moreover we are focusing on fundamental rights as opposed to ordinary ones. This stipulative definition, however, is not immediately self-explanatory. The present chapter aims to clarify various questions related to the notion of FLRs I have put forward. I believe the only way to know more about conflicts of FLRs is to accurately examine the objects that clash.

In the vast literature on rights, it is often the case that rights are presented through the looking glass of a selected aspect. One may choose, for example, to study rights from the point of view of their role or scope in legal or moral reasoning. I will attempt to study FLRs from four different angles: their structure, their point, their content, and their function. By structure, I mean the basic ingredients that constitute FLRs. By point, I mean the reasons that make FLRs so important. By content, I mean the scope of actions and behaviours to which FLRs apply. By function, I mean the tasks FLRs perform within legal systems.

The present chapter mirrors the questions just raised. Therein, I provide an outline of the structure, point, content and function of rights, and an explanation of FLRs as distinguished from ordinary rights. Section 2 will discuss some forms of reductionism in rights discourse. Section 3 will provide a historical overview of the debates on the structure and point of rights in general. Section 4 will focus on the scope (or content) of FLRs in particular. Section 5 will present the function of FLRs within institutional frameworks. Finally, section 6 will offer a conclusive explanation on the stipulative definition of FLRs I use throughout this book.

2. A Preliminary Problem: Reductionism

The structure of rights is a very complex matter. Most of the scholars confronted with this problem propose a formula, with the aim of reducing the structure of rights down to one simple idea. There are two broad types of reductionism: a philosophical, and an analytical reductionism of rights.

Philosophical reductionism: this form of reductionism is inspired by the rejection of utilitarianism, a widespread political philosophy that attempts to maximize happiness. This collective aim prevails over individual interests. Rawls, Nozick, and Dworkin expressed their criticisms of utilitarianism in the clearest terms. In order to do this, they developed conceptions of rights that were expressly opposed to the utilitarian calculus. Rights are thus considered, either as 'trumps' over utility (Dworkin), or as 'side constraints' to utility (Nozick). These two very simplified presentations of the theories stem from a fundamental criticism of utilitarianism: it did not reflect the separateness of people.

Utilitarianism is commonly depicted as rejecting the rhetoric of rights. Bentham's and Austin's invectives against moral rights are all too well-known, and need no rehearsal here.

For our purposes, it is sufficient to recall that the project of social reforms defended by utilitarianism was grounded on the central concept of utility, as opposed to the notion of rights favoured by certain partisans of the French and American revolutions.

Analytical reductionism: 'Law' and 'rights' are the most controversial concepts of legal and moral theory. In English they are linguistically kept separate, but in French (Droit), German (Recht), Italian (Diritto), and Spanish (Derecho) 'law' and 'right' are expressed by the same term. This linguistic issue alone points to a very difficult problem for legal theory; namely, the reduction of the language of rights to the language of law.[1] The question is whether we can meaningfully distinguish between 'subjective rights' and 'objective law' or whether we should simply merge the two linguistic systems. At the outset, there seems to be little overlap between the language of 'subjective rights', that talks of interests, will, need etc . . . and the language of law that refers to obligations, prohibitions, and permissions. The two languages belong to entirely different groups, according to Georg von Wright, who distinguishes between deontological, axyological, and anthropological concepts.[2] According to him, the language of law belongs to the deontological group, whereas the language of subjective rights belongs to the anthropological group.

A recent study suggests that the idea of 'subjective rights' and that of 'objective law' cannot coexist. The suggestion is that constitutional rights are often presented as shields around certain actions, but they would better be understood

---

[1] On this issue, see Alf Ross, *On Law and Justice* (1958), ch V. See also Richard Tur, 'The leaves on the trees', (1976) Juridical Review. More recently, Bruno Celano, 'I diritti nella jurisprudence anglosassone contemporanea. Da Hart a Raz', in Paolo Comanducci e Riccardo Guastini, *Analisi e diritto* (2001). For a recent debate in the USA, see Matthew Adler, 'Personal Rights and Rule dependence' 6 Legal Theory (2000) 337–89.
[2] Georg von Wright, *The Logic of Preference* (Edinburgh: EUP, 1963) 7.

as shields against rules.³ Constitutional adjudication is overwhelmingly rule-dependent, it is held, and that is the manner by which rights should be understood also. This viewpoint claims originality, but in fact it merely reproduces continental debates on the reduction of 'subjective rights' to 'objective law'.

A second form of analytical reduction of the concept of rights is based on the supposedly axiomatic correlative relation between rights and duties. In this context, 'correlative' means that, for each right of a person X, there exists a corresponding duty of a person Y, and vice versa. If this were true, then it would be easy to say that a right of X exists, if and only if, a duty has been imposed on Y. Since a legal duty is always established by legislation, it is possible to tie the existence of a right to the existence of a duty, in a way that signifies the logical priority of the duty. Thus, a reduction of a right into a duty occurs.

3. The Structure and Point of Rights[4]

The 20th century saw the seminal work of Wesley Newcomb Hohfeld, *Fundamental Legal Conceptions*.[5] Hohfeld believed in the possibility of breaking down into basic elements all legal concepts in order to help eliminate a certain amount of logical errors committed by practitioners. In addition, he provided lawyers with useful tools, with which legal problems could be more easily dealt with.[6] Hohfeld believed that, when we refer to a right, we are in fact conflating four different terms: claim, power, privilege, and immunity.

Hohfeld presents a very valuable attempt to explore the deeper structure of rights. After breaking rights into four different concepts, he claims that these are basic elements of every jural relation. The evolution of legal theory on rights saw the criticism of Hohfeld on the basis that those concepts were not as basic or as accurate as he had presented them. Moreover, Hohfeld's theory was most criticized for not providing a unifying viewpoint (the *point* of rights), which is what HLA Hart attempts to do by introducing a normative layer into the analytical theory of rights. Subsequently, Hart was criticized for not having provided a theory general enough to embrace all types of rights.

We will now examine three kinds of theories of rights that have emerged at different historical periods. This general picture reflects an Anglo-American debate, but, where possible, some parallels will be drawn between it and the

---

[3] Matthew Adler, 'Rights against Rules: The Moral Structure of American Constitutional Law', 97 Mich LR 1 (1998). See also Matthew Adler, 'Rights, Rules and the Structure of Constitutional Adjudication: A Response to Professor Fallon', 113 HLR 1321 (2000).

[4] Here I focus on the question of the structure of FLRs exclusively. This issue must be distinguished from the question of the structure of norms of FLRs, on one hand, and from the problem of the articulation of FLRs, on the other.

[5] WN Hohfeld, *Fundamental Legal Conceptions as Applied in Judicial Reasoning*, new edition by D Campbell and Philip Thomas (Aldershot: Ashgate/Dartmouth, 2001). First published as two separate articles in (1913) 23 Yale LJ 16 and (1917) 26 Yale LJ 710.   [6] Ibid, 4.

European/Continental debates. The first set of theories reflects an analytical concern for the misuse of rights. Hohfeld's view is the cornerstone of that debate and his theory is (not very accurately) characterized as purely analytical. Hart shares the same analytical concern, but goes beyond this by showing that a philosophical theory can be developed—with the starting point being analysis. The second set of theories insists on the normative side of rights, and inverts the Hohfeldian perspective, insofar as it suggests that the normative element is prior to the analytical. The third tries to go beyond both the interest and the will theories.[7]

A. From Hohfeld to Hart: From Analysis to Theory

(i) Hohfeld's table of jural relations

Hohfeld begins his essay by distinguishing between legal and non-legal conceptions. He insists that most of the legal confusion stems from conflating legal with mental and physical relations (eg 'X is under a duty' establishes a legal relation. 'X has an interest in something against Y' is a mental relation. 'X can exercise his force against Y' is a physical relation). In addition, Hohfeld denounces the looseness of legal language. For instance, property sometimes refers to a thing (X's property is Z), and sometimes refers to an interest (X's property is his right over Z). Then, a second distinction is made, in order to dispel another set of ambiguities. Here we are concerned with the distinction between operative and evidential facts. Operative facts are the conditions set out by rules, for the purpose of modifying a legal relation. Evidential facts are those under which other facts can be deduced.

After making these two preliminary points, Hohfeld presents his table of fundamental jural relations that is reproduced below. The purpose of setting out this table is to shed light on difficult topics such as trust, equity, and other legal disciplines. Hohfeld fears that the complexity of these issues results from the ambiguity of the concepts used, namely the lack of clarity as to the relation between right and duty. There are four fundamental pairs of concepts that can be organized under the headings of jural opposites or jural correlatives. Jural opposites are simply the negation of each other (right/no-right; power/disability). Jural correlatives are mutually related, that is, each one entails the other (the existence of a duty in X corresponds to the existence of a right in Y).

Jural Opposites	right	privilege	power	immunity
	no-right	duty	disability	liability
Jural Correlatives	right	privilege	power	immunity
	duty	no-right	liability	disability

[7] It has been suggested that the debate between interest and will theories of rights ended in a standoff. See Leif Wenar, 'The Nature of Rights', Philosophy and Public Affairs 33 (2005) 223–52. I agree with this general point, although I am not convinced that Wenar advances a genuine third way in theories of rights.

Hohfeld holds that the term 'right' is often used in legal language in a very broad sense corresponding to four different concepts: right, privilege, power, and immunity. Hohfeld proposes to use right only as the first basic conception, that which is correlative to duty, and is opposite to 'no-right'. Hence, the conditions for a right to exist are: the existence of a relation between two persons, and the existence of a duty for one of those two persons (the other party will be the right-holder). For instance, if X has a right that Y stays off X's land, the correlative is that Y is under a duty toward X to stay off the land. Hohfeld also adds that it could be possible to replace the word 'right' with the word 'claim' in this relation.

The second correlative relation is privilege/no-right. Yet again, one term helps to define the other, and the relation is between two persons. If X has a privilege over Y, then Y has a no-right against X. Privilege can also be defined by its opposite—duty. Privilege occurs in a situation in which there is an absence of duty on X, in his relation with Y, who has a no-right vis-à-vis X. Thus, in Hohfeld's example, X has a claim against Y for him to stay off the land, but X has the privilege of entering the land.

The third correlative relation is power/liability. Whoever holds a legal power, in Hohfeld's scheme, can alter legal relations. The closest synonym to legal power is legal ability, and that is the opposite of legal disability. Hence, whoever is under a liability, must abide by the changes of a legal relation. In Hohfeld's example, X has the power to enter into a contract with Y and to grant him the right to enter the land, in exchange for Y's duty to work for X. In this case, the exercise of X's power entails Y's liability.

The final correlative relation is immunity/disability. Immunity acts as a shield against liability; that is a shield against obedience to the change in legal relations. If X is immune, this means that X will not be affected by any legal change, as enacted by the holder of a legal power in a given context. In other words, X is free from any change brought about by Y's legal power. Immunity is the most useful concept in constitutional law. It is possible to imagine that Y (for example, the parliament) has the legal power to change X's relations. In this sense, X is liable. But in certain cases, X may have an immunity from change (this case depicts how a FLR protects an individual against the state), where X's immunity from change corresponds to Y's disability. For instance, Y (the parliament) may be disabled to create a burden on X's immunity with regard to free speech.

Hohfeld concludes by stating that those four pairs of attributes are the lowest common denominators within the law. This may prove very valuable, as reducing issues to their simplest level, may help in discovering similarities in different areas of law. This, in turn, can help jurists in their use of arguments and precedents from all areas of law, and in their application of them to other areas. Thus, hidden similarities can appear thanks to the analysis provided in Hohfeld's basic legal conceptions.

It is helpful to make some observations here. First, Hohfeld's scheme depends on the correlativity between certain concepts. Hence, if a right is correlative to a duty, then the existence of a right is dependent on the existence of a duty. Second, Hohfeld's scheme applies only to any relation between two persons. Third, the legal relations that may help us understand FLRs is that of immunity. This will be dealt with in a later chapter. Let us turn to HLA Hart's theory of rights.

(ii) HLA Hart: the structure of rights and the choice theory of rights

In his *Essays on Bentham*, Hart argues that Bentham is far more thought provoking than Hohfeld on the topic of legal rights.[8] Bentham distinguishes three types of rights that roughly correspond to Hohfeld's 'claim-right', 'privilege', and 'power'—although he does not identify a category close to 'immunity'. Unlike Hohfeld, who refers to a right *stricto sensu* only in terms of a claim-right, Bentham does not use such a disclaimer.

Bentham, from the outset, outlines a fundamental distinction between rights grounded in an obligation imposed by the law (1), and rights grounded in the absence of legal obligation (2). The latter is defined as a right (of the right-holder) to do or to abstain from doing an action. The former is defined as a right to services; that is a right to the action or the forbearance of the duty-bearer. Permissive laws are the source of the latter, while coercive laws are the source of the former. Permissions can be active, inactive or silent. It is active when a law permits what was previously prohibited; it is inactive when the law simply declares that an action is permitted, even though it was not prohibited before. The permission is silent when the law does not make any express prohibition. The permissive type of right (2) Bentham identifies corresponds to a silent permission and Hart calls this 'liberty-right'. The right stemming from an obligation imposed by the law can be called 'right correlative to obligation (1)'. Hart starts with an analysis of the 'liberty-right'.

A liberty-right is a negative notion and many thought of it as empty of legal significance. In fact, as Hart explains, it is a crucial notion in understanding many legal relations, such as ownership or economic competition. Hart adds two important rejoinders. First, Bentham often refers to a bilateral liberty when he thinks of liberty-rights. That is, a man is neither under an obligation to nor is he under an obligation not to—he can make up his mind as to whether to do something. For instance, X is at liberty to look Y in the eyes. But, Y has no duty to be looked in the eyes. Y can wear sunglasses to prevent X from looking into his eyes. But, more generally, Y has a duty of non-interference with X's liberty-right, insofar as Y cannot punch X in the face, if X wishes to look into Y's eyes.

A right correlative to an obligation is a right to a service to be performed by a duty-bearer. Every duty imposed by law has a correlative right (with two minor exceptions that are of no interest here). Hence, to have a right correlative to an obligation is to be the person intended to benefit from the performance of the

---

[8] HLA Hart, 'Legal Rights' in HLA Hart, *Essays on Bentham* (Oxford: Clarendon Press, 1982) 162–95.

obligation. This is the *point* of a 'benefit theory of rights' as expounded by Bentham.

The third type of rights identified by Bentham is a legal power. Hart identifies two ways in which Bentham speaks of legal power. First, Bentham defines legal powers when a person can interfere with, or physically control, things or bodies. Second, and more interestingly, Bentham describes legal powers as being 'investitive' or 'divestitive'. These are powers to alter legal relations; this definition coincides with Hohfeld's legal conceptions. Bentham specifies that laws generally impose duties, or else they are permissive. Laws granting powers are labelled as 'imperfect laws', and these leave a blank to be filled by the power-holder.

Having brushed a general picture of Bentham's three fundamental conceptions, Hart proceeds to a criticism of Bentham, and to the elaboration of his own theory. This, in contrast with Bentham's benefit theory, is a will (or choice) theory of rights.

First, Hart comes back to the notion of liberty-rights to explain why he considers it so important, and indeed central, to any account of legal rights. Hart explains that even if a liberty-right is negative, it entails nonetheless a perimeter of obligations that make it a real right. For instance, if I walk down the street, my liberty-right implies a duty of non-interference, as well as some other duties, that the state has to protect. Hart insists that both the liberty and the perimeter are important notions and, as such, they must be kept separate. He then provides an example in relation to economic competition. Two men, who, walking down the street, see a purse, may engage in a competition to win the purse (they are at liberty to do so in this sense). However, both enjoy a perimeter of protection consisting of a duty of non-interference with each other's race to the purse. One cannot knock down the competitor while running toward the purse.

To sum up, the existence of a liberty-right has two separate requirements. First, its core is a bilateral liberty, that is, a liberty to, or not to do something. Second, the liberty-right must be secured by a perimeter of non-correlative duties. On this second point, Hart insists that Bentham was ambiguous and confusing. This criticism is made on the basis of Bentham's claim that a liberty could either be 'vested' or 'naked', that is either protected by a perimeter of obligation or not, and yet still be a right. Hart makes it clear that only a 'vested liberty' can be a right.

Hart also criticizes Bentham's benefit theory of rights on the very idea of benefit. According to Bentham, every obligation is correlative to the right of a person who is intended to benefit from the performance of the obligation. Thus, if a duty-bearer does not perform his obligation, he violates a right. There are two types of breach: one is private, and the other is public. The former is the breach of a duty towards an individual (assignable person). The latter is the breach of a duty towards the community (unassignable person). An assignable person is an individual duly identified by name or by description. Even if deeply unclear, that notion helps us distinguish between offences to assignable persons, and offences to the public (intended as a collection of individuals who benefits from the compliance with the law by the duty-bearer). A second feature of Bentham's benefit theory is precisely concerned with benefit (or its opposite, detriment). A benefit is loosely related to Bentham's utilitarian distinction between pleasure and pain. But more generally, a benefit corresponds to the maintaining of a treatment that is regarded as desirable. Therefore, every single breach of the law is necessarily of detriment to individuals and in this way the respect of the law is a benefit. Finally, within such a framework, we can understand the phrase 'intended by the law to benefit' as merely meaning that a breach of the law entails a detriment to individuals. This final point constitutes the last element of a 'strong benefit theory', and is the primary target of Hart's attack.

Bentham's benefit theory of rights correlative to duties brings us back to the fundamental problem of reduction of rights in another language. Indeed, it would seem that an accurate account of duties would provide all the information, and therefore rights would amount to a pleonasm. The charge of redundancy that a benefit theorist faces, Hart explains, can be met by introducing a distinction between absolute and relative duties. In the broadest sense, absolute duties pertain to criminal law, whereas relative duties pertain to civil law. The main difference is one of standing: the right-holder of a civil law right is considered as having mini-sovereignty over the correlative duty of the duty-bearer. That is, the right holder has a measure of control that amounts to his legal powers to waive performance, take steps after the breach, and waive compensation. Instead of a benefit, Hart sees that measure of control as central to every right, and this is also the *point* of Hart's will theory. A second major advantage of Hart's theory is the explanation of contracts that benefit a third party. According to Bentham's benefit theory, the third party is considered as being the right-holder. Yet this is not the case, as the third party is only the beneficiary of a service, and he has to be distinguished from the right-holder, who has stipulated the contract with the duty-bearer, and has control over the performance of the contractual duty.

Unlike both Hohfeld's and Bentham's theories, Hart's will theory has the main advantage of providing a unifying core concept (the point of rights) for the explanation of various categories of rights (ie that of control, or bilateral liberty): especially considering bilateral liberty is the core of a liberty right in the same way that it is central to a legal power. Equally, it is the core of a right correlative to a duty, which, in Hohfeld's theory, is merely a subcategory of a legal power.

However, Hart points to the main limit of his own theory; that is, it does not account for constitutional freedoms and benefits, as protected by bills of rights. An explanation of this lies in the focus of both Bentham's and Hart's theories. They are designed to explain the concept of rights at work in ordinary law, such as civil or criminal law. Fundamental rights, however, belong to the realm of constitutional law, and amount to a limitation of the state's power to make the law, when such a change would abridge or excessively limit any fundamental right. In order to explain such a right, both theories would have to bring in the concept of immunity, as explained by Hohfeld, but neglected by both Bentham and Hart.

The avowed limits of Hart's theory are illuminating for our purpose; namely, a working definition of FLRs. Hart confirms that the concept of immunity, as Hohfeld identified it, is a preliminary candidate for the explanation of FLRs.[9] Hart also points out that both his and Bentham's theories are not fit for explaining the notion of a FLR. Although this is only half way to the goal, it is very important to know what a theory of FLR is *not* concerned with. Also, this helps in understanding subsequent criticism of Hart's theory on the grounds that he simply did not explain the notion of FLRs. It is mainly to these criticisms that we now turn.

B. Carl Wellman: The Will Theory as Applied to FLRs

An Approach to Rights[10] provides a developed analysis of a will theory as applied to rights entrenched in bills of rights. Wellman starts his analysis by pointing to the fact that the text of constitutions defines our constitutional rights in terms of mere labels or short descriptions. Hence, in order to guide or regulate our legal practices, we ought to define the meaning of those phrases in much more detail. Moreover, we have to interpret the expression 'the right to' within the constitution, as well as in court decisions. Thus, for instance, in the statement 'the right to life', it is important to know the scope of 'life', but it is equally important to know what 'the right to' means. Wellman explains that if we take Hohfeld's theory, then a right is a claim against others. In his example, therefore, one's right to life is a claim against others not to take one's life. Accordingly, the right to life will correspond to a duty of a physician not to kill a terminally ill patient. If, on the contrary, we take Hart's stance, then the right will be interpreted as a freedom of choice; as a consequence, the right to life will amount to one's freedom to choose whether to continue living or not.

Wellman regards Hohfeld's categories as very valuable in understanding constitutional rights, although he does not share Hohfeld's normative suggestion as to which claims are the only rights strictly speaking. This, Wellman explains, would simply overlook some of the most important features of certain rights. For instance, freedom of speech is a claim against both the government and other individuals, but actually the central element is the liberty of speaking out in public.

The only theorist who shares in Hohfeld's normative account of rights, as Wellman points out, is Feinberg.[11] Feinberg accepts the idea that, strictly speaking, a right is a claim, and also that to 'have a claim' is to be in a position to claim. However, not every claim is a right; there exists conflicting claims where only one of them is a right. This is established after having decided which claim has priority over the other. As a consequence, only valid claims are real rights. Feinberg's account stresses the value of rights to individual right-holders. But his account is

---

[9] Of course, immunity should be understood as 'immunity in a constitutional law' context.
[10] Carl Wellman, *An Approach to Rights—Studies in the Philosophy of Law and Morals* (Dordrecht: Kluwer Academic Press, 1997).
[11] Joel Feinberg, *Rights, Justice, and the Bounds of Liberty* (Princeton NJ: PUP, 1980).

fraught with the same problem as Hohfeld's: it forces all rights into the same mould of valid legal claims.

Hohfeld's and Feinberg's weaknesses strengthen Hart's position. Hart acknowledges the diversity of rights, while striving to spot the common features within this diversity. A legal right is a legally protected choice, he claims. At its core is a bilateral liberty, and it is surrounded by a protective perimeter of the duties of others not to interfere with the right holder's exercise of a bilateral liberty. Even though Hart's theory may be valuable in understanding that rights are concerned with the distribution of freedom, he himself recognizes the inability of the theory in explaining certain (unwaivable) immunities, such as the fifth Amendment of the US Constitution (not to be put in jeopardy twice). Wellman suggests that his own outline of legal rights could be more helpful in understanding constitutional rights. Hart's limit lies in the fact that his concept of right distributes freedom, but does not guarantee dominion over another party. Now, in the case of a conflict of rights, one of the two clashing rights must enable one right holder to claim dominion over the other. A right is 'a system of Hohfeld's positions that, if respected, confer dominion on one party in a potential confrontation over a specific domain.'[12]

I do not share in Wellman's idea of dominion. It is based on a legal realist understanding of law, according to which a right is nothing more than an *ex post* statement of the outcome of a particular lawsuit. According to that understanding, every case involving constitutional rights is a conflict of rights in a loose sense, since a court's decision is commonly seen as the solution of a conflict.

C. MacCormick and Raz: Non-Hohfeldian Interest Theories of Rights

Hohfeld was exclusively concerned with the problem of the structure of rights. As a good chemist, he wanted to boil down the ambiguous concept of rights into a set of basic elements that would be more intelligible. Hart shares in part of that endeavour, but he adds a second fundamental dimension to the enquiry on rights: he seeks to define the *point* of having a right. That is, what kind of normative justification we appeal to when we hold that we ought to have a right to x. Hart's answer is that, when law protects a right, it seeks to give to the individual a power of choice; that is the unifying *point* of 'having a right'.

A number of subsequent theorists have focused mainly on the normative dimension highlighted by Hart, and dismiss Hohfeld's analytical contribution as being reductive of the notion of rights to that of duty.[13] However, these theorists

---

[12] Carl Wellman, *An Approach to Rights* (n 10 above) 26.
[13] Neil MacCormick, 'Rights in Legislation' in PMS Hacker and J Raz (eds), *Law, Morality, and Society—Essays in honour of H.L.A. Hart* (Oxford: OUP, 1977) 189. Joseph Raz, *The Morality of Freedom* (Oxford: OUP, 1986).

oppose Hart's notion that choice is at the core of rights. Instead, the more recent rights theorists insist that the proper *normative justification* for having a right is to be found in the idea of interest. Someone has a right if his interest is important enough to hold someone else under a duty to fulfil that interest. This idea of interest is broader than that of choice, since it treats the notion of choice as one among many interests an individual can have. From the viewpoint of the interest theory, a right is always prior to a duty, since a right is defined as the reason that justifies imposing a duty upon someone else.

Concentrating on the normative justification (the point of rights) gives theories of rights a broader perspective: in this, they are not only concerned with legal rights alone, but also with moral rights. If there really exists a normative justification for a person to have a right, then this must be the same justification for both legal and moral rights. This marks a fundamental shift in jurisprudence. Legal theory is not solely concerned with the analytical enquiry of law anymore. It aims to unravel the normative foundations of the social phenomenon called law. In what follows, I will briefly sketch the argument against Hart's choice theory, and then I will outline the main tenets of interest theories.

(i) MacCormick: the interest theory of rights as a criticism of Hart

MacCormick's arguments are simple and powerful.[14] First, he attacks Hart's choice theory, and then he explains the gist of his interest theory of rights: (1) Hart's choice theory cannot explain why certain categories of people, such as babies, have rights.[15] (2) The interest theory is easily stated: 'the essential feature of rules which confer rights is that they have as a specific aim the protection or advancement of individual interests or goods'.[16] The argument against the choice theory is clear: children have rights. Hence, the claim of Hart's theory must be confronted with that question. However, the choice theory fails this test and must therefore be abandoned. To be more precise, children have, for instance, the right to food and assistance. As such, we cannot give an account of these rights in terms of children's power to enforce, or to waive parental duties in this context. Thus, either we hold that children have no rights, or we reject the choice theory.

The argument for the interest theory is more complex. To have a right, for MacCormick, means to assert reasons in favour of a treatment (T) for a certain category (C). 'To ascribe to all members of a class C a right to treatment T is to presuppose that T is, in all normal circumstances, a good for every member of C, and that T is a good of such importance that it would be wrong to deny it to or withhold it from any member of C.'[17] Hence, generally speaking, rights are goods

---

[14] Thanks to Neil MacCormick for his comments on this chapter. MacCormick goes beyond his interest theory and formulates a theory of constitutional rights. See for example his forthcoming revised edition of *Institutions of Law* (Oxford: OUP, 2007).

[15] Neil MacCormick, 'Children's Rights: A Test Case for Theories of Rights', (1976) *Archiv für Rechts und Sozialphilosophie*, 62.   [16] N 13 above.

[17] Neil MacCormick (n 15 above) 311.

which ought to be secured by individuals. Thus, the difference between choice theory and interest theory regards the reasons for attribution of rights. The choice theory insists on the protection of a limited sovereignty of the individual, while the interest theory insists on the individual's well-being.

At the outset, the interest theory is appealing, especially when it is read against the background of utilitarianism. Thomas Scanlon summarizes it: 'in attacking utilitarianism one is inclined to appeal to individual rights, which mere considerations of social utility cannot justify us in overriding. But rights themselves need to be justified somehow, and how other than by appeal to the human interests their recognition promotes and protects?'[18] The interest theory places itself in opposition to a number of points made in Hohfeld's approach. First, a right does not only concern the relation between two individuals. Second, there is a common core to all rights. Third, there is no necessary correlation between duty and rights. Fourth, rights are prior to duties insofar as rights are reasons to hold someone else under a duty.

The most important point, in my opinion, concerns the logical priority of rights over duties. Hart makes the same point against Hohfeld, when he argued the language of rights could not possibly be reduced to the language of duties (redundancy thesis). Hart then suggested that the language of right had a unity, and a priority, insofar as it embeds the idea of choice. Interest theorists argued that their theory is superior to the choice theory, as it can fully explain the reasons for attributing rights to people. We do consider that a person has a right, when the person has an interest of certain importance or weight.[19]

(ii) Raz: an interest theory of constitutional rights?

In *Morality of Freedom*, Raz provides an extensive account of how freedom is defined by the fundamental rights that individuals hold. He first develops his own version of the interest theory of rights, and in a later chapter he draws some conclusions as to the constitutional role of fundamental rights. It is to the constitutional role of rights that we now turn.

A person has a fundamental (moral) right when he has an interest of ultimate value, ie inasmuch as the value of that interest does not derive from some other interest of the right-holder, or from other persons.[20] Thus far, Raz applies what we already know about the interest theory to a special type of rights. Later on, Raz questions the role of rights in constitutional democracies. His position

---

[18] TM Scanlon, 'Rights, Goals and Fairness' in Waldron (ed), *Theories of Rights* (Oxford: OUP, 1984) 137.

[19] Note that this idea echoes of Dworkin's idea of rights as principles having a dimension of weight or importance. Interestingly, the interest theory is explicitly pluralist, as it accepts any interest as a ground of rights provided that it has a certain importance or weight in achieving a person's well-being (Joseph Raz, *The Morality of Freedom* (Oxford: OUP, 1986) 192). On the contrary, Dworkin's theory of rights is distinctively monist, since every right is ultimately grounded in the idea of equal respect and concern.   [20] Joseph Raz, *The Morality of Freedom* (Oxford: OUP, 1986) 192.

is a peculiar one, since he does not believe that rights serve the purpose of articulating fundamental principles, nor does he think that they protect a personal interest of absolute weight. 'The role of rights is to maintain and protect the fundamental moral and political culture of a community through specific institutional arrangements'.[21]

It would seem that rights oscillate between the common good of the community, and the individual interest of the right-holder. However, Raz explains that this opposition is not a real one, as the value of the right holder's interest is partly determined by the usefulness of the right in enhancing the common goods that are provided by the community. In other words, in order to fully enjoy the benefits provided by rights, the right holder must regard his interest as partly shaped by the common goods protected by the community. Hence, there is no necessary conflict between individual rights and common goods. A conflict can occur, but it is far from being necessary, since the existence of a common culture, providing common goods, is a precondition for the enjoyment of individual rights. Thus, an intellectual's interest in having an environment which is conducive to free speech, but in which the intellectual cannot participate, is greater than the interest of the intellectual to speak within an environment not conducive to free speech.[22] The important point, as Raz puts it, is that a right is meant to foster a public culture that enables people to take pride in their identity as members of a society.[23]

The importance of these rights is therefore justified by their service to the public good. But why then should we give a constitutional status to those rights? The answer could lie in their moral strength, but Raz points out that there are some important institutional considerations that are worthy of being stressed. In particular, he affirms that constitutional rights are devices in effecting a division of power between various branches of government.

Thus, for instance, the existence of constitutional rights means that they are removed from the exclusive control of the ordinary legislature. It should be noted here that the previous consideration does not depend on the existence of a written constitution. It suffices that a legal culture protects certain civil liberties (as in the UK) to understand that courts have a role in protecting those liberties.[24] Hence, some constitutional rights are institutional means to protect some collective goods inasmuch as damage to them is caused by harming the interests of identifiable individuals.[25]

The upshot of this outlook of rights is a particular institutional arrangement that places the courts at the centre of rights protection. It is argued that these specialized institutions are suitable places for evaluating the weight of the interests,[26] which correspond to the strength of a right.[27]

[21] Ibid, 245.
[22] Joseph Raz, 'Freedom of expression and personal identification', (1991) 11 OJLS 303.
[23] Joseph Raz, *The Morality of Freedom* (Oxford: OUP, 1986) 254.
[24] This point can be debated, especially in light of further development of the human rights protection in the UK. [25] Raz (n 23 above), 258.
[26] Ibid, 261. [27] Ibid, 262.

D. Kamm and Nagel: Status Theory of Rights

The interest theory provides a less-than-satisfactory account of the stringency of rights. On one hand, Raz holds that the strength of rights corresponds to the weight of the right holder's interest. On the other, the importance of the interest to the right holder is also determined by the interests of others, who equally benefit from the performance of a right. For instance, a journalist's right to free speech is important as it serves the interests of his audience, and not only because it serves the journalist's own interests. But then, this means that the strength of the right is not directly dependent on the interest of the right holder.

An alternative account of what constitutes the stringency of rights was suggested by Frances Kamm[28] and Thomas Nagel.[29] Kamm asks whether a right can be justified on grounds other than the interests of persons. She argues that rights are based on the very nature of persons *qua* persons, and independent from their well-being.[30] Thomas Nagel helps us to understand this idea further. First, he defines rights as 'universal protections of every individual against being justifiably used or sacrificed in certain ways for purposes worthy or unworthy'.[31] Then he states that rights can be more accurately understood as aspects of status—that is, being a member of the moral community. Moral status, as conferred by moral rights, Nagel explains, 'is analogous to legal status, as conferred by legal rights, except that the former is not contingent on social practices'.[32]

Further, he defines the ground of rights as a moral status, conferred on all human beings, by the design of a non-consequentialist morality.[33] Moral status, he holds:

is that of a certain kind of *inviolability*, which we identify with the possession of rights. . . . Being inviolable is not a condition like being happy or free, just as being violable is not a condition, like being unhappy or oppressed. To be inviolable does not mean that one will not be violated. It is a moral status: It means that one *may not* be violated in certain ways: Such treatment is inadmissible, and if it occurs, the person has been wronged. So someone's having or lacking this status is not equivalent to anything's happening or not happening to him. If he has it, he does not lose it when his rights are violated.[34]

The stringency of inviolability seems to be detached from the idea of the interests of the right-holder. The stringency of a right does not depend on what actually happens to an individual. On the contrary, a right sets a number of things that can constitute a violation of the inviolability of a person's life, action, and thought. Rights are strict deontological requirements and not merely trumps against

---

[28] Frances M Kamm, 'Rights' in Jules Coleman and Scott Shapiro (eds), *The Oxford Handbook of Jurisprudence and Philosophy of Law* (Oxford: OUP, 2001).
[29] Thomas Nagel, 'Personal Rights and Public Space' in Thomas Nagel, *Concealment and Exposure & Other Essays* (Oxford: OUP, 2002) 31–52.
[30] Even if, as a result, it is in a person's interest to have that nature, 'the right derives from their nature not their interest in having it'. Frances M Kamm (n 28 above) 485.
[31] Thomas Nagel (n 29 above) 31–52.   [32] Ibid, 33.   [33] Ibid, 35.   [34] Ibid, 37.

utilitarian calculus. In words more familiar to lawyers, rights are strict rules and not principles that need to be balanced. It is one thing to say, in a rule-like fashion, that torture is not permitted. It is another to say that torture is not permitted, unless it may assist in saving a thousand lives. The former does not mean that torture will never happen, but it means that whenever it does happen, a person will have been wronged and therefore will have lost something of importance. As such, a tragedy will have ensued. Similarly, the latter statement does not mean that torture will be more frequent. Yet, it does mean that in some extraordinary situations torture will not only be practised, but it will also be considered as justified: this is the really unbearable thing.

E. Constitutional Status as a Ground of FLRs

My suggestion here is that FLRs can be understood in an analogous way to Kamm's and Nagel's understandings of moral rights. The point of departure is Nagel's remark on the analogy between moral and legal status. I argue that the constitutional status, as conferred by FLRs, is dependent and contingent on the institutional setting.

The deontological structure of fundamental moral rights can only be translated into law by the deontological structure provided by constitutional rules.[35] It is interesting to note that the notion of inviolability is compared to that of immunity.[36] In this sense, we can find a common thread that brings together Hohfeld, Hart, and the status theorists. However, Hohfeld would define immunity only in relation to its correlative (disability) and its opposite (liability). In other words, an individual would only have constitutional immunity when the legislator is under a disability to modify the legal relations of the individual. Hohfeld's correlativity implies that one term is perfectly reducible to the other. Also, in Hohfeld's scheme, it is impossible to understand the independent value of immunity. Kamm and Nagel explain why immunity (inviolability is a type of immunity, I would suggest) is indeed an independent value and it is therefore prior to its correlative—disability.

The priority of immunity over disability can be used to justify the existence of the constitutional protection of FLRs. The constitutional status (of persons) is maintained if FLRs are protected from the arbitrary intrusion of the government. But what exactly does this mean?

Constitutional status is contingent on social practices, and hence, different practices can be eligible for this status. The rights set out in a bill of rights are selected according to social contingencies. This is dependent on there being a written constitution. If this is the case, then the borders of constitutional status can be seen as very thin. The vast majority of constitutions contain bills of rights. Even the UK

---

[35] Jurgen Habermas, *Between Facts and Norms*, passim.
[36] Thomas Nagel (n 29 above) 41.

recently incorporated, into the domestic legal system, the European Convention of Human Rights (ECHR). A special court to police the area protected by the constitutional status is not a necessary condition. The American Supreme Court is not a specialized constitutional court such as the *BundesVerfassungGericht*. Nor is there a necessity for special procedures of invalidation. The power of the court can range from invalidation through the 'interpretation in conformity with'.[37]

I would like to suggest a general distinction that, I hope, can elucidate the functioning of constitutional status. A status may be passive or active. It is passive when the individual uses it in order to protect his inner citadel from the interference of either the state or other individuals. A passive status works like a *shield* that protects each individual's action. To infringe this screen, one would have to produce a stringent countervailing argument. The shield confers both negative and positive FLRs. It is a mistake, however, to think that the individual has no positive claims. On the contrary, it may be necessary to ask the state to intervene, in order to prevent others from infringing on the passive status. For instance, an individual may request that the state undertake expenditures, in order to challenge the breach of electronic privacy, which is constantly threatened by other agents.

Constitutional status can also be active. Thus, individuals can also operate their FLRs as *swords*. This is the case, for example, when an individual wants to use his FLR in order to express his thoughts and beliefs. Free speech is a good example. When an individual or a group decides to exercise their FLR to free speech, it is done in order to assert their presence, and their message, to a public audience. Even the active status gives rise to both positive and negative FLRs. Sometimes, one may simply ask that the state and other individuals do not interfere. But other times a right holder may request the intervention of the state in order to protect their use of the right.

The constitutional status of individuals can be compared to the constitution of the society. Both can be threatened by external agents, and by internal problems. The constitutional status has both internal (the scope) and external (the functions) limits.[38]

4. The Scope (or Content) of FLRs

In order to understand what constitutional status amounts to we have to examine the scope of FLRs in legal systems. The constitutional status, as conferred by FLRs, protects an individual sphere of inviolability. As such, it covers a grey area between a purely negative and a positive conception of inviolability. We will begin by characterizing the opposing ends of the spectrum, and then we will try to define the contours of the sphere of inviolability itself.

---

[37] See Art 3 of the Human Rights Act 1998 for an example of such a clause.
[38] Andrei Marmor, 'On the limits of Rights', *Law and Philosophy* 16 (1997) 1–18.

What kind of protection can FLRs afford? Are FLRs shields that protect individual action, or are they swords that empower people fulfilling their needs? In other words, are they negative or positive? The answer to this is not easy, simply because there is little agreement as to what constitutes a purely negative and a purely positive protection. Roughly, we could argue that a negative protection implies that the state is not empowered to intervene in any case where a constitutionally protected liberty applies. That is, a negative protection amounts to a mere omission. For instance, the state cannot intervene in preventing someone from airing his views publicly on political or religious issues. Equally, it could be argued that a positive intervention of the state amounts to some kind of entitlement on the part of the individual. For instance, the state may invest a certain amount of money in providing education or health facilities.

The orthodox view is that FLRs only concern the negative dimensions and that there are no grounds for justifying the existence of entitlement-rights. This is simply because these rights cannot be guaranteed in the case of a shortage of economic resources. But, are negative liberties protected by FLRs completely cost free? A recent publication, *The Cost of Rights*, argues that all rights entail cost and thus, from this viewpoint, all rights are positive.[39] This argument is refreshing, and instigates a rethinking on the distinction between negative and positive rights. Nonetheless, I think this view ultimately fails to illuminate the importance of the negative role of FLRs.[40] Here is why.

Positive rights are understood in *The Cost of Rights* in two different ways. First, positive is placed in opposition to moral. In this sense, positive refers to the fact that certain rights are legally recognized and implemented, as opposed to moral rights that are deemed as pure aspirations of moral theories. The authors of this work insist on the importance of legal enforcement as a precondition to the existence of legal rights. This, however, does not illuminate our understanding of the positive/negative distinction. Second, positive rights are opposed to negative. The authors refer to this distinction by simply describing the kinds of duties that are entailed by rights. They are seen as negative if the government has a requirement not to interfere—and positive if the government is required to invest in resources, in order to fulfil its obligation. However, the thesis is that this distinction grossly misrepresents reality, and that it is based on fundamental confusions.[41] The misrepresentation concerns the effective costs that the government pays to protect all kind of liberties (and this is buttressed by an empirical analysis of the data). Therefore, to say that a right is negative does not give account for the expenses that that right involves.

The fundamental confusion rests, in the authors' mind, on the fact that the orthodox view applies the distinction between forbearance/performance concerning

---

[39] Stephen Holmes and Cass R Sunstein, *The Cost of Rights: Why Liberty Depends on Taxes* (New York: WW Norton & Co, 2000).
[40] My position is largely inspired by Alan Gewirth's, 'Are all rights positive?', Philosophy and Public Affairs 30 (2001) 321–33.   [41] *The Cost of Rights* (n 39 above), 43.

individual actions, to the activity of government, which is distinctively positive. Now, the question is whether we can meaningfully characterize the governmental role in the protection of FLRs as negative. Holmes and Sunstein answer no to this question. But, then, how can we define the object of the FLR to free speech or religion? It seems to me that in this case, an individual has the right to speak his mind, and the government has the correlative duty to refrain from intervening with the object of the right. The fact that sometimes the government does intervene positively, in order to stop individuals from breaching the FLR of another individual, is another issue. This situation is explained through the idea of associated duties that make the central object of negative FLRs possible. This means that the government has a primary duty not to interfere, and this is correlative to the immunity-rights of the individual. The government is primarily required not to censor, or indeed to take any other positive step in order to curtail the FLR to free speech. Of course, if the threat of censorship, or other limitations on the right, does not come from the state but from other individuals, or groups, then the state will have an associated duty to stop those interferences from curtailing the immunity-rights of the right-holder.

Thus, the role of governmental action can indeed be characterized as being negative. In this sense, the distinction positive/negative is meaningful, and not fraught with confusion, as is suggested by Holmes and Sunstein. Furthermore, it can also be argued that the negative trait of a right logically comes prior to the positive one. If our idea of constitutional status is correct, then it is possible to argue that to have a FLR to x is to belong in a legal system that guarantees, through its institutions, a *sphere of inviolability* for each individual. This sphere of inviolability requires the compliance of all institutions, including representative institutions. So what really makes the difference in a legal system with FLRs is the fact that the sovereign is limited in its power to alter the rights of individuals.

A sphere of inviolability, in my view, is therefore constituted by two differing sets of considerations. First, a sphere of inviolability is negative in character insofar as it involves the forbearance of the state from interfering in important aspects of the individual domain. Thus, the life, thoughts, and actions of individuals are protected from interference by the state. These three areas constitute the sphere of inviolability, although it may be argued that they are circoncentric spheres around the individual. To give examples, bodily integrity is within the inner sphere; then, brain activity—consisting in whatever formation of opinion—is in the second sphere (even chronologically); and then, actions expressing in whatever form the identity of the individual, belong in the third sphere.

The boundaries between the three spheres are not clear-cut, and often one depends on another; sometimes, one cannot exist without the other. For instance, the FLR to free speech cannot be meaningful if the expressive action is not supported by the necessary thought process preceding it. Also, it can be argued that a life free from bodily violation, but devoid of free expression, is not a valuable life after all. In my opinion, the division of the three spheres acquires meaning in terms of potential irreversibility of the wrong. That is, if the state interferes on individual bodily integrity, for example by forcing a person to donate his kidney for transplant, then the wrong that is committed is irreversible. If the state interferes with the freedom of thought, say by imposing a certain ideology using public education, then, while the wrong committed is serious, it can still be redressed over a period of time by exposing individuals to competing views, and informed opinions that falsify the ideology. If the state interferes with the action of the individual, say by limiting his free speech on a given occasion, then the wrong committed is serious, but it can be immediately redressed by compensating the individual, and giving him the chance to speak his mind in a public context.

A sphere of inviolability, however, does require the existence of positive obligations on behalf of the state, and this is the major teaching of our discussion on the positive/negative distinction. Nowadays, in Western societies, the encroachment from the state is limited because of the immediate reaction that any potential interference would immediately entail. The state therefore, has found a new role as a regulator of liberties when their exercise by different individuals leads to an abuse or clash of liberties. The state has two different tasks. First, it must define liberties in such a way so that they are neither abused, nor excessively limited. Therefore, for instance, state institutions do single out certain categories of speech that are not worth protecting. Also, state institutions must make sure that an individual can safely air his message, without being silenced by a crowd. Second, there is a distinct possibility that an individual or a group will impinge on someone else's liberty while exercising theirs—in the case, for instance, where an individual wants to distribute leaflets on private property (eg a shopping mall). Of course, the activity itself is duly protected by the FLR to free speech, but is it possible to carry on that activity on someone else's private property—thereby violating the FLR to private property? The state has to keep both concerns in mind, and must take positive steps in deciding whose right to protect, and with what means.

FLRs create a constitutional status for individuals, which can be explained in terms of a sphere of inviolability, involving both negative and positive action by the state. It should be noted that the sphere of inviolability has internal limits and, even when we define these limits, the likelihood is that individual spheres of inviolability do intersect. Therefore the risk of a conflict of liberties is very high. FLRs have a second set of limitations imposed upon them by the fact that they involve a complex web of relations. These will be examined in the following section.

5. The External Dimension or the Function(s) of FLRs

The main function of FLRs is that of separation of powers.[42] FLRs are not immunities in a vacuum. They involve complex relationships between individuals

---

[42] I maintain that this is the case from a historical perspective also. Historically, it suffices to take Art 16 of the French Declaration of Human and Civic Rights 1789, as an example. Art 16 states: 'Any

and institutions. They may be concerned with relationships between individuals themselves or between them and institutions. Similarly, they encompass relationships between the state as an entity, and individuals. Finally, they cover relationships between different institutions. I distinguish three types of duties: directional, general, and institutional. Each of these duties involves an aspect of separation of powers.

First, the *directional duty* links the right-holder with one, or many duty-bearers. So, for instance, when a FLR to free speech is at stake, there is a right holder, who is the person who wants to exercise his freedom of speech. The right holder's FLR entails direct duties. In this example, the FLR to free speech creates duties for the individuals gathering the audience to refrain from interfering with the speaker's expression. In turn, this may generate duties for public order officers to make sure that nobody interferes with the FLR of the speaker.

Second, a FLR generates general duties that shape the relationship between the government (*lato sensu*) and individuals. Individuals are right holders and the government is the duty-bearer. The duty of the government is to refrain from enacting general laws that may abridge, in any way, the core of FLRs. Thus, for instance, the government has a general duty not to exercise its legislative power in order to limit the FLR to free speech.

Third, there may be institutional duties that inform the relationship between two or three branches of government. The disability of the legislative power must be enforced by a specialized body, ie a constitutional court. This is generally an indirect, or mediated, type of relationship. It is indirect as the specialized body will only intervene if triggered by an individual demand, or else by another body enabled to do so.

All of these relationships are mediated by law. For the purposes of litigation, law defines right-holders and duty bearers. Law also names the institutional bodies that are charged with the task of policing the boundaries of FLRs. Finally, law outlines the procedures to follow in case of violation, or non-respect of FLRs.

FLRs are concerned with the allocation of freedom between individuals; the right balance between government intervention and the individual's sphere of inviolability; and the distribution of power amongst institutions. Roughly, directional duties are concerned with the horizontal distribution of freedom amongst individuals. General duties determine the private/public divide; that is, the degree of interference of the state over private business or, in other words, the vertical distribution of freedom. Finally, institutional duties are those involving the distribution and separation of powers. It is helpful to recall, on this point, Article 16 of the French Declaration of Human and Civic Rights 1789: 'Any society in which no provision is made for guaranteeing rights or for the separation of powers, has no Constitution'.[43]

---

society in which no provision is made for guaranteeing rights or for the separation of powers, has no Constitution'.

[43] Art 16, Déclaration des Droits de l'homme et du citoyen: 'Toute société dans laquelle la garantie des droits n'est pas assurée, ni la séparation des pouvoirs détérminée, n'a point de Constitution'.

The sphere of inviolability, or constitutional status as conferred by FLRs, is therefore not only limited internally, as we saw in the previous section, but also externally. This is the case as, in order to work out the FLRs of individuals, we also need to determine the right distribution of freedoms among both the individuals themselves, and between the state and the individuals. The precise boundaries of FLRs would also depend upon the interplay between the different institutions.

6. FLRs: A Stipulative Definition

At this point it is useful to reflect on some issues that have been covered thus far. The difference between the language of law and that of rights was the starting point where the explanation was not very clear. Looking at the structure, point, scope and functions of rights, showed us that rights have various complex layers, and that it is often difficult to disentangle them. Overall, however, exploring these issues aid in providing a greater understanding of how FLRs actually work.

A stipulative definition is necessary, as it is impossible to define FLRs by merely observing the way they work in different legal systems.[44] The discourse on rights is vast and incoherent. Virtually every legal dispute lends itself to the question of definition of rights if we adhere to Carl Wellman's definition of rights as giving dominion to one right holder over another. I do not share in this position, for I believe in a strong, but limited, role for rights. Any stipulative definition must help to shape the field of research by defining the objects that make up the area. FLRs are the 'objects' that I propose to examine here, in particular in situations where FLRs conflict. I will outline six main features of FLRs.

First, 'right' is a highly plurivocal term, as we learned from Hohfeld's analysis. A right may refer to a claim, a privilege, a power, and immunity. Hohfeld's analysis provides some useful insights. Moreover, I believe that constitutional practice of rights is better explained using his concept of immunity together with its correlative (disability) and opposite (liability). However, I do not share Hohfeld's view that immunity is perfectly correlative to disability, and therefore that one is reducible to the other. Instead, I firmly believe that the immunity-right has a logical priority over its opposite. I have discussed this point in relation to the negative core of the state's duty to refrain from interfering with an individual FLR.

Second, FLRs are often framed in very broad statements, contained in bills of rights. I have suggested that these statements should be interpreted as rules, as opposed to principles,[45] for the dimension of principle undermines the inherent strength of rights. Yet, they are a particular type of rules, namely they are 'constitutional permissions'. The domain covered by constitutional permissions is what we

---

[44] For a discussion on the importance of virtuous stipulation in relation to the concept of rights, see Andrew Halpin, *Rights and Law—Analysis and Theory* (Oxford: Hart Publishing, rep. 2001) 13–16.
[45] On rights and rules see Tom Campbell, *Rights: A Critical Introduction* (Oxford: Routledge, 2006) 27–30.

call constitutional status. The extent of the status depends not only on a liberal understanding of the scope of FLRs, but also, on the institutional setting provided by each legal system.

Third, constitutional permissions encompass what I refer to as the constitutional status of individuals. Every individual is guaranteed an equal constitutional status by FLRs.

Fourth, the coverage of this constitutional status coincides with the sphere of inviolability that requires from the state a combination of negative and positive obligations, also covering obligations depending on other individuals and institutions more generally.

Fifth, constitutional permissions are hierarchically superior to legislative and infra-legislative norms produced by legislators or other bodies. This means that the legislator is disabled, insofar as it cannot alter legal positions determined by FLRs. This disability entails a corresponding power of the court to invalidate, or to interpret in conformity, legislative and infra-legislative norms that breach FLRs.

Sixth, FLRs must be guaranteed in a way that takes into account their tripartite functions. These are the distribution of freedom horizontally and vertically, and the distribution of power amongst institutions.

In conclusion, FLRs are constitutional permissions that determine a constitutional status, whose scope coincides with an individual sphere of inviolability, and whose function is to distribute freedom and power. It is only when we know what FLRs are about that we can start understanding how they interact and conflict with each other.

3
The Anatomy of Conflicts of Fundamental Legal Rights

1. Introduction

Conflicts of Fundamental Legal Rights (FLRs) have been conceptually explained so far by both a necessary 'choice' and a necessary 'loss'; these need to be studied in more detail. The notion of choice allows speculation as to the existence of inconsistencies in legal sytems, while the notion of loss refers to the consequences of normative inconsistencies, which are referred to as either trade-offs or sacrifices. In this chapter, I address both notions and conclude with a suggested typology of conflicts of FLRs, which, I hope, can improve our understanding of the phenomenon.

In other words, I will explain what I mean by conflicts of FLRs. The very expression 'conflict of FLRs' is ambiguous, as a FLR can conflict with another FLR, but it can also conflict with other constitutional norms that protect collective goals, or indeed with other norms that protect relevant private or public interests. In this work, I limit myself to genuine conflict between FLRs. But, first, in section 2, I will offer an explanation as to what this expression actually excludes: that is, what I am not interested in. Following from this, in section 3, I will present the concept of normative inconsistencies to try and explain the basic notion of choice between the two essentials that lie behind the idea of genuine conflicts. In the fourth section, the question of conflicts of FLRs will be tested against the constitutional status theory of FLRs, and compared to the interest or will theories of rights. In section 5, I explore the way in which rights theorists attempt to avoid the deadlock of conflicts. I will conclude with section 6 and that attempts to present a typology of genuine conflicts of FLRs.

2. *Lato Sensu* and Spurious Conflicts of FLRs

FLRs can conflict with all the norms of a legal system. While some conflicts are relatively easy to solve, others give rise to deadlocks. To start, conflicts of FLRs should not be confused with the phenomenon of disagreement.[1] Conflicts arise in

---

[1] For a different perspective see Samantha Besson, *The Morality of Conflict—Reasonable Disagreement and the Law* (Oxford: Hart, 2005).

adversarial circumstances.² There is, certainly, disagreement on certain issues of rights; it is a necessary, but insufficient, condition for conflicts to exist. In order for there to be a conflict, one norm must make it permissible to do x, and the other norm must deny the permission to do x. In other words, the actions permitted by both rights are not jointly performable. This, however, is not a peculiarity of conflicts of FLRs. Any norm can conflict in such a way. Hence we have to distinguish between conflicts between the norms supporting two FLRs, and conflict between such norms and other types of norms (of constitutional or inferior ranking).

When FLRs' norms conflict with other norms then we have what I label as *lato sensu* conflicts. On one side you have a FLR, on the other you have a norm that protects a collective goal, or another special interest which is not embedded in a FLR. A constitution, for example, can contain both FLRs and collective goals. Moreover, a constitution may well create a relation between the two through either a general or specific clause. A general clause may stipulate that, in case of a threat to national security, the government may take measures that are likely to infringe upon the FLRs of individuals. For instance, the USA policy against terrorism prioritizes safety over certain individual rights.³ Thus, suspect individuals could be detained incommunicado for an indeterminate length of time, denying them their right to a fair trial. There may also be specific clauses that create a relation between a FLR and a collective goal.⁴ Thus, national security, territorial integrity, public safety, or other grounds can prevail over a specified number of rights.

The question of conflicts of rights should also be distinguished from the question of limits of rights. Of course the two are interrelated but they are not the same thing. They are intertwined because it may be possible to define the scope of a FLR in such a way as not to conflict with another FLR. Yet, this is not always possible. There are cases where two FLRs are jointly incompossible. As HLA Hart puts it:

> Before we can say so, we have to fill out with specifications of the agents and victims and times to which the rules related. If the same agents are required by one rule to do, and by another rule to abstain from, the same action at the same time, this will be reflected in the corresponding obedience statements, which would be logically inconsistent. Joint obedience to the rules would be logically impossible.⁵

Ronald Dworkin's conception of rights as trumps allows only the possibility of *lato sensu* conflict.⁶ From that point of view, individual rights resist, and prevail

---

   ² Hillel Steiner, 'Working Rights' in Kramer, Simmonds, and Steiner *A Debate over Rights*, (Oxford: OUP, 2000) 236–37.
   ³ Whether that policy is constitutional or not is a very controversial matter. See for example, Ronald Dworkin, 'Terror & Attack on civil liberties', *New York Review of Books*, 6 November 2003.
   ⁴ You find examples of these specific clauses of rights limitation in the ECHR.
   ⁵ Hart, 'Kelsen's doctrine of the unity of law', in Paulson and Paulson, *Normativity and Norms* (Oxford: Clarendon Press, 1998) 567.
   ⁶ Ronald Dworkin, 'Rights as Trumps' in Jeremy Waldron, *Theories of Rights* (Oxford: OUP, 1984) 153.

over, collective goals; the importance of which is calculated by appealing to utilitarian arguments that deny the equal importance of every individual. Two remarks stem from this position. First, what happens when collective goals take the equal worth of individuals duly into account? Second, why isn't there a discussion of what happens when trumps conflict?[7]

Lato sensu conflicts of FLRs involve all types of clashes between one FLR and other norms. This is not the place to explore this category of conflict in more detail. However in this book, I am concerned with *stricto sensu* conflicts of FLRs; that is, the conflicts that arise between two or more instantiations of one or more abstract general FLRs. A further distinction is central at this stage.

A conflict between FLRs can be spurious or genuine. The main difference is that genuine conflicts of FLRs involve normative inconsistencies. It may be useful to list a certain number of spurious conflicts to illustrate the distinction.

Confusion arises as to conflicts involving equality. Often, these cases are treated as paradigmatic examples of genuine conflicts. I wish to argue that this should not be the case. Some writers present, for instance, matters of redistributive taxation, or matters of affirmative action, under the headings of conflict of rights.[8] I do not think that these are instances of genuine conflict of rights. They may instead be defined as instances of identification of right-holders. Should black people have a right to be hired in preference to any other? That is a potential question, and a very serious one, especially with regard to affirmative action policy. And yet, the question of the identity of right-holders should be kept separate from the question of conflict between FLRs. The central problem this work addresses concerns the situation in which a right makes something permissible while a competing right makes it impermissible, thereby creating a joint incompossibility. I am not stating that the FLR to equality cannot conflict with another right. All I am saying is that sometimes issues involving the FLR to equality are misleadingly described as genuine conflicts of rights.

Likewise, the redistribution of taxes does not concern a conflict between FLRs. Of course the FLR to private property for some people is at stake. By the same token, there is a collective goal, namely the problem of selecting the policy that the state should fund with the taxation returns. If this can be seen as a conflict, then it is only a *lato sensu* conflict. Hence, by redefining a right as a collective goal, it brings us back to the more general case of conflicts *lato sensu* that were already excluded here.

A second type of spurious conflicts of FLRs is that which occurs as a consequence of scarce resources (or of a technological advancement). Genuine conflicts

---

[7] In Dworkin's theory trumps never conflict because to have a right (a trump) is precisely to have a strong claim to something against someone. Why, though, would it be impossible that both parties have a strong claim? Take for instance the case in which the FLR to privacy of a public person clashes with the FLR to free expression of the press.

[8] John Rowan, *Conflict of Rights—Moral Theory and Social Policy Implications* (Oxford: Westview Press, 1999).

of FLRs exist despite scarce resources or other external elements. It may well be that scarce resources make conflicts more visible, but this alone does not constitute a conflict. This is the case because, as we have already pointed out, matters of conflicts of rights do not concern questions of distribution of resources. Thus, for instance, the fact that a hospital cannot help cure a patient, because of the lack of money—it has been used to build a new school—is not a situation of *stricto sensu* conflict between the right to health and the right to education. The choice between the two is a matter of policy. Every time that resources are allocated a similar choice is made, but this does not correspond to a situation of conflict of rights.

The same can be said for technological developments. It is sometimes said that new technologies, facilitating the acquisition of information, breach privacy. Thus, a right to free expression, which is based on the disclosure of certain information as acquired by new methods, is sometimes seen as clashing with the right to privacy. What makes it impermissible to disclose certain information is the content; not how the information was gathered. Of course on certain occasions individuals go beyond the accepted boundaries and use illegal ways of acquiring information. However, this is not the point since I am concerned here with cases in which a genuine conflict of FLRs arises. So far we have examined what genuine conflicts of FLRs are not. In the next section I will discuss the central features of genuine conflicts of FLRs.

3. The Core of Conflicts of FLRs

The problem that makes conflicts of FLRs so daunting is the spectre of normative inconsistency. A normative inconsistency arises when two norms are jointly incompatible. Either we follow one or we follow the other; but there is no logical possibility to conciliate the two, since they contradict one another. We can only choose one or the other; and that choice will entail an inevitable loss. Some scholars suggest that, in order to safeguard the unity of the legal system, it is necessary to apply a principle of non-contradiction to norms.[9] The challenge therefore is to establish the extent to which a legal system, and more precisely a system of FLRs, can cope with the existence of normative inconsistencies. Kant first introduced the dilemma when, in discussing his doctrine of right, he argued that to make an act inconsistent with moral law permissible, amounts to stating the doctrine of right is in contradiction with itself.[10]

---

[9] This idea is deeply controversial and Hans Kelsen, for one, retracted his original viewpoint on it. See on this point Bruno Celano, 'Norm Conflicts: Kelsen's view and a rejoinder' in Stanley and Bonnie Paulson, *Normativity and Norms* (Oxford: Clarendon Press, 1998) 343–61. See also HLA Hart 'Kelsen visited' and 'Kelsen Doctrine of the Unity' in HLA Hart, *Essays in Jurisprudence and Philosophy* (Oxford: OUP, 1983).

[10] Immanuel Kant, *The Metaphysics of Morals* (Cambridge, Mass: CUP, 1991) (trans Mary Gregor).

When applied to FLRs, the problem of inconsistency resonates throughout the entire legal system. The reason is that FLRs are part of the constitutional essentials upon which the legitimacy of the whole structure rests. If constitutional essentials happen to contradict each other, then it is difficult to determine the real constitutive role of FLRs. These are meant to provide reasons for supporting certain actions carried out by individuals. But, if a certain action is both permissible and forbidden, then the function of reason giving seems to be undermined; individuals would have to rely on something else in order to decide whether they can act upon their FLRs or not.

A. Permissiveness and Conflict

Commonly, theoreticians argue that the central case is that of conflict between duties. This can be exemplified by taking the example of a speaker wishing to distribute leaflets on private property. The speaker has a right to his FLR to free speech, but the owner of a shopping mall, for example, has a FLR to private property. The speaker can claim that other individuals are under a duty to refrain from interfering with his speech, while the owner can claim a duty on behalf of the distributor to refrain from trespassing on his property.

The question that we encounter next is whether different permissions can conflict. After all it is far from evident that a permission to speak one's mind can conflict with the permission, say, of protecting one's property. Hart, for instance, states that: 'permissive rules cannot conflict, but joint conformity with two permissive rules may be logically impossible (for example, "Opening the window is permitted", "Shutting the window is permitted").'[11] Does this mean that permissions never conflict? HLA Hart explains that the joint-conformity test of conflict only works if all rules, or all but one, either require or prohibit an action.[12] If correct, this would seem to mean that FLRs understood as permissive rules cannot conflict because they do not directly require or prohibit actions. However, this does not apply to FLRs. In order to understand conflicts of FLRs we have to consider also the prohibitions or obligations set out by the correlative duties of FLRs. Once we acknowledge this necessary correlativity between rights and duties, we can better understand how FLRs can conflict.

The normative structure of FLRs that we are interested in is twofold. FLRs state, on one hand, permissive rules to do or refrain from doing something; on the other, they impose on a number of duty bearers an obligation to respect the permission granted. A conflict can arise either between two duties, or between a duty and a permissive rule. The latter case can be exemplified with a hypothetical case, where two groups of people claim the FLR to free speech in order to stop the other from exercising their FLR.[13] Imagine that, for example, a neo-Nazi group wants

[11] HLA Hart, 'Kelsen's Doctrine of the Unity of Law' (n 5 above), 568–69, n 42.
[12] Ibid, 568.
[13] Jeremy Waldron, 'Rights in Conflict' in J Waldron, *Liberal Rights* (Cambridge: CUP, 1993) 203.

to exercise its FLR to free speech. Their opponents, the post-communist group, organize a counter-demonstration, which is aimed to respond to the Nazi group. The time, place, and manner are exactly the same. Both groups have a FLR that involves a duty not to interfere in the free speech of others. Both groups are permitted to demonstrate, and to express their own ideas, but at the same time both groups are required to refrain from interfering with the other's FLR to free speech. The conflict here is between the permission to demonstrate and the duty to refrain from demonstrating.

The actual extent to which two norms may conflict depends on how we identify the agents, the time, the place, and the manner in which the rules should be applied. Law places constraints on each of those features. We know, for instance, that a right holder must fulfil certain conditions in order to be able to redress the breach of his FLR (capacity, etc). Equally, law can impose duties on either general or specified duty-bearers. The state is generally considered a primary duty-bearer, while individuals are secondary duty-bearers.

Once FLRs are duly articulated, their conflict becomes more apparent. From this point of view, we can say that FLRs do conflict by virtue of the assumption of correlativity that they carry with them. This problem is central to the notion of conflict. Moreover, the possibility of normative inconsistencies cannot be denied on the basis that it undermines the unity of the legal system. This is because a legal system cannot impose *a priori* principle of non-contradiction.[14]

B. Empirical Proof of Normative Inconsistencies

Legal systems aim to minimize, as much as they can, the risk of normative inconsistencies. This explains why they have all developed rules for the solution of conflicts, which are based on formal properties of rules. Hence, we can identify rules such as *lex posterior derogat priori*, or *lex specialis derogat generalis*, or *lex superior derogat inferior*. However, conflicts of FLRs are a particular threat to the 'unity' of legal systems, because neither of these rules of conflict applies to them. First, FLRs are all enacted at the same time in the same bills of rights, declarations, or charters. Second, all FLRs are stated in very broad terms and, as such, they cannot be considered to prevail on grounds of specificity. Third, FLRs belong to the same formal category of norms, that is, the category of constitutional rules.

What is interesting to note here is that legal systems are filled with normative inconsistencies, and that in order to survive they had to develop tools for the resolution of conflicts. FLRs have never been studied from this angle, and the reasons for this are manifold. To begin with, FLRs' adjudication is relatively recent. Moreover, there is a powerful rhetoric on FLRs that tends to present them as the primary resource in solving legal problems. Finally, FLRs' adjudication is a source of legitimacy for supreme courts. If courts were to acknowledge that some cases

---

[14] HLA Hart, 'Kelsen visited' (n 9 above).

can only be solved by creating *ex novo* rules, prior to FLRs themselves, then the legitimacy would be somehow undermined. Yet clearly, new rules for the solution of conflict of FLRs are required in order to resolve the problems created by the existence of normative inconsistencies.

4. Theories of Rights, Normative Inconsistencies, and Incommensurability

The norms of FLRs may involve normative inconsistencies. In chapter 2 I suggested that the best way of understanding FLRs is by elaborating a theory of FLRs in terms of a constitutional status. In this section, I argue that the constitutional status theory of a FLR is a preferred model for the explanation of the problem of conflicts.

From a conflict of rights viewpoint, the interest and will theories lie at opposite ends of the spectrum. The interest theory, as developed by MacCormick and Raz, and taken up by Waldron[15] and Marmor,[16] involves an increasing number of conflicts, given its dynamic nature. In the opposing case, the will theory, as presented by Hart, and defended by Wellman[17] and Steiner,[18] aims to present rights in a way that removes conflicts from the stage. For, if rights were the coronation of a power of individuals over their own domains, then any conflict would as such amount to the negation of the existence of these domains.

Jeremy Waldron provides an interesting discussion on how the interest theory can cope with the problem of conflicts. Waldron's overall attempt is to elucidate the meaning of conflict, while playing down their disruptive effects as to the theory of rights. To be more accurate, the interest theory is presented against the background of utilitarian philosophy. Hence, the main point of the interest theory is that certain individual interests are sufficient to justify the existence of a right of a person. This goes against the idea that interests have to be aggregated in order to be calculated. Waldron explains that rights conflict when their correlative duties conflict; or to put it in another way, when their duties are not compossible.[19] This idea can be articulated into four different stages. First, Albert has an interest that holds Carl under a duty X. Second, Bonnie has an interest that holds Carl under a duty X. Third, Albert's and Bonnie's interests hold Carl under the *same* duty. Fourth, Carl cannot perform his duty to both simultaneously.

The problem is the following: on which grounds does Carl make a choice, given that his decision will either fully or partially frustrate either interest?

---

[15] Jeremy Waldron, 'Rights in Conflict' in J Waldron, *Liberal Rights* (Cambridge: CUP, 1993) 203.
[16] Andrei Marmor, 'On the Limits of Rights', Law and Philosophy 16 (1997) 1–18.
[17] Carl Wellman, *Real Rights* (New York: OUP, 1995).
[18] Hillel Steiner, *A Debate over Rights* (Oxford: OUP, 2000).
[19] Jeremy Waldron, 'Rights in Conflict' in J Waldron, *Liberal Rights* (Cambridge: CUP, 1993) 203.

Waldron explains that for a long time the attraction of utilitarianism was that it provided *one single rule* in order to solve conflicts. However, what makes utilitarianism unpalatable is the fact that it involves trade-offs. If two courses of action are possible, then the one which harms only Albert, and prevents Bonnie and Carl from being harmed is preferable. Rights, Waldron explains, were conceived of in order to avoid trade-offs. That is, rights make some basic interests unattainable. But when rights conflict, then the spectre of trade-offs may reappear. Hence, an individual may feel aggrieved if his rights are traded with those of another person, where the choice has been made according to the overall goal of maximizing satisfaction.

One point needs to be made here. Waldron presents the problem as a choice between two interests, and then goes on to stress the matter of trade-offs. But, as pointed out earlier, the problem is, first and foremost, one of inconsistency. Having said that, it is appropriate to examine how Waldron proposes to reduce the threat of trade-offs. First, he holds that the proponents of trade-offs have no responsibility for the existence of conflicts. Conflicts are a given, and they have to be solved. Second, Waldron proposes a distinction between utilitarian trade-offs, and trade-offs in rights conflicts. In the former case, the problem is to combine trade-offs with a doctrine of quantitative commensurability. This may mean that unimportant interests of the multitude may overrule the more important interest of an individual.

Conflicts of rights arise because their corresponding duties are incompatible. This highlights the special relationship between rights, interests and duties. It needs to be stressed here that protecting an interest involves a large number of duties. For instance, the interests in free speech involve a duty not to censor, but also to allow public speech, to keep order during speeches, etc. Even if a clear duty is strictly associated to a right (eg a right not to be tortured entails a duty not to torture), it is clear that the general duty generates a wave of sub-duties. For instance, the FLR not to be tortured implies the duty to inform public opinion as to the wrongness of torture, or the duty to find the identity of the torturers, etc.

The question for Waldron is whether associated duties that stem from a given right all possess the same strength as the first duty. In fact, his answer to this is negative. Some duties are more central than others in the protection of a right. Hence, we can establish an internal comparison between the duties associated with rights in conflict, and to evaluate which one is more important. But there is a problem in this: intuitively, we may think that certain duties are indeed more important than others, but we have no reason to support this statement.

At this point, Waldron suggests that the priority of duties depends on an internal consideration of the right being defended. For example, JS Mill's conception of freedom of speech, where the central point was to shake conventional understanding of people, would support a strong duty to refrain from interfering with unpalatable speech. On the contrary, it can be argued that a neo-Nazis claim to a FLR to free speech can be interpreted as a claim to exclude other forms of expression. Therefore, this claim should be limited on the grounds that it is incompatible with the very right that they claim to exercise. Waldron concludes that the role of internal relations of reasons within rights is insightful if we aim to explain the qualitative precedence of rights. However, the role played by certain quantitative arguments can be highlighted in other contexts.

Waldron's position is helpful in different respects: it correctly points out that an interest theory has to recognize the widespread existence of conflicts. Moreover, Waldron demystifies the notion of trade-offs. He does this by distinguishing between those implying an aggregation of interests, and those that keep individual interests separate. Finally, Waldron suggests a stimulating defence of the idea of lexical priority as a description of an internal relation between the reasons provided by rights.

However, such a viewpoint has drawbacks that we must examine here. An interest theory, such as Waldron's, does not focus on the conditions of existence of conflicts, but instead focuses on their consequences. In other words, to adhere to an interest theory means to accept, as a given, that interests of various types do in fact conflict. There is, therefore, no need to account for the problem of inconsistencies. Rather, the aim is to demonstrate that trade-offs are not as serious a threat as they first appear to be. I disagree as I think that the problem of normative inconsistencies should be explained and not taken for granted. In addition to that, it is crucial to understand that there is a possibility for dramatic trade-offs to arise. Waldron seems concerned with downplaying this possibility. I do not think he succeeds, however.

Waldron may have shown that some conflicts are not dilemmas. But this alone does not prove that, in other circumstances, conflicts between central duties will arise and result in dramatic trade-offs. Waldron may say that the vast majority of cases do not involve dramatic trade-offs. However, my point is that in certain hard cases the choice inevitably undermines an important right, and this fact should not be underestimated, but should be taken seriously and duly explained.[20]

The main difference between Waldron's explanation of conflicts and mine lies in the role of incommensurability.

It is now time to move to the opposing end of the spectrum. Certain versions of the will theory reject the existence of conflicts whole-heartedly. The best example of this is provided by Hillel Steiner's theory of rights. The point of a will theory of rights, according to Steiner, is to establish a mini-sovereignty for the individual.[21] This mini-sovereignty corresponds to what he calls discretionary domains. These are constituted by all the duties owed to the right holder, *minus* the duties he owes to others.[22] This notion of domain is in itself controversial. The challenge for Steiner's idea of domains is when domains intersect; that is, when conflicts of

---

[20] Moreover, the distinction drawn by Waldron, between utilitarian and qualitative trade-offs, is not unquestionable.
[21] Hillel Steiner, 'Working Rights' in M Kramer, N Simmonds, and H Steiner, *A Debate over Rights* (Oxford: OUP, 2000). [22] Ibid, 262–63.

rights arise. Steiner holds that we need not despair. The fact that two duties are incompossible does not mean that the right holders are adversaries. Right holders may well see the difficulty of such a situation, and opt for a solution that dispels the conflict. For instance, a right holder may choose to waive his right. This kind of solution is referred to as an internal solution. An external solution, on the other hand, arises when a third party has the power to modify the relations between two right holders. Steiner suggests that external solutions are a complete negation of rights: they are what Hart calls the nightmare.[23] This is the case where the rights of people are replaced by the will of a third party who determines the extent and scope of individual rights. From this perspective, will theories of rights constitute an attempt to dispense with external solutions.[24]

Steiner's theory is illuminating from various viewpoints. His theory clearly grounds rights on a strong conception of autonomy, which explains the central role of individual will. As a result we can understand why, and in what circumstances, an individual may opt to waive his rights, when the rights may undermine an attempt to coordinate with others. In addition, it places a responsibility on right-holders in the solution of conflicts of rights. This is an important aspect and it should not be underestimated.

Steiner's approach avoids suggesting that a qualitative precedence can be easily evaluated, as interest theorists seem to do. However, there are major drawbacks to the will theory that must be underlined. At the outset it is far too optimistic as a doctrine. The fact that right holders may, and should, be willing to cooperate in order to minimize the occurrence of conflicts cannot possibly mean that all right holders, in every given situation, will in fact do this. Moreover, Steiner's theory does not account for those rights that are inalienable without being un-waivable.[25] For instance, one can waive the right to bodily integrity in order to allow a kidney transplant. However, one cannot waive that right if it causes the death of the person as a direct effect.

Finally, and more generally, I disagree with the idea that to call for an external solution jettisons rights. At least insofar as FLRs are concerned, rights adjudication amounts to effective protection in many legal systems. As such it must be accounted for and explained. Moreover, an internal position that carefully draws lines between individual domains is not always available. Right holders may strongly disagree to the point of rejecting communication. We should not exclude an external party to the conflict who may in fact succeed in bringing the two parties in the conflict to conciliation.

We are therefore left with two very different viewpoints. On one hand, the interest theory acknowledges the existence of conflicts, without believing in their disruptive effect on the normative system. On the other, the will theory minimizes

[23] Ibid, 264. [24] Ibid, 267.
[25] See Joel Feinberg for this distinction, 'Voluntary Euthanasia and the Inalienable Right to Life,' Philosophy and Public Affairs 7 (1978) 102.

the confrontational aspect of conflicts. From the perspective of FLRs, I believe that neither theory is fully satisfactory. The interest theory does not offer a very meaningful distinction between fundamental and simple rights. Rights only exist, according to the interest theory, when they contribute to the protection of an important individual interest. Yet, this is quite a difficult task; it is doubtful whether such a theory offers an explanation of the distinction between fundamental and simple rights in terms of degree of importance. The will theory, as Hart himself acknowledges,[26] cannot fully explain FLRs.[27] This is because it does not factor in certain important aspects of rights that lie outside the exercise of one's own will or dominion (it does not take into account institutional factors for example).

I suggest that the constitutional status theory is more suitable to illuminate the problem of conflicts. How does one explain conflicts of FLRs then? The constitutional status theory attempts to elucidate both the problem of normative inconsistencies and that of trade-offs. In this way, it claims to be superior to the interest theory. Moreover, it attempts to explain conflicts but avoids making the suggestion that the only available solution is internal. And from this point of view it claims to be more far-reaching than the will theory.

When FLRs conflict both rights are real. Put otherwise, conflicts of FLRs do not boil down to conflicts of their duties. Imagine that, in order to save the life of two persons, a very rare medicine is required. Now, only an indivisible portion of that medicine is available. Both persons have a FLR to the medicine, but both have a duty not to interfere with another's right. In this case, the rights conflict, rather than their duties. More precisely, each person is at liberty to take the medicine, but has a duty to refrain from taking it. This is a right/duty internal conflict, rather than a duty/duty external one.[28] Here we see that the domain of the individual, as described by Steiner, is empty. If the scope of the liberty is defined by the right, then that very liberty is denied by the existence of a duty not to exercise that liberty. If the same is used in applying the interest theory, difficulties arise in measuring which right is more important than the other. Also, Waldron's argument to minimize the tragic element of trade-offs could not apply here. Both persons are equally entitled to the medicine to save their life. It is difficult to imagine any calculation that is not quantitative in this case, since the qualitative elements are identical. And even still, the quantitative calculation alone does not seem to yield a satisfactory result. As a consequence, a tragic sacrifice is inevitable in this case.

This example confirms once more that the will and the interest theories must be combined in order to provide a richer understanding of rights, or at least of FLRs. Namely, a satisfactory theory of FLRs should be able to elucidate the

---

[26] HLA Hart, 'Legal Rights' in HLA Hart, *Essays on Bentham* (Oxford: Clarendon Press, 1982).
[27] Hart talks about constitutional rights.
[28] For this example, see Francis Kamm, 'Rights' in Coleman and Shapiro, *The Oxford Handbook of Jurisprudence and Philosophy of Law* (Oxford: OUP, 2002) 499.

central problem of conflicts. The interest theory focuses on the role of trade-offs, whereas the will theory rests on the dangers of normative inconsistencies. The constitutional status theory deals with both issues, as both constitutive of conflict, and as being crucial to understand the way in which a system of rights works. The constitutional status theory has a second aspect: it stresses the importance of contingent institutional mechanisms in enforcing FLRs (function).

Institutional devices include both formal and material norms of solution of conflicts. This is because institutions solve conflicts of FLRs by developing a definition of the domain covered by FLRs. They couple this with an evaluation of the importance of each FLR when they clash. Both of these activities involve a level of discretion as exercised by the relevant institution. Moreover, both formal and material norms create a framework for the adjudication of conflicts of FLRs.

Officials should remember that their discretion must be deferential to the way individuals wish to exercise their rights. The material process should also be exercised so as to avoid basic errors. Waldron has suggested a way by which a 'lexical priority' can be established by reference to internal relations between rights. Although this idea is interesting, it may be based on a relation between incomparable things—such as between actual and foreseen results.[29] For instance, it is extremely difficult to link the foreseen satisfaction of protecting free speech versus the actual frustration of not preventing a breach of privacy. It amounts to comparing an abstract with a concrete weight, and this is obviously problematic: a concrete weight is burdened by the actual difficulties of enforcing a FLR.

To conclude, sometimes institutions will have to recognize that individuals may waive their rights in order to promote another interest (eg euthanasia). On other occasions, institutions will have to question their own understanding of the interests promoted by certain rights, while furthering others (eg privacy v free speech). To sum up, a constitutional status theory attempts to elucidate the *real* problems involved in cases of genuine conflicts. It does this in order to provide a better framework to deal with them from many perspectives, including the institutional one.

5. Beyond Absolute or Prima Facie FLRs

FLRs are sometimes misleadingly portrayed. The idea of them being either absolute or prima facie is by far the greatest myth. To understand this, look at what is meant by FLRs as being either absolute or prima facie. FLRs are said to be absolute when they do not admit to being overruled. Absolute rights are meant to win every competition, and there is no reason that can outweigh them. But, what if two absolute rights conflict with another? Does this mean that the same right can be both stronger and weaker simultaneously? 'Absolutists' would argue that

[29] Ibid, 502.

there is only ever one right at stake and that is the one that prevails. They do not regard the alternate right as a *real* FLR. But, what if the same right is real, as in the previous example of the life-saving medicine?

Prima facie theorists, on the other hand, hold that a right is always susceptible to being overridden by countervailing rights. The real significance of rights is dependent on its *scope*: although the reason that a right provides is always relative, this right always provides a reason that we have to balance with others. Hence, absolutists believe in maximum *strength* but limited scope, whereas prima facie theorists believe in relative strength but general scope.

In my opinion FLRs are neither absolute nor prima facie. FLRs are relative both in strength and in scope; although their strength may be very firm, and their reach very broad. But both these attributes depend on the way FLRs further a constitutional status for individuals. What is absolute, and inalienable, is the status of individuals. And, as constitutive of the constitutional status, FLRs have a double dimension: a static and a dynamic one. The static dimension determines a set of important interests that have to be respected by creating adequate institutional arrangements. The dynamic aspect depends on the capacity of each right holder to elect how to operate his FLRs. For example, a FLR to free speech held by a journalist is near absolute—if the journalist is in the pursuit of true and correct information for the public.

The opposition between absolute and prima facie conceptions of rights concerns their very foundations. The absolutist conception corresponds to a Kantian view of rights, while the prima facie conception can be traced back to Bentham. A famous example will be used to illustrate the different approaches: the 'two men on a plank' case.[30] Imagine that after being shipwrecked two men are fighting for survival; there is only one plank, and it can only support one man. Kant argued that in such a case, to push a man off the plank cannot be justified on the basis of rights. It can only be excused, or pardoned. But to state that there is a conflict of rights in this situation would render morality inconsistent. An interest theory, however, would identify the interest in survival as being held by both men. As a result, an interest of one individual would hold the other under a duty to refrain from interfering with the right holder's right. Since the duty is the same for both, and both have the same right, there is a conflict of duties, which requires a trade-off. It is difficult to see how a trade-off, in this case, could be made less dramatic simply by establishing internal relations between the duties, as Waldron would have it.

A similar case was decided by the House of Lords in 1884.[31] A crew of five, who had been shipwrecked, were left on a lifeboat without food and water. In order to survive they killed and ate the ship's cabin boy, who was in the worst condition. The House of Lords, adhering to a Kantian view of rights, displayed some sympathy,

---

[30] Claire Oakes Finkelstein, 'Two Men on a Plank', Legal Theory 7 (2001) 279–306.
[31] *Regina v Dudley and Stephens* [1884] 14 QBD 273 DC.

but concluded that the crew did not have the right to kill, and that no excuse was acceptable. This 19th century case can be used in contrast with more recent cases. Recently, the Supreme Court of the United States had to decide a case in which a woman, who was carrying twins, was advised by her doctor to have a caesarean in order to save both children. She refused to do this, and this led to the death of the twins. The debate in the court revolved around the possibility of accusing the woman of murder. The court rejected this, holding that there were conflicting rights at stake, and therefore the choice of the mother could be accepted.

Why compare the caesarean case and the shipwreck case? These two cases present two opposing conceptions of rights. In the shipwreck case, the House of Lords assumed that rights allowing a normative inconsistency are not rights. Therefore, there were no rights at stake. In the caesarean case, the US Supreme Court is not afraid of the spectre of normative inconsistencies. As a result, it is *a priori* possible to suggest that both the mother and the unborn twins have rights. This, in turn, leaves a scope to the right holder, who cannot be accused of having acted in an incompatible way to his right. But what is the teaching of these cases? It seems that we cannot construe rights in order to avoid normative inconsistencies. Also, if rights lead to inconsistencies, then we must think harder about the implications of these issues for law and morality.

Conceptions of rights are constantly adjusted and refined, in order to meet or to avoid the problem of conflicts of FLRs. The distinction between absolute and prima facie conceptions is merely nominal. The cabin case, as used by Feinberg, may help us understand how theorists tackle the problem of conflicts. He writes:

Suppose that you are on a backpacking trip in the high mountain country when an unanticipated blizzard strikes the area with such ferocity that your life is imperilled. Fortunately, you stumble onto an unoccupied cabin, locked and boarded up for winter, clearly somebody else's private property. You smash in a window, enter, and huddle in a corner for three days until the storm abates. During this period you help yourself to your unknown benefactor's food supply and burn his wooden furniture in the fireplace to keep warm. Surely you are justified in doing all these things, and yet you have infringed the clear rights of another person.[32]

This example is laden with normative inconsistencies and this is more apparent if you consider the following three propositions:[33] (1) Paul, the cabin's owner, has a FLR to private property; (2) if Paul has a FLR, then Stephen, the backpacker, has a correlative duty not to infringe Paul's FLR to private property; (3) Stephen may permissibly infringe Paul's FLR to private property on the grounds of his FLR to life.

---

[32] Joel Feinberg, 'Voluntary Euthanasia and the Inalienable Right to Life', Philosophy and Public Affairs 7 (1978) 102.
[33] Cristopher Heath Wellman, 'On Conflict Between Rights', Philosophy and Public Affairs 24 (1995) 271–95.

Rights theorists are concerned with the assumptions that characterize the cabin case. Some attack the idea that to have a right to X entails a permission to do X.[34] Others suggest that to have a right is not incompatible with having a duty related to the same action we have a right to.[35] A situation of conflict permits us to rethink assumptions of rights. However, we always return to the same fundamental ideas: either it is not the case that two conflicting FLRs can coexist, or else, it is possible to override a right.

In my opinion, as far as FLRs are concerned, neither strategy seems to me unassailable. First, I do not think that either the absolutist or the prima facie view correctly depict FLRs. Second, neither position elucidates conflicts of FLRs. Third, it seems to be very difficult to disentangle one position from the other. From the legal point of view it is important to keep in mind two central questions: the generality of rights, and the attribution of rights.

A right is general if it exists independently from, and prior to, its concrete application. Carl Wellman disagrees on this point; he believes that a right is real only if it is upheld by a court.[36] That is, a right exists, if and only if, a court favours one claim over another. The recognition of a right is the upshot of a legal process, and not a feature of the reasoning leading to a given result. To say that Wesley has a right amounts to a description of his actual legal positions and relations, as worked out by the court. From this point of view, the reality of a right coincides with its particularity, in that the right belongs to a given individual. A competing view is that rights are first and foremost general.[37] They exist prior to any actual confrontation and they shape the way decisions are taken. I prefer the second approach.

Second, the question of the attribution of rights concerns the problem of who is a right holder. There is a general agreement as to the fact that every human being is a right holder. However, there is no agreement on the concept of human being. This issue relates also to the problem of capacity, and often concerns what we call the edges of life. Is a foetus a right holder?[38] Is a comatose person a right holder? Moreover, legal systems often draw a distinction between the FLRs of human beings and those of citizens.

Why are the reality of rights and their attribution relevant here? Because they qualify, from the legal point of view, certain claims of absoluteness of FLRs, and other claims of the prima facie character of rights. To start with, they qualify the idea of absoluteness as it is extremely difficult to conceive of a system of rights where FLRs are simultaneously broad and strong, while never in conflict. It is

---

[34] Philip Montague, 'When Rights conflict', Legal Theory 7 (2001) 257–77.
[35] Claire Oakes Finkelstein, 'Two Men on a Plank', Legal Theory 7 (2001) 279–306.
[36] See Carl Wellman, *Real Rights* (NY: OUP, 1995). Frederick Schauer explains that Hohfeld's theory is underlined by an American realist concern, 'The Generality of Rights', Legal Theory 6 (2000) 323–28.
[37] Frederick Schauer, 'The Generality of Rights', Legal Theory 6 (2000) 323–36.
[38] Carl Wellman, 'The Concept of Fetal Rights', Law and Philosophy 21 (2002) 65–93.

always the case that, the stronger the right, the more its scope needs refinement. Similarly, the broader the reach of a right, the lesser its strength in peripheral applications.

The prima facie character is equally qualified, as the universal character of a FLR is contested. The reason is that their attribution is limited to certain categories of right holders. In addition, the prima facie conception would have it that, no matter how strong a FLR is in a certain case, it could still be susceptible to overruling by another FLR. But this is a sort of infinite regress that can also undermine the central core of FLRs.

What if, instead of maintaining that FLRs have fixed properties, we changed our perspective and argued that their features depend on their role within every individual's constitutional status? Let me explain. I think that what can be considered as an absolute is the fact that each individual has a constitutional status. By absolute I mean that the constitutional status is inalienable. This means that an individual cannot, even if he consented to, decide to dismiss his constitutional status in exchange for other sorts of benefits. For example, an individual could never decide to enslave himself, and therefore become less equal; even if he was determined that that was his own free choice. The constitutional status is inalienable, but this does not mean that FLRs conferred by the constitutional status are not waivable. On the contrary, it is up to each individual to decide whether, and how, to demand the implementation of his FLR. In some cases an individual will consider that even though one of his FLRs has been breached it is *not* in his interest to insist for the strict respect of his FLR. Hence, a terminally ill patient may think that a doctor, by refraining from doing everything to keep the patient alive, is breaching the patient's FLR to life. Yet, the patient can also believe that to do this rests on a superior interest, namely the interest of having a good death.

What I want to stress here is that, within each individual's constitutional status, every FLR is constitutive, and yet the relative importance of each FLR is determined by the way the individual applies them. This should demonstrate clearly how both the will and the interest theories come together, despite the reality that both interests are factored in differing ways. But the will of an individual is not always central because it may well be that an individual has a constitutional status without being able to decide for himself (ie a child). Also, the theory of constitutional status points out that the only absolute aspect of FLRs is the inalienability of constitutional status (in other words a constitutional status is externally static, but internally dynamic). Within that status, it is possible that individuals consider some of their FLRs as prima facie requirements, and these can in fact be waived.

6. A Typology of Conflicts of FLRs

There are two fundamental aspects of FLRs that have emerged so far. First, FLRs protect aspects of the constitutional status of individuals. This corresponds, as we saw in the second chapter, to a series of circoncentric spheres, which span from innermost thoughts to expressive actions. The protected aspects depend on many contingent features of bills of rights. To be sure, FLRs need to be instantiated in each case; in order to do this officials have to undertake a complex interpretation of abstract permissions. It is now possible to say that conflicts of FLRs take place at the level of their instantiation. We can encounter either conflicts of different FLRs, or conflicts between two instantiations of the same FLR. The former is an inter-right conflict, while the latter is an intra-right conflict. Second, the scope of the actions protected by FLRs in each case depends on the way in which agents operate their FLRs.

In order to build a typology of rights I will use here the notion of constitutional status. A conflict can be either internal or external to one's own constitutional status. The internal conflict occurs when one individual experiences a difficult choice between various FLRs. An external conflict occurs when an agent operates his FLRs in a way that impinges on the constitutional status of another individual. We can actually refine the latter category by using the distinction between active and passive status. Hence, we could have conflicts between two agents claiming protection that stems from their passive status; their active status; or a combination of both. It is also possible to further distinguish between negative and positive FLRs, and between negative and positive duties.

However, the basic structure is as follows:

	Inter-rights	Intra-rights
Internal	FLR to life v FLR to decisional privacy	FLR to life v FLR to life
External	FLR to free speech v FLR to informational privacy	FLR to free speech v FLR to free speech

Determining the correct type of instantiations depends on the guidance given by charters of FLRs, and in the manner in which officials interpret them. The way internal or external conflicts of FLRs are shaped depends on the way FLRs are operated by agents.

In order to explain further the table above I will provide some examples. Internal conflicts of FLRs may take different forms. The most general is either conflicts between instantiations of the same FLR, or conflicts between instantiations of different FLRs. Take, for instance, an individual with a terminal illness. It may be the case that his FLR to life protects an aspect of his existence that is in conflict with his FLR to privacy in supporting his choice to end his life. The fact that the conflict is internal does not mean that there are no duty bearers. On the contrary, the state may be considered as a duty bearer, insofar as it has to refrain from interfering with the choice of the individual. Equally, the physician who treats the patient should be considered a duty bearer. Possibly we can observe the reality of internal conflicts by focusing on the relationship between the individual and the physician. On one hand, the FLR to life of each individual commands that the physician does his best to improve the patient's standards of living. The FLR to decisional privacy, however, may lead the agent to make certain choices that may result in the suppression of his FLR to life.

The problem does not arise, however, from the fact that the individual is willing to waive his FLR to life. The difficulty is that in doing this, the individual alienates his constitutional status by taking such a decision. In other words, by deciding to opt for a good death, the patient is placing in the hands of the physician the entire power in determining the constitutional status of the individual. The internal conflict therefore, is alternatively represented by the conflict of duties on the physician. On one hand, the doctor is required to follow the individual's choice, while on the other, he is forbidden to take away his life.

The second illustration concerns an external type of conflict. In this case we have one agent operating his FLR in a way that conflicts with the way another individual operates his.

The aim of this chapter was to elucidate, as far as possible, the main features of conflicts of FLRs. If the features identified are relevant, then the typology will offer a framework that can help in interpreting, in more illuminating ways, conflicts of FLRs. However, as already suggested, there is ample scope for further exploration since the way FLRs conflict depends on the way bills of rights frame them, and also on the way officials interpret them. The next chapter will present the basic features displayed by legal systems in an attempt to deal with conflicts of FLRs.

4

A Framework to Deal with Conflicts of Fundamental Legal Rights

1. Why a Framework?

In order to deal with genuine conflicts of Fundamental legal Rights (FLRs) we need a constitutional framework. By constitutional framework, I mean a set of institutions and procedures that are set up with the aim of producing decisions of constitutional importance. The framework is comprised of constitutional rules and the practices that stem from them. The problem with a framework is that we always tend to exaggerate the role of an institution, or of a procedure, and therefore neglect other aspects. This is illustrated by modern theories of constitutional adjudication that focus exclusively on the role of constitutional courts and neglect the role of other institutions or procedures.

This chapter is the *clef de voûte* in the architecture of the book. It attempts to bring together the theoretical arguments developed to this point along with their illustration taken from the French, the US, and the English legal systems. As such, it paints a very broad picture of the way each legal system deals with the question of conflict of FLRs. At this macro-level, the aim is to identify some basic differences and similarities that underlie different constitutional frameworks. I believe that the conceptual problem of conflicts of FLRs arise in every system. However, it acquires different forms, and informs different answers, according to certain contingent arrangements that vary from system to system.

A comparative glance may help to dispel certain assumptions that are based entirely on contingent arrangements of legal systems. That is why, in this chapter, I present four main aspects of constitutional frameworks. The four aspects are very broad and are meant to give an overview of the kind of arguments that are advanced in legal reasoning to tackle the problem of genuine conflicts of FLRs. First, I outline the role of a constitution in relation to conflicts of rights. This sounds like an awfully general question, but it is important in introducing some points on the kind of choices that are made by constitutions. Second, I present the vexed question of constitutional interpretation. This is an equally difficult question and I can only aim to sketch what I regard as a proper interpretation of FLRs. Third, I deal with the issue of deference in matters of conflicts of FLRs.

In other words, I discuss which institution is best-placed to formulate an answer to constitutional dilemmas. Fourth, the matter of balancing in legal reasoning is examined.[1] Balancing is often described as the best procedure to help judges reach decisions that involve apparently irreconcilable values.[2] I will argue that this view deeply misrepresents the notion of genuine conflicts of FLRs.

2. Conflicts and the Constitution

Several genuine conflicts of FLRs can arise in constitutional settings. What kind of directives can the constitution (and the charters, declarations, and bills of rights) give as to the resolution of these conflicts? In other words, what does it mean to follow the constitution in these cases? In this section, we will merely point out the way in which constitutional essentials are identified. To be able to pinpoint these sources is already a very important step towards the resolution of the problem of conflicts.

However the issue is a very complex one. It may well be that constitutions do not give clear guidance as to genuine conflicts of FLRs. This is for two reasons. First, constitutions do not provide an answer to every question. From this point of view a constitution is itself a framework and not a foundation.[3] That is, a constitution is not like a 'genome', containing all the relevant information that is there to be unpacked (foundation); it is a legal instrument that defines procedures and institutions that help in reaching decisions.

The document in which these institutions and procedures are set out is the constitution. We have no trouble in identifying the constitution with the document that it is supported by. However, we do have problems when it comes to determining what it is that constitutional norms stand for. From this point of view we can distinguish a constitution *qua symbols* (s) and a constitution *qua norms* (n).[4] The framers of constitutions have clearly intended (s), but there are also certain constitutional norms (n) that they have not intended. Thus, for instance, both in France and in the US the framers did not intend to establish a judicial review of legislation on the grounds of FLRs. Yet both the Supreme Court and the Constitutional Council exercise control over legislation on those grounds.

Bills of rights, charters, and declarations are peculiar objects in the body of a constitution. They do not give any firm guidance on how they ought to be

---

[1] Aleinikoff, 'Constitutional Law in the age of balancing', 96 *Yale LJ* 943 (1986).
[2] David Beatty, *The Ultimate Rule of Law* (Oxford: OUP, 2004).
[3] This is a well known distinction in German constitutional law. See on this point Robert Alexy, 'Postscript' in Robert Alexy, *A Theory of Constitutional Rights* (Oxford: OUP, 2002). There, Alexy refers to the distinction that Böckenförde and Forsthoff draw.
[4] Larry Alexander, 'Introduction' in Larry Alexander (ed), *Constitutionalism: Philosophical Foundations* (Cambridge: CUP, 2001) 6–7. See also in the same volume, Michael J Perry, 'What is "the Constitution" (and Other Fundamental Questions)', 99–151 and Richard S Kay, 'American Constitutionalism', 16–63.

administered, yet they have a very central place. Through bills of rights, constitutions make choices between conflicting schemes of justice. A set of rights is selected and sometimes some rights are given a more prominent position within a set. But, mostly, a set of rights is very uninformative as to the relationship between the different rights.

The distinction previously drawn for the constitution also applies to rights' documents. In order to understand what bills of rights (s) mean, we have to rely on the interpretation of the text. The same does not always apply in consideration of bills of rights (n). For instance, the US Constitution does not clearly mention a FLR to privacy; yet this FLR becomes increasingly important in US constitutional law.[5]

It is now important to return to the issue of conflicts of FLRs and constitutional guidance. Is it the symbolic constitution that we refer to when we try to decide between free speech and privacy? Or is it the normative constitution? In addition, we have to know what difference law makes in cases of conflicts of FLRs. The beginning of an answer is that law is the last resort. It frames the conflict in a simplified way: one party against another fighting for a well-defined claim. Presented this way the conflict has a necessary solution in that either one or the other wins; from this point of view law has to solve the question once it has 'accepted' it.

Conflicts of FLRs are shaped by constitutional rules and practices. We have two broad types of constitutional rules: material and formal. Material rules are those that make it obligatory, prohibited, or permitted to do, or to refrain from doing something. Formal rules are concerned with institutional arrangements. They define the role of institutions and limit their power; moreover, they set up the procedures through which they can achieve their goals. Thus, solving conflicts of FLRs amounts to clearly understanding the complex interplay between constitutional rules, whether formal or material. To this extent constitutions do provide guidance in solving conflicts of FLRs. However, in order to deepen our understanding of these rules, we have to look at how different legal systems flesh out formal and material constitutional rules.

France, the US, and the UK deeply differ as to their constitutional arrangements and practices. A broad outlook shows that the US has a constitutional text which is correlated to a series of amendments. The most important of these amendments came in two separate waves. France has one constitutional text (1958) with no charter or declaration of rights included. The UK does not have a constitutional text and has a spurious bill of rights since the enactment of the Human Rights Act 1998 (HRA 1998).[6] Hence, from the viewpoint of the

---

[5] Lawrence H Tribe, 'Lawrence v. Texas: The Fundamental Right that dare not speak its name', 117 Harv L Rev 1893. Cf ch 5.

[6] It is spurious in the sense that it is not a genuinely British bill of rights, but it is the result of the incorporation of an international document, ie the European Convention of Human Rights. On this point see Sir Sydney Kentridge QC, 'The Incorporation of the European Convention on Human Rights', in University of Cambridge Center for Public Law (ed), *Constitutional Reform in the United Kingdom*, ch 7, 69.

symbolic constitution, it is already difficult to compare these three systems. However, we will see that the constitution *qua* norms (n) do shed some light on the similarities and differences of how these systems create a framework for dealing with conflicts of FLRs.

In the USA, the Constitution of 1787–89 and the Bill of Rights of 1789–91 are viewed as works of genius. Their achievements are the object of veneration and pride. But what exactly is the US Constitution? Is it just the text as approved by the framers, or is it the text as interpreted by generations of constitutional actors up to this point in time? In other words, is the US Constitution a static or a dynamic document? The debates on this question are clearly divided between 'originalists' and 'interpretativists'. In this section I am only concerned with the problem of what both parties recognize as the constitution, and the consequences of this on conflicts of FLRs. In the next section I will deal with the connected topic of constitutional interpretation.

When it comes to how we should understand the constitution we face vigorous disagreement. On one hand, originalists, mainly represented by Justice Scalia[7] and Judge Bork,[8] claim that in order to correctly understand the meaning of the constitution, we have to construct a constitutional history, and to locate the intentions of the framers in a proper historical context. It is not the subjective intentions that we seek, but the objective meaning of clauses, as understood at the end of the 19th century. Contrary to this interpretativists argue that the meaning of the constitution must be expanded in a way that produces the best moral results; in any event, there is no way to establish its original meaning.[9]

I believe that the distinction between constitution (s) and constitution (n) can prove very useful in eliminating misunderstandings. Constitution (s) does bear a meaning that is intelligible, and can be explained. However, in order to understand how the constitution works, we must also ask what is the meaning of the constitution (n); this may well be independent from the former, and yet be constitutional bedrock.[10] The constitution may well be constituted of norms that had never crossed the framers' mind but established themselves as successful constitutional practices (ie judicial review). This simple point assists in an understanding of why originalists cannot maintain their position throughout. They themselves acknowledge that non-originalist precedents bind the interpretation of the constitution.[11]

Interpretativists argue that the constitution (s) can only be a starting point for justice-seeking interpretations. It is a starting point only in a trivial sense since the main aim is to find solutions that morally justify the outcome of constitutional cases. From this perspective our distinction between constitution (s) and constitution (n)

---

[7] Antonin Scalia, *A matter of interpretation: Federal Courts and the Law*, The University Center for Human Values Series (Princeton, NJ: PUP, 1997) 37–41.
[8] Robert Bork, *The Tempting of America* (New York: Free Press, 1990) 218–20.
[9] Ronald Dworkin, *Freedom's Law* (Oxford: OUP, 1996), 1–38.
[10] Michael J Perry (n 4 above), 104–107.
[11] See on this point Richard Fallon, *Implementing the Constitution* (Cambridge, Mass: HUP, 2001) 17.

becomes irrelevant, given that the constitution is what the best moral interpretation says it is. Hence, it would be as good to have a bill of rights that simply states: 'do what is morally best'. This is not fully accurate, however, because justice-seeking interpretations claim that they want to *fit* precedents, as much as they want to *justify* new decisions. But of course, in hard cases, it is probable to have moral reasons that go against previous constitutional practice. Under such conditions the moral dimension obviously takes precedence. This position is not so much wrong as it is incomplete, as it does not fit the practice very well. Likewise, it tends to completely underestimate the role played by strategic and institutional arguments as developed by the Supreme Court.[12]

Both originalists and interpretativists fall short of providing a full explanation as to what the constitution is and how it can actually give guidance in dealing with conflicts of FLRs. No doubt the original meaning of the constitution is helpful in order to understand the constitutional text. It provides information about its aims as sought by the authors of the text. On the other hand, interpretativists undoubtedly present the constitution in an attractive way; this is because of the 'best light's device' that they require from decision-makers. However, they fail to give a proper account of what happens when no 'best light' can be shed. That is, in cases of genuine conflicts of FLRs. It could be suggested that the distinction between constitution (s) and constitution (n) should be kept, in order to understand both the original meaning of the text and the implications of its modifications.

France, as noted, does have a constitution (s), but has no declaration, charter, or bill of rights in the body of the constitution (s). It is only in the preamble that there is a reference to past declarations of rights. However, it is clear that the constitution (s) did not intend to incorporate a declaration. Yet, the constitution (n) only makes sense if it is understood in light of the decision of the Constitutional Council.[13] Then it was decided that the texts referred to in the preamble are a source of judicial review of legislation. The preamble of the 1958 Constitution reads as follows:

The French people solemnly proclaim their attachment to the Rights of Man and to the principles of national sovereignty as defined by the Declaration of 1789, confirmed and complemented by the Preamble to the Constitution of 1946.

This short text refers to the historical Declaration of Rights (1789). Moreover, it refers to the Preamble of the Constitution of 1946 which contains a certain number of social and economic rights. As a result, France not only has one but it has at least two declarations of rights. The French Constitution did not contemplate a judicial review of legislation on grounds of FLRs. This is the result of a famous decision made in 1971 which created a '*bloc de constitutionnalité*', that is, a set of texts serving as a basis for review. What is striking is that the two main documents composing the '*bloc*' originate from very different philosophical and historical

---

[12] Ibid, 28.   [13] *Conseil Constitutionnel*, 71–44 DC *Liberté d'association*.

contexts; thus, they are quite different in content. The Declaration of 1789 contains classical rights and it is inspired by a liberal philosophy. The Preamble of 1946 is inspired by a threefold political source as influenced by communist, socialist, and centrist politics. It also displays rights that are more socially oriented. To the two texts already cited we have to add a third source of rights that is named by the 1946's Preamble: the fundamental principles recognized by the laws of the republic.[14] This category of principles has been developed by the Constitutional Council, with reference to the statutes of the third Republic, and created a protective regime for some liberties such as the right to free association,[15] and the right to freedom of education.[16]

The heterogeneity of bills of rights raises doubts as to how to identify the sources of constitutional rights. One of the main problems in relation to the Constitution (s) is how to know whether any document on rights is superior to another. Most authors regard this issue as one having a possible bearing on the question of FLRs conflicts. If it were possible to determine the superiority of one text over another, then this would provide a means to interpret rights in either one sense or another. Unfortunately the arguments for the primacy of the first or the second texts are fraught with great difficulties.

To begin with, a hierarchy of texts cannot be established through the principle of the *lex posterior*, as the documents are recognized simultaneously in the Constitution of 1958 by its Preamble. Thus, it is difficult to show that the Preamble of 1946 is superior to the Declaration of 1789 simply because it is posterior to it. Similarly, there is no decisive reason for the primacy of the Declaration of 1789 over the Preamble of 1946. Roughly, the arguments on this point have attempted to show that the text of 1789 is a universal and a-temporal Declaration, whereas the Preamble of 1946 is the product of a precise political context. Therefore the latter is seen as being more contingent, and hence inferior. However, it is difficult to understand this argument. Both texts (1789 and 1946) have been recognized by the Constitution of 1958 as being at the foundation of the French polity. Moreover, it remains hard to show how the formulation of any one text has a more stringent value than another. Both are couched in rather general terms and, in all likelihood, neither is thought to be sufficiently precise to guide the work of a judge. From a political philosophy perspective it may be argued that some principles fit better with certain substantive philosophical positions, but this does not constitute an argument for the ranking of the texts.[17]

The impression is that the debate over the formal hierarchy of the texts is sterile. In 1958 the *pouvoir constituant* took the decision to refer to both texts;

---

[14] '*Principes Fondamentaux reconnus par les lois de la République*'. For a study of these principles see Véronique Champeil Desplats, *Les Principes Fondamentaux reconnus par les lois de la République* (Aix-Marseille: PUAM, 1998). [15] Cf *Conseil Constitutionnel*, 71–44 DC.
[16] *Conseil Constitutionnel*, déc. 77–87 DC, *Liberté d'enseignement et de conscience*.
[17] For an impressive argument in favour of sifting, and ranking, constitutional principles see Alan Brudner, *Constitutional Goods* (Oxford: OUP, 2004).

therefore they have to be read as a whole. Of course this whole is far from being coherent. Also, it is far from exhausting the sources of constitutional rights. However to cast the problem in terms of a hierarchy of texts is somehow misleading. At best, the latter could be seen as a conflict of ideologies underpinning the declaration and the preamble, but not an interesting conflict from a legal point of view; namely, one that commands a hard choice between two competing statements of rights. For the purposes of our enquiry this might prove particularly interesting as it points to the lack of explicit norms dealing with clashes between FLRs. French doctrine, however, turns to futile arguments of formal hierarchy, which prove to be of little help.

Some authors suggest that a Constitution (n) should show the existence of a material hierarchy of rights. This hierarchy stems from a supposedly statistical assessment of the decisions of the Constitutional Council. This however is often a pretext for authors to put forward their personal view on the primacy of rights. Thus, some argue for the primacy of classical liberties.[18] Others hold that dignity and pluralism are the overarching principles of the system; and even if those are not, strictly speaking, rights they may be seen as rights to have rights.[19] Still others insist on the degree of protection afforded by certain decisions, and then draw conclusions as to the hierarchy of rights from that. Favoreu gives a prominent position not only to freedom of thought and of conscience, but also to the freedom of association and to academic freedom. Finally, some revive a natural law tradition by appealing to the primacy of natural rights such as liberty, property, and disobedience.[20]

To distinguish between the Constitution (s) and the Constitution (n) proves again useful. It helps elucidate the extent of the Constitution (s) and the way it is modified by the Constitution (n). Also, it helps locate different types of arguments and evaluate their relevance for the structure of the *bloc de constitutionnalité*.

In the UK there is no written constitution. Hence, it is not possible to identify a constitution (s). However, it is often said that England does have an unwritten constitution, which we can refer to as a constitution (n). The latter is often presented in the way Albert Venn Dicey systematized it in his seminal work.[21] Since 1998 England has a written Bill of Rights; the Human Rights Act 1998 (HRA).[22] However, the Bill of Rights (n) is wider than the HRA—understood as the Bill of Rights (s). This is so for two reasons. First, it is often argued that the UK protected

---

[18] R Badinter and B Genevois, 'Normes de valeur constitutionnelle et dégré de protection des droits fondamentaux'. Rapport présenté par la délégation française à la VIII conférence des Cours constitutionnelles européennes (Ankara, 7–10 May 1990) in RFDA 6 (3), May–June 1990.

[19] Dominique Rousseau, *Droit du contentieux constitutionnel* (5th edn, 1999).

[20] Turpin, *Contentieux constitutionnel* (Paris: PUF, 1994).

[21] Albert V Dicey, *The Law of the Constitution* (Boston: Adamant Media Corp, 2000). To present the constitution this way is paradoxical because it seems to confer to it a certain rigidity which by definition an unwritten constitution lacks.

[22] John Wadham and Helen Mountfield, *Blackstone's guide to the Human Rights Act 1998* (London: Blackstone Press Limited, 1999).

certain FLRs long before the incorporation of the ECHR.[23] Second, the HRA not only incorporates the text of the ECHR, but also requires domestic courts to take into account the relevant case law of the Court of Strasbourg. Section 2 of the HRA requires doing so, 'so far as, in the opinion of the court or tribunal, [the case law] is relevant to the proceedings in which that question has arisen'. It is therefore up to domestic courts to state the criteria according to which Strasbourg's case law should be taken into account.

To add to this difficulty, the HRA is not endowed constitutional status. It is an ordinary Act of Parliament and, as such, it is difficult to understand how it can really impose itself on other Acts at the same hierarchical level.[24] Moreover, the HRA does not create a free-standing system of judicial review of legislation. Judges can only interpret legislation, in a way that makes it compatible with the requirements of the HRA. In cases of flagrant incompatibility, the judge has no explicit power to void legislation incompatible with the HRA.[25]

Our distinction once more plays an important role. It allows us to identify both constitutional law and FLRs and to put them in relation. Arguably this relation has not yet been fully explained. However, we can start by observing how judges deal with hard cases and in particular with cases of conflict of FLRs.

3. Interpretation and Conflicts of FLRs

The broad texture of constitutional norms requires intensive interpretative work.[26] However, interpretation cannot be perceived as the only means in solving constitutional problems. FLRs that are seen as being in conflict can sometimes be interpreted in a way that explains away the conflict. But, at other times, interpretation can only shed light on the existence of a conflict, without being able to define it away. The latter distinction underlies the difference between modest and comprehensive interpretations.[27] Comprehensive interpretations view the truth of both the interpretation of a norm and of the scheme of justice within which the

---

[23] Murray Hunt, *Using Human Rights Law in English Courts* (Oxford: Hart Publishing, 1998).

[24] Nicholas Bamforth, 'Parliamentary Sovereignty and H.R.A.1998' [1998] Public Law 572. Contra, David Feldman, 'The Human Rights Act 1998 and Constitutional Principles' Legal Studies 19 (1999) 165–206.   [25] I will come back to this point in the next section.

[26] The literature on this point is enormous. I will give but a few examples for each country. Robert Alexy, *Theorie der Grundrechte* (1985); Dorf and Tribe, *Reading the Constitution* (Cambridge Mass: HUP, 1991); Robert H Bork, *The Last Tempting of America—The Political Seduction of The Law* (New York: Free Press, 1990); Richard H Fallon Jr, *Implementing the Constitution* (Cambridge, Mass: HUP, 2001); Ronald Dworkin, *Freedom's Law* (Oxford: OUP, 1996); Andrei Marmor, *Positive Law and Objective Values*, (Oxford: OUP, 2001); Bertrand Mathieu and Michel Verpeaux, *Contentieux Constitutionnel des Droits Fondamentaux* (Paris: LGDJ, 2001); Otto Pfersmann, 'Esquisse d'une théorie des droits fondamentaux' in Favoreu et al., Droits des libertés fondamentales (Paris: Dalloz, 2000); Joseph Raz, *The Morality of Freedom* (Oxford: OUP, 1986); Antonin Scalia, *A Matter of Interpretation*, n 7 above.

[27] Andrei Marmor, *Positive Law and Objective Values*, ibid, 133.

interpretation is performed. A comprehensive interpretation claims that free speech should be understood in a certain way and from a certain perspective. Moreover, this perspective is the only possible viewpoint from which free speech can be apprehended. A modest interpretation, on the contrary, would simply claim that within a given perspective there is one truthful interpretation. Of course, other interpretations are possible from different perspectives.

To anticipate, it will emerge that modest interpretations are best suited to the understanding of constitutional practices. The main reason for doubting comprehensive interpretations is that they totally obscure the existence of conflicts of FLRs. Indeed, the superiority of the scheme of justice advanced by comprehensive interpretation lies in the fact that it always offers right answers; thereby removing the possibility of genuine conflicts. On the contrary, modest interpretations acknowledge the existence of a plurality of perspectives. Hence, a conflict of FLRs may very well be the reflection of a truthful interpretation of constitutional practice.

Interpretation includes two different aspects, which I will call *stricto sensu* interpretation, and specification.[28] *Stricto sensu* interpretation attempts to understand the meaning of FLRs, while specification attempts to determine the object to which a FLR applies. Therefore, when we say that we have a new case in front of us, we do not want to imply that the meaning of a FLR must be changed. In this sense, whichever interpretative process is used, it has to guarantee a certain consistency. What we mean by 'new case' is that we are unsure as to whether it falls within the protective scope of a given FLR. Is, for instance, the right to die an instantiation of a right to life? This is the kind of problem that specification is concerned with.

Having drawn this distinction, it is easier now to understand the role of modest interpretations. They are mainly meant to elucidate the meaning of the text entrenching FLRs. In a sense, we can say that it is mainly a looking backward exercise that attempts to understand why and when a value has been selected as a constitutional essential. Specification, however, plays a role in modest interpretations, albeit a contested one. Specification can be described as a forward looking exercise. It aims to grasp the actual context and understand whether a FLR can explain its reading. Specification amounts to a form of discretion requiring from the relevant institution a set of value choices. The question is whether those value choices are somehow constrained. I believe that specification is subordinated to *stricto sensu* interpretation that set boundaries to the possible value choices. Moreover, specification is also to be understood within institutional constraints. A new hard case is never taken in a vacuum. It must instead be placed within a line of cases and prior interpretations. In order to better understand these distinctions it is useful to analyse them in context. The debate about *stricto sensu* interpretation and specification of FLRs is forthright in every country. I will start with the debate in the UK as it proves quite problematic.

---

[28] The latter aspect of interpretation is referred to in various different ways: specification, concretization, instantiation, articulation, etc. I will use the word specification for the sake of uniformity.

Under the HRA, judges in the UK have an obligation to interpret legislation by conforming to Convention rights: 'So far as it is possible to do so, primary legislation and subordinate legislation must be read and given effect in a way which is compatible with the Convention Rights'.[29] The very interpretation of this rule of interpretation raises a host of problems.[30] In particular, the meaning of 'possible' is very hard to grasp. By deciding what is possible, the judge will determine the intrusiveness of his control. Likewise, it is already quite clear that judges will not only intervene when the meaning of the legislation at stake is ambiguous; but, they are also willing to stretch that meaning when seeking reconciliation between the HRA and any conflicting piece of legislation.[31] To do that, two techniques are envisaged: 'reading in' and 'reading down'.[32] 'Reading in' consists of adding to the legislative text a word that will make the text consistent with the HRA. 'Reading down' means narrowing the possible meanings of legislation down to a number of options that are compatible with the HRA.

However, there are other problems that fall within the category of interpretation. To understand this, we have to distinguish between three types of interpretation as required by the HRA either explicitly or implicitly.[33] First, as mentioned above, it requires the interpretation of the rule of interpretation. Second, it requires the interpretation of the legislation at stake. Third, it requires the interpretation of Convention rights. These three interpretations are intertwined.

What we are concerned with here is the interpretation of Convention rights. At this stage, the distinction between *stricto sensu* interpretation and specification can be a partial relief for the judge. Interpretation, at this level, is constrained by the interpretations that the Strasbourg Court has already given in previous cases.[34] Not to pay adequate attention to the Strasbourg Court would be a big risk, since a plaintiff could always claim that Convention rights have not been duly interpreted. The domestic judge could however focus on the task of specification of Convention rights, since Strasbourg leaves a notable 'margin of appreciation'. Specification, as previously stated, requires a considerable amount of discretion, directed at making some value choices that will have an impact on the decision of a case.

Statutory interpretation, as stated in section 3(1), has to be subordinated to *stricto sensu* interpretation and specification. To recap, *stricto sensu* interpretation of Convention rights are constrained by a backward looking process. Courts should pay attention to previous case law, as decided either domestically or internationally. This does not completely restrict the discretion of the UK judges, who still need to embark on the exercise of specification; this requires value choices as

---

[29] S 3(1), HRA.
[30] Geoffrey Marshall, 'Interpreting Interpretation in the Human Rights Bill', Public Law (1998) 167.   [31] *R v A* [2002] 1 AC 45, para 97 *per* Lord Clyde.
[32] David Feldman, *Civil liberties and Human Rights in England and Wales* (Oxford: OUP, 2002) 80–112.
[33] Aileen Kavanagh, 'Interpretation under the Human Rights Act 1998', (2004) 24 OJLS 259–85.   [34] S 2(1), HRA.

constrained by proper *stricto sensu* interpretation. Once reaching this point, the judge is able to evaluate his role, in the 'possible' interpretation of statutory law, and how far it wishes to go before making it compatible with convention rights.

In the US, the issue of interpretation of FLRs is a primary focus in the debates. Justice Scalia, for instance, deems constitutional adjudication a matter of interpretation.[35] He argues that the common law creative methodology has a disruptive effect when applied to the interpretation of the broad clauses of the Constitution. Most US constitutional lawyers are aware of the difficulties with the interpretation of FLRs; many of them distinguish between the question of interpretation and that of specification.[36] Some authors suggest that the best method in deciding how to specify FLRs is the 'constitution-as-a-whole' method. From that perspective FLRs are regarded as displaying a 'rational continuum'. It is useful to quote from one of these authors:

In particular, the Court gave short shrift to the notion that it was under some obligation to confine its implementation of substantive due process to the largely mechanical exercise of isolating 'fundamental rights' as though they were a historically given set of data points on a two-dimensional grid, with one dimension representing time and the other representing a carefully defined and circumscribed sequence of protected primary activities (speaking, praying, raising children, using contraceptives, and the like).[37]

In this passage Laurence Tribe comments on the exercise of specification, as carried out by the Supreme Court when expanding the due process clause. What is important to note is that it is possible to have different methods of specification. The boundaries of specification are open-ended. When the court proceeds to specification, it makes two types of value choices. First, it determines the method. Second, it clarifies the application of the method.

Another way to deal with the problem of interpretation is offered by Richard Fallon. He seeks to overcome the problems related to interpretation by expanding the notion of constitutional implementation.[38] Implementation is concerned with two processes: the first is the search for constitutional meaning; the second is pragmatic insofar as it amounts to the working out of doctrines capable of responding to more pressing problems. In other words, Fallon distinguishes between interpretation and specification. However, he defines specification as a practical exercise that takes into account institutional and strategic concerns that the Supreme Court must face. This will have different implications in ordinary and extraordinary cases. In ordinary cases, implementing the Constitution will require the correct application of precedents: in extraordinary cases, it will call on

---

[35] Antonin Scalia, *A Matter of Interpretation*, passim.
[36] To take but one example, see Michael Dorf and Laurence Tribe, (n 26 above) *On Reading the Constitution* (Cambridge, Mass: HUP, 1991). They do refer to it as the problem of 'levels of abstraction'.
[37] Laurence Tribe, 'Lawrence v. Texas: The Fundamental Right that dare not speak its name', 117 Harv L Rev 1893 at 1898 (2004).
[38] Richard Fallon, *Implementing the Constitution* (n 11 above).

creating new methods for the resolution of hard cases. By using the notion of implementation, Fallon perceives a need to move the debate onto a platform that is not as heavily influenced by the often-misleading concept of interpretation.[39]

The move from holistic interpretation to more practical concerns of the Constitution may help us understand why constitutional scholars should opt for modest interpretation rather than comprehensive ones. In the past, the battle has often been conducted on the grounds of those possessing the best overall theory of interpretation. Thus, a list of general guidelines was set, and from them we are supposed to draw every possible answer. Increasingly however, constitutional scholars point to the limited insight provided by general theories of constitutional interpretation.

In France interpretation is the object of deep disagreement.[40] As applied to FLRs, interpretation covers a range of activities that have little in common with one another. First, the Declaration of 1789 and the Preamble of 1946 are interpreted in order to understand their underlying philosophy.[41] This proves particularly difficult because the Declaration of 1789 was informed by a liberal background while the Preamble of 1946 has a socialist flavour. Given the impossibility of reconciling those schemes at the conceptual level, the most intense interpretive task takes place at the level of application of the norms. But, once more, it is advisable to distinguish different types of operations falling within the broad label of 'interpretation'. The previous distinction between understanding the meaning and specifying FLRs' requirements can apply in this case too. However, in the French system the task of specification is much less important than in the previous two cases. This can be explained very easily. French constitutional review takes place exclusively before the enactment of a statute and it is therefore always a control *in abstracto*. The *Conseil Constitutionnel* never decides on concrete cases, so the necessity of specifying the range of application of FLRs is less important.

Second, interpretation also serves the purpose of discovering FLRs in the shape of fundamental principles recognized by the Laws of the Republic. Hence, FLRs are found in the statutes of the Third Republic, by way of interpreting them and evaluating their importance at the constitutional level. Third, when deciding issues of constitutionality, the court has to interpret legislation in order to decide whether it complies with FLRs. In many ways the *Conseil Constitutionnel* strains the meaning of legislation, and suggests ways to amend it in order to make it comply with FLRs.[42]

What we are interested in is the interpretation of the constitutional texts. France, from this point of view, is an interesting example as it shows that comprehensive

---

[39] I can only agree with this point. However, in this chapter I tried to make sense of 'interpretation' as it is used in constitutional law and practice.

[40] Otto Pfersmann, 'Esquisse d'une théorie des droits fondamentaux' in Louis Favoreu et alii (n 26 above).

[41] Stephane Rials, *La déclaration des droits de l'homme et du citoyen* (Paris: Hachette, 1988).

[42] Alexandre Viala, *Les réserves d'interprétation dans la jurisprudence du Conseil Constitutionnel* (Paris: LGDJ, 1999).

interpretations are simply not conceivable here. How could we possibly hold that there is an underlying scheme of justice that guides the right interpretation when the founding texts stem from different, if not opposite, philosophical backgrounds? Instead of comprehensive interpretations, the *Conseil Constitutionnel* acknowledges the importance of institutional and practical concerns.

Interpretation plays a central role in constitutional adjudication. Unfortunately, it is hard to pin down its exact role and scope. But a useful distinction between *stricto sensu* interpretation and specification can be drawn in order to define better what is required by interpretation itself. Moreover, I argue that it is advisable to resort to modest interpretations of the constitution as opposed to comprehensive interpretations, which often misrepresent the reality of constitutional practice.

4. Deference and Conflicts of FLRs

Genuine conflicts of FLRs provoke, as argued before, disagreement coupled with deadlock. Agents involved in a conflict hold competing views, and there is no way of solving the disagreement without a sacrifice. It is often said that in such cases, courts should defer the matter to more representative institutions. But does this solve the problem? The short answer is no, since we are left with no directives as to when deference should apply. In fact, it is deeply unclear what we mean by deference *tout court*.

Deference is a very multi-layered concept. Commonly, judicial institutions have to display a certain amount of deference towards more representative institutions. But deference need not be exclusively an institutional business. Judges may pay deference towards individuals too. This is the case when, in some cases, a norm protects individuals' autonomous choices. Moreover, deference is not unilateral. It may well be that a legislative body would defer to the court for a certain decision; for example, in the case of repartition of competences. Finally, deference could be intra-branches, in the sense that a lower court may defer to a higher court or vice versa.

In this section, what I am interested in is whether constitutions do openly address one of the many facets of deference, with the purpose of solving certain conflicts of FLRs. A quick overview suggests that constitutions are silent about this, but constitutional practices do seem to display considerable concern for the question of deference. Similarly, the subject of deference has produced a vast amount of literature. The crux of this issue concerns the place of the judicial power within the constitutional setting. It is interesting to compare the USA—where judicial supremacism is a widespread conviction—with France and the UK—where the principle of sovereignty of the legislator is stronger than in many other European states. However, deference does not boil down to the recognition of either doctrine. Within each framework the question of deference concerns the extent to which, and the principles according to which, a court should leave the decision to the representative body or decide for itself. When applied to a dilemma concerning FLRs, the issue of deference acquires considerable importance.[43]

In the UK, the enactment of the HRA upset the balance of powers within the British constitution. In order to moderate judicial power, both the judges[44] and academics have developed a concept of deference that is meant to secure room for manoeuvre for the Government. The concept of deference has already stimulated a number of commentaries that attempt to make sense out of an elusive and controversial notion.

Nonetheless, its nature remains unclear and its definition ambiguous. On one hand the normative grounds for such a notion have not been spelled out. There is no mention of it either in the HRA or in the European Convention of Human Rights. Of course, the European Court of Human Rights (EctHR) uses the notion of margin of appreciation in order to limit its supervision over rights issues that need to be assessed within the national dimension. However, the doctrine of a margin of appreciation is an international doctrine that does not fit easily into the national picture. On the other hand, deference seems to have no added value in contrast with more classical notions such as discretion or separation of powers. Laws LJ, for example, refers to deference and discretion as two sides of the same coin:

> the principles now being developed by the courts for the ascertainment of the *degree of deference* which the judges will pay, or the scope of the *discretionary area of judgement* which they will cede, to the democratic powers of government in fulfilment of the courts' duty to decide in any given case whether there has been a violation of a Convention right.[45]

However, I believe that the question of conflict of FLRs goes beyond the mere repartition of competences, or the area of discretion exercised by each institution. Is it really possible to hold that, whatever the decision of the elected body, it will fit the requirements of the system of rights' protection? Is the question of conflict of rights only a matter of exercizing authority? The short answer to this is negative. A more in-depth answer depends on more thorough investigation, which delves into the rationales of the doctrine of deference in matters of rights.

In the case of *Roth*,[46] Laws LJ gave four rationales for the deference doctrine. First, he states that deference is based on democratic grounds. The court should vary their deference according to the decision-maker who takes the decision. The deference to parliament, for instance, should be greater than that owed to a minister, or to another governmental authority. Moreover, 'the parliament, and not a written constitution, bears the ultimate mantle of democracy in the state'.[47] From

---

[43] A very good illustration of deference in the context of ethical dilemmas is provided by the ECHR case, *Evans v UK* (Application No 6339/05), 7 March 2006.
[44] *R v DPP, ex parte Kebilene* [2000] 2 AC 326. *R (Alconbury Developments Ltd) v Secretary of the State for the Environment, Transport and the Regions* [2001] 2 WLR 1389.
[45] Ibid.
[46] *International Transport Roth GmbH v Secretary of State for the Home Department* [2003] QB 728. *Per* Laws LJ §81. [47] Ibid at §83.

this point of view, it seems that rights are subordinated to a principle of democracy. This would seem to uphold the idea that the final decision of conflict of rights is a matter of democratic authority. But this is still not sufficient. Just because parliament has scope for discretion, does not mean that it can reach whichever decision.

Second, deference depends on the right at stake. Laws LJ distinguishes between qualified and unqualified rights. A qualified right is simply a right that has been enunciated in the ECHR with a limitation clause (§2). All others are deemed as unqualified. The consequence of deference is that 'there is more scope for deference where the convention itself requires a balance to be struck, much less so where the right is stated in terms which are unqualified'.[48] The interpretation of this statement is quite difficult. Does it mean that only the parliament can balance qualified rights? Of course this is not the case. Does it mean that unqualified rights are absolute? And if so, what happens if they conflict? Does it mean that the only institution competent enough to balance is parliament? And what about the review of proportionality as exercised by the courts? The distinction between qualified and unqualified rights begs more questions than it solves.

Third, deference will be greater where the subject-matter is within the responsibility of democratic powers. For instance, defence is a government prerogative, and as such its exercise cannot be reviewed. It may, however, be doubted as to whether this doctrine really concerns the protection of constitutional rights. For instance, if the government were to torture people because it was persuaded that they threatened the security of the state. This would still be an insufficient justification in granting the government a wide discretion on whether to torture or not. The discretion allowed should be lesser, not greater.

Fourth, deference depends on the level of expertise of the institution that implements it. This rationale is strictly linked with the previous one. It means that a decision must be located within a bigger policy framework that requires a certain expertise. For instance, if parliament takes a decision that fits within a macro-economic framework, it is less likely that the judge will be in a position to decide whether the decision fits into the broader scheme. This last rationale is less controversial and does not require much in the way of comment.

The impression is that the rationales for deference do not give any guidance as to who has the final word on rights' conflict. Indeed, it is difficult to square the existence of such a broad area of discretion, with the idea that the courts are the guardians of human rights: 'the court's role under the 1998 Act is as the guardian of human rights. It cannot abdicate this responsibility'.[49]

The tension between the idea of deference and the idea of the judge being the guardian of constitutional rights is at the core of the UK scheme of the protection of rights. Much ink has been spilled in attempting to 'dress-up' the tensions in reasonably acceptable clothes. I think there is a major flaw; namely, the illusion that the sovereignty of parliament can be preserved in the face of constitutional rights.

[48] Ibid at §85. [49] Ibid *per* Brown LJ at §27.

In the US or in continental Europe, the understanding of constitutional rights implies that the legislature itself is bound to respect them. To say the contrary leaves a gap that the judiciary or the doctrine tries to fill by the notion of deference. But a tool as underdeveloped as deference is simply unfit to provide responses to hard questions. It is impossible to draw a line to discriminate between the actions that the elected body can or cannot do, irrespective of their impact on constitutional rights. To give even a preliminary answer would require a fully-fledged theory of rights, which carefully sets out a hierarchy of rights, and outlines the respective roles of the institution. As it is presented, deference seems merely to be a useless tool which has little normative ground and does not perform any specific role.[50]

In France, the institutional question also seems to have been resolved in favour of the legislator. Art 34 of the Constitution states that the parliament is competent to enact the rules concerning civil rights and the guarantees of public liberties. Moreover, the *Conseil Constitutionnel* has held that the legislator has a wider power of appreciation than the 'council'.[51] Also, it is the task of the legislator to balance competing rights.[52]

However, the *pouvoir discrétionnaire de conciliation* of the legislature is under the control of the Constitutional Council. Indeed it provides some directives that the legislator has to follow in order to not exceed its power: 'Considering that the legislature can only regulate the exercise of fundamental liberties to make it either more effective or to reconcile it with other rules or principles of constitutional value.'[53]

Here, we have two conflicting guidelines. First, the court refers to the '*jurisprudence du cliquet*'.[54] '*Cliquet*' is a metaphorical expression for the principle of the 'always more', in matters of rights protection. This means that if the legislator wishes to modify the protection of a right, it can only do so if the protection is equivalent to, or superior to the initial one. The second guideline, concerns the discretionary power of balancing competing constitutional principles. Thus, the former imposes on the legislator a duty to intervene, for the sake of either maintaining the same level of protection or enhancing protection. The latter principle gives the legislator the competence to conciliate different rights. There is an explicit contradiction between the two principles. The former confers an exclusive competence to the legislator, while the latter considerably limits its competence. On a deeper level, it is hard to understand how the legislator can always enhance a right, if this right conflicts with another. At least one of those rights must be sacrificed. But then '*conciliation*' leads to the lowering of a right.

However, the Constitutional Council, while reconciling, cannot lower the degree of protection of a right to a level where the right would be denied.[55] It is

---

[50] As such it can be filled with whatever one wants. See for instance Trevor Allan, 'Human Rights and Judicial Review: A Critique of "Due Deference"' CLJ 65(3) (2006) 671–95.
[51] *Conseil Constitutionnel*, 81–132 DC (author's translation).
[52] Ibid, 80–127 DC (author's translation).
[53] Ibid, 94–345 DC (author's translation).
[54] Ibid, 79–105 DC (author's translation).
[55] Ibid, 84–181 DC (author's translation).

difficult to apply this last requirement with the '*cliquet*' doctrine; the case law does not display much consistency. The main reason for this, is the protean nature of the term '*conciliation*', which may apply both to a legislative and to a judicial competence as understood by the proportionality principle.

An attempt has been made, within the doctrine, to expand some of the criteria guiding '*conciliation*', still, they seem to be as broad and open ended as those applying to deference. Badinter and Genevois proposed three criteria: (1) the degree of precision of the principles; (2) the degree of attachment of the dominant opinion; (3) the extent of the control that the judge can exercise.[56] These three criteria are quite interesting and also confusing. One wonders what really should be understood by the term 'dominant opinion'. Moreover, it is partly because constitutional rights are stated in broad terms that they create the problem of conflict between them. Finally, the extent of the control of the judge is not fully determined *a priori*. The judge himself has scope when it comes to determining his control. Thus, the fact that a court is willing to exercise stronger control over certain cases, does not make it more competent on the issues of rights-conflict. Viewed in this light, the third criterion is in this context entirely question-begging. Therefore, the question that I originally set out to answer—who decides conflicts of rights?—would depend on the way the judge controls the activity of the legislator. However, this contradicts with the general principle of legislative competence.

The tension between the scope of parliamentary discretion and the extent of protection of constitutional rights appears both in France and in the UK. This is quite surprising, given the fact that in the UK this tension stems from the very notion of rights that forms the debate there. In France, the notion of constitutional right would seem to establish the legitimacy of constitutional review. However, the question of conflicts of rights throws a new challenge to the legitimacy of judicial supervision of the constitution. In any event, both the French and the UK systems grant, in matters of rights conflict, a certain degree of legislative discretion that sits uncomfortably with the intrusive principles of rights adjudication.

In the USA, the doctrine of judicial supremacism shadows the issue of deference. In fact, the notion of judicial supremacism obscures the problem, rather than elucidating it. When confronted with difficult constitutional decisions, and indeed conflicts of FLRs, one thing is to say that the Supreme Court is the final arbiter of who has to take the decision. It is a wholly different thing to ask to what extent the court itself should go on deciding. In fact, the Supreme Court may well be the final arbiter, while at the same time be very deferential to other institutions.

There are three interesting issues here. First, is the Supreme Court supreme? Second, does the Constitution require deferential attitudes? Third, do institutions have substantive views on deference? The obvious implication for conflicts of FLRs

---

[56] R Badinter et B Genevois, 'Normes de valeur constitutionnelle et degré de protection des droits fondamentaux' Rapport présenté par la délégation française à la VIII conférence des Cours constitutionnelles européennes (Ankara, 7–10 May 1990) in *RFDA* 6 (3), May–June 1990.

has both a formal and substantive aspect: is there a single institution charged with the resolution of conflicts? If so, on what grounds is the decision taken?

First, the Supreme Court is indeed considered to be the final interpreter of the Constitution. This is part of the USA doctrine of judicial review developed since *Marbury v Madison*.[57] The Constitution itself does not address the issue, however, it may be argued that the supremacy of interpretation flows from a possible reading of the Constitution which takes the enforcement of the Constitution as an important feature.

Second, the Constitution does not address the question of deference. No institution is deemed better placed to deal with conflicts of FLRs from the point of view of the Constitutional text. Here, we may even wonder as to whether it is desirable to explicitly mention it. The question of deference is a serious substantive one and not simply a matter of courtesy. It involves the establishment of a proper understanding of the role of the court. This means, for the court, setting the boundaries of permissible decision within which the legislature will take a decision. The court will intervene when a dubious case requires clarification. The court is not there to undo the errors made by the legislature, but it does hold the legislative power or the government responsible for their tasks. In this sense, the judge is the ultimate arbiter of what is rational and permissible.

Third, does the court bow to other institutions if a case raises disagreement? I think not; but here again we need clarification. There are some issues that raise considerable disagreement, without ending up in a deadlock. Genuine conflicts of FLRs are not only fraught with disagreement but characterized by a deadlock. In my opinion, courts are there to judge whether we are facing a genuine conflict of FLRs. If they do this, however, they are implicitly acknowledging that their decision is not going to be more just than any other institution's decision. In this case, it may be desirable to consider a greater degree of deference.

5. Balancing and Conflicts of FLRs

Balancing is often perceived as the tool that can help us to solve all those tough constitutional problems, which include conflicts of FLRs. If we can't apply a norm straightforwardly without breaching another fundamental norm, then we can at least try to apply them both—albeit to a partial extent.[58] The language of balancing is a holistic doctrine that attempts to provide us with answers to all the problems raised previously in this chapter. Thus it provides a way of working out

---

[57] *Marbury v Madison*, 5 US 137 (1803); *Cooper v Aaron*, 358 US 1 (1958); *Dickerson v United States*, 530 US 428 (2000).

[58] Guillaume Drago, 'La conciliation entre principes constitutionnels', *Recueil Dalloz-Sirey*, 1991, Chron., 265–69.

the best set of rights⁵⁹; a type of reasoning within the constitution⁶⁰; an explanation of the relation between institutional branches; and finally, a judicial test that we apply in order to reach legal answers.⁶¹

However, can balancing be really useful in the decision of conflict of FLRs? The main criticism comes from the notion of incommensurability.⁶² When two incommensurable values embedded in rights conflict, how is it possible to force them into a measurement of their weight or importance? Jeremy Waldron suggests a distinction between strong and weak incommensurability. He argues that strong incommensurability is the stuff of tragic choices: Agamennon facing the choice between his daughter and his expedition.⁶³ Strong incommensurability leads to agony and paralysis, and it does not offer any criterion of choice other than personal preference. Weak incommensurability, on the contrary, is merely expressed in terms of a 'simple or straightforward priority rule'. This means that, instead of a quantitative utilitarian-like balancing, decisions are taken by playing trumps or enforcing the priority. However, sometimes it will be necessary to choose between trumps. At that point we will resort to balancing albeit a qualitative type of balancing that tries to work out the internal relationship of the values at stake, by way of philosophical reasoning.

The latter view suggests the existence of a fluid moral life where every decision should be carried out by way of unpacking moral considerations. It then compares them one to another in order to discover which values deserve to be better protected. Weak incommensurability is deemed to be central to this kind of moral and constitutional life, and indeed the most prominent theoreticians are deemed to subscribe to this view. In short, weak incommensurability still allows a certain form of moral comparison and therefore moral justification after appropriate reasoning.

I think that some decisions presented to judges are made of strong incommensurability. Waldron, on the contrary, says that this may be the case in certain cases. But he believes implicitly, that constitutional, and moral thinking, exclude strong incommensurability from the scene. This is far from obvious, and no argument is provided with this intent. I would agree that there are certain constitutional cases

---

⁵⁹ David Beatty, *The Ultimate Rule of Law—A study of balancing* (Oxford: OUP, 2004).
⁶⁰ Robert Alexy, 'Constitutional Rights, Balancing and Rationality', Ratio Juris 16 (2003) 131–40.
⁶¹ Alexander Aleinikoff, 'Constitutional Law in the age of balancing', 96 Yale LJ 943 (1986). Richard Fallon, *Implementing the Constitution* (Cambridge, Mass: HUP, 2001).
⁶² On this notion, there is a burgeoning literature: see for example the symposium held at the Univeristy of Pennsylvania Law School and published at 146 U Pa L Rev 1169. See in particular the contributions by Matthew Adler, 'Law and Incommensurability: introduction' 1169; Eric A Posner, 'The strategic basis of principled behaviour: A Critique of the incommensurability thesis', 1185; Frederick Schauer, 'Instrumental Commensurability' 1215; Matthew Adler, 'Incommensurability and Cost-Benefit Analysis' 1371; Ruth Chang, 'Comparison and the Justification of Choice' 1569; Larry Alexander, 'Banishing the Bogey of Incommensurability' 1641. Stephen Gardbaum, 'Law, Incommensurability, and Expression' 1687; Brian Leiter, 'Incommensurability: Truth or Consequences?' 1723. See also Jeremy Waldron, 'Fake Incommensurability: A response to Professor Schauer', (1994) 45 Hastings LJ 813.
⁶³ Jeremy Waldron, 'Fake Incommensurability: A response to Professor Schauer', (1994) 45 Hastings LJ 816

where a strong form of incommensurability applies. It is better to ponder whether these cases would be better left to judges, or whether they should start a social conversation that can lead to a better shaping of social preferences. Also, to acknowledge that some genuine conflicts of FLRs do exist can help in understanding the limits of constitutional adjudication, and of the strategies it applies in order to reach decisions. Balancing, for instance, can only perform a limited role, and not all the way up to conflicts of FLRs. When a genuine conflict of FLR arises it may be necessary to resort to second order type of reasons that may range from coherence to other types of considerations.

In an age of balancing most of the conflicts are dealt with by appealing to the process of weighing competing interests, in order to come up with a reasonable solution.[64] But, to hold that rights can be balanced implies a very complex groundwork involving the identification, quantification, and comparison of the interests protected by constitutional rights. Even if this were possible, one wonders whether, in case of conflicts, the interests can be composed or conciliated as the idea of balancing suggests. In other words, by the act of weighing, one uses the same metric—that is he considers rights to be commensurable and therefore composible. Now, the question is whether that assumption is compatible with the definition of rights conflicts, as entailing two actions that cannot be performed simultaneously.

In the framework of rights conflict, the idea of balance seems more apt to avoid conflicts rather than adjudicate them. To avoid conflicts is prima facie more appealing. It gives the impression that there are fewer hard decisions concerning rights. Moreover, even if hard decisions exist, the notion of balance gives the illusion of providing a reasonable method to take all the interests into account and to come up with a fair solution. But the language of balance begs more questions than it solves. What interests go in the balance? What is the value of the outcome of a balance? Despite the pretended reasonableness provided by the balancing process, hard decisions persist. Rights conflicts cannot be defined away, they have to be taken seriously. This requires, on one hand, that we cast the question of conflicts in a clear way, and on the other, that we adjudicate the conflict by stating the prevalence of one right over another.

Legal systems oscillate between the language of balance and conflict. As most of the assumptions beyond these languages are implicit, legal actors cannot flag an explicit commitment to either one or the other. As a consequence, there are many inconsistencies in the language of legal and political actors. On top of that, the rights discourse that is produced is unclear and confused. When we look closer, we can, arguably, find some signs of primacy in the language of balance. This can be explained by the reasons which were put forward earlier; namely the attractiveness of such a language when it comes to justifying hard decisions. In all three countries here examined, balancing occupies an overarching role in constitutional law.

---

[64] A Aleinikoff, 'Constitutional Law in the age of balancing', 96 Yale LJ 943 (1986).

Unfortunately, the language of balancing is often so broad that many different things are encompassed under the label. In what follows, we will try to make some distinctions that may help elucidate the role of balancing. Moreover, we will suggest in the conclusion that balancing, as properly defined, plays only a marginal role in the question of conflicts of FLRs.

An examination of the constitutional discourse post-HRA in the UK shows that balance is used in four different senses. A good illustration of this is given by *Roth* where Laws LJ uses the four features simultaneously.[65] First, balance is used, in general, to define the peculiar UK system of rights protection; this seeks a balance between parliamentary sovereignty and constitutional rights. '[The HRA's] structure, as has more than once been observed, reveals an *elegant balance* between respect for Parliament's legislative supremacy and the legal security of the Convention rights'.[66]

Second, balance defines the action of the courts when dealing with issues of limitations of rights. In this case, a balance will be struck between the general interest, and the interests as protected by constitutional rights.

'The court must determine whether a fair balance was struck between the demands of the general interest of the community and the requirement of the protection of the individuals' fundamental rights. The search for this balance is inherent in the whole of the Convention'.[67]

Third, Laws LJ refers to an institutional balance between elected bodies and the courts. This is the question of judicial deference, to which I shall return. For the moment it is sufficient to note that the court will have to pay a varying degree of deference, depending on whether the rights at stake are qualified or not. If the rights are qualified, then the parliament will have to strike its own balance. To the contrary, if the rights are unqualified, the courts are especially well placed to assess the needs of protection. 'It will be easier for such an area of judgement [a discretionary area of judgement] to be recognised where the Convention itself requires a balance to be struck, much less so where the right is stated in terms which are unqualified.'[68]

Fourth, balance is referred to in its usual legal-technical way, that is the proportionality test. Here, balance refers to the intensity of the review exercised by the courts. 'Being a domestic tribunal, our judgement as to deference owed to the democratic powers will reflect the culture and conditions of the British State. . . . The importance of this is to emphasise the fact that our courts' task is to develop an autonomous, and not merely an adjectival, human rights jurisprudence.'[69]

All four definitions are intertwined, and do not contribute to enhancing the clarity of the debate. Balance is presented as the solution for a certain number of tensions introduced by the HRA in the UK legal system. Thus, the tension

---

[65] *International Transport Roth GmbH and others v Secretary of State for the Home Department* [2002] EWCA Civ 158.   [66] Ibid, at § 71. Emphasis added.
[67] Ibid, at § 81.   [68] Ibid, at § 80.   [69] Ibid, at § 82.

between parliamentary sovereignty and constitutional rights has shaped the entire debate about rights.

The most general impression is that balance constitutes an ideology that permeates all judicial reasoning. It creates the illusion that all human rights' decisions can, in the end, harmoniously promote all interests at stake. This is patently not the case. It suffices to think of hard decisions, such as those of the Supreme Court in abortion cases. The fierce reactions confirm that the decisions did not harmoniously balance the rights at stake; on the contrary, they roused those involved.

The question is: what does it mean to strike a balance when the conflict is such that one constitutional right has to be turned down? For instance, when a terminally ill patient seeks permission for assistance with suicide, the question is often framed in a way that opposes the right to life (Art 2, ECHR) to the right to respect private and family life (Art 8, ECHR). In this case, it is difficult to see what a balance between rights would really mean. Also, it would be difficult to characterize any decision, in this context, as an exercise of balancing. Would this hold as a balancing exercise, or is it an exercise of authority?

In France constitutional discourse about rights-conflict is dominated by the idea of 'conciliation'.[70] As balance, 'conciliation' is a highly plurivocal term. It overlaps at least with the last three meanings of balance described above. Of course, it does not apply to the balance between parliamentary sovereignty and constitutional rights. This is because in France the concept of constitutional rights implies a limitation on the legislature. Otherwise, 'conciliation' may refer to the tension between general and private interests[71]; but, it may also concern the institutional balance between the judiciary and the parliament since:

Considering that it is permissible at any moment for the legislature, deciding in the province reserved to it by article 34 of the Constitution, to amend previous texts, or to repeal them and substitute for them other provisions, as the situation requires; that, in order to achieve or reconcile objectives of constitutional values, it is no less permissible for it to adopt new methods, of whose appropriateness it is the judge, and these may include the amendment or repeal of provisions that it considers excessive or unnecessary; that, however, the exercise of this power cannot lead to the removal of legal safeguards for requirements having constitutional value.[72]

Finally, it obviously refers to the degree of scrutiny exercised by the *Conseil Constitutionnel* through the proportionality technique. Thus, for instance, one author defines 'conciliation' as follows: '*concilier des principes c'est les appliquer partiellement l'un et l'autre*'.[73] Further on, he adds that conciliation amounts to varying the degree of protection of a constitutional norm in relation to the objects to which that norm applies.[74] In other words, '*conciliation*' is an exercise dependent

---

[70] V Saint-James, *La conciliation des droits de l'homme et des libertés en droit public français* (Paris: PUF, 1995). See also Guillame Drago n 58 above, 265.
[71] *Conseil Constitutionnel*, 78–174 DC (the right to strike is balanced with the general interest).
[72] Ibid, 84–181 DC §2 (translation from J Bell, *French Constitutional Law* (1992) 328).
[73] See G Drago (n 58 above) 265.   [74] Ibid, 266.

upon the circumstances of the case. All liberties have the same value, but their protection may vary as to the degree of conciliation. Finally, he holds that the general tendency is to appeal to the proportionality principle in the constitutional case law.[75]

The plurivocal nature of the concept '*conciliation*' raises a number of inconsistencies within French constitutional discourse. For instance, some authors conflate limitation and '*conciliation*'.[76] More precisely, they consider '*conciliation*' as a species of limitation. Indeed they talk of limitation as aiming at the '*conciliation*' of two rights, or of a right with a general interest. This position is underlined by a commitment to a very peculiar type of rights theory. This is neatly encapsulated in the two following statements of principle: Proposition 1: '*Fundamental rights and liberties are by their very nature reconcilable*'. Proposition 2: '*The recognition of human dignity leads to both the limitation of one's own liberty as well as that of others. That said, with the exceptions of the principle of dignity, fundamental rights and liberties can be derogated*'.[77]

Those two propositions give a clear idea of the implicit theory of rights put forward here. The authors believe in a harmonious system of rights. Yet this very statement is qualified when it comes to the principle of dignity (Proposition 2). However, as we will see, the principle of dignity is eminently ambiguous. They give a very contestable definition of dignity, as being in contrast with individual liberty.

One of the many paradoxes is that these authors hold that '*conciliation*' is always made *in concreto*. However, they themselves hint at the existence of very strong *a priori* principles that are likely to shape the way the question is posed and thus the way it is solved. In the end, to hold that the solution is taken *in concreto* is mere window-dressing, serving to hide the substantive theory of rights proposed by the authors in question.

In the USA, the language of balancing is no less debated. Both judges and scholars disagree fiercely on the matter. The underlying belief is that either we consider FLR as absolutes or we balance them.[78] Judges, who are against balancing, hold that the framers had done all the balancing *a priori*, when they selected a certain number of rights.[79] Opponents to that approach hold that a genuine weighing of competing interests is more desirable than the existence of absolute rules. This is because absolute exceptions to rules would, in the end, corrode rights themselves (eg Justice Frankfurter).[80]

It is not entirely clear as to what extent these sharp oppositions are really meaningful. Often the debate is triggered by lack of understanding of what balancing really amounts to. A helpful explanation of balancing is offered by Richard Fallon

---

[75] Ibid, 267.
[76] B Mathieu et M Verpeaux, *Contentieux des droits fondamentaux* (Paris: Montchretien, 2001) 474.
[77] Ibid, 472–73 (author's translation).
[78] Kathleen Sullivan, *Constitutional Law* (New York: Foundation Press, 2001) 965.
[79] *Konigsberg v State Bar of California*, 366 US 36 (1961) (Justice Black, dissenting). See also Balck, 'The Bill of Rights', 35 NYU L Rev 865 (1960).
[80] *Dennis v United States*, 341 US 494 (1951) at 517–61.

in his book, *Implementing the Constitution*.[81] Fallon draws a distinction between balancing in the shaping of tests, and balancing as a constitutional doctrine. Balancing as shaping judicial tests is seen as positive, since it mirrors some pragmatic concern; namely, the fact that the court resorts to a number of strategic tools in order to reach a decision. Moreover, it shows the limits of originalism and interpretativism, for they do not take into account multifactor-based tests. According to this first definition, balancing simply means that the court takes into account a number of different reasons when deciding cases. This is perfectly acceptable. However he goes on to say that, under conditions of reasonable disagreement, balancing within constitutional doctrine may not yield optimal results because of reasons concerning notice, predictability, and excessive litigation. In other words, when the decision is fraught with disagreement, balancing may lead to outcomes that are not predictable. Therefore, balancing cannot be understood as being particularly helpful when we face questions of conflicts of FLRs.

Thus, in the first case, the criticism of strong incommensurability is not applicable because in tailoring tests justices are always bound to take together factors that are heterogeneous. But in the second case—when a strong non-deferential attitude is required on a case by case basis—balancing becomes less than optimal since it does not further predictability. In conclusion, balancing is, and should indeed be, used in shaping certain judicial tests. But it does not help in dispelling fundamental disagreements, outside of cases of conflicts of FLR. These cases, when they arise, require special constitutional argumentation that delves into the question of the shape of constitutional essentials.

6. The Rule of Conflict as the Ultimate Rule of Law

What is wrong with balancing, then? The problem is that it allows limiting the value of basic liberties on the grounds of public interests that are not recognized as FLRs. This is wrong, because it fails to respect the priority of FLRs. Priority, here, means that when we rightfully claim the protection of a FLR, this creates a strong presumption that governmental or other interests are trumped by the value protected by FLRs. Rawls, for one, criticizes this understanding of balancing, and he strongly argues for the priority of basic liberties in precluding such an exercise.[82] A French author strongly criticized a similar argument from the *Conseil Constitutionnel*.[83] It is argued that the French Constitutional Council strongly favours the *intérêt général* to the detriment of basic liberties. This is done by using different techniques of interpretation of the Constitution as applied to cases where the public interest conflicts with FLRs.[84] The *Conseil Constitutionnel*

---

[81] Richard Fallon (n 11 above), 82–85.
[82] John Rawls, *Political Liberalism* (New York: Columbia UP, 1993) 357–58.
[83] Nicolas Molfessis, *Le Conseil Constitutionnel et le Droit Privé* (Paris: LGDJ, 1997).
[84] Ibid, 20–49.

displays two different attitudes. Either it talks of reconciliation of different interests at stake in a very pragmatic way, or it reads conflicts between FLRs and the public interests in a 'voluntarist' fashion. This means that the Council construes the case as if it involved a conflict in order to justify the limitation of a FLR.

I believe that the overall priority of FLRs rules out the possibility of genuine conflict between FLRs and public interests. From this point of view, the priority of FLRs as a family over public interests is clear, as well as other considerations. But what is the implication for the family of FLRs? Are we saying that FLRs are absolutes that can never be limited, and are not susceptible to being trumped by considerations stemming from other FLRs?

Some authors have defended the idea of FLRs as absolutes. As a consequence, a binary logic applies to these FLRs; either they fall within the category of protection, or they fall within that of unprotected interests, and can therefore be limited. In the US this has applied to freedom of speech rulings. Scanlon, for example, argued for the existence of mutually exclusive categories.[85] One category did not admit limitations; the other was open to such arguments.

In order to find a middle ground between balancing and absolutes, Rawls suggests a distinction between regulating and restricting liberties.[86] Within the family of basic liberties it is always possible to regulate their enforcement, but it is not possible to restrict them. To illustrate this distinction, it suffices to think about the rules of time, space, and manner, which make communication between people possible. These rules are always open to further regulation. However, the content of the message can never be restricted.

Rawls believes that a mutual adjustment of basic liberties, along the lines of regulation, is always possible. He also asserts that this produces a harmonious family of rights where the central range of application of those liberties is always guaranteed. I disagree. There is nothing to prevent the possibility of a conflict between the central elements of basic liberties. Rawls perceives this problem when he argues that:

'It is wise, I think, to limit the basic liberties to those that are truly essential . . . The reason for this limit on the list of basic liberties is the special status of these liberties. Whenever we enlarge the list of basic liberties we risk weakening the protection of the most essential ones and recreating within the scheme of liberties the indeterminate and unguided balancing problems we had hoped to avoid by a suitably circumscribed notion of priority.'[87]

The failure to acknowledge the possibility of sacrifices between constitutional essentials can be accounted for by the underlying liberal philosophy. This is grounded in a faith in human rationality, and in its capacity to reconcile different values in tension.

---

[85] Thomas Scanlon, 'A Theory of Freedom of Expression', Philosophy and Public Affairs 1 (1972) 204.
[86] Rawls takes this distinction from Laurence Tribe, as he acknowledges in *Political Liberalism* (New York: Columbia UP, 1996) 295.
[87] John Rawls, *Political Liberalism* (n 86 above), 296.

This is in fact the assumption of constitutional constructivism as inspired by Rawlsian philosophy, which aims for a 'Constitution perfecting theory'.[88]

The framework I have briefly sketched in this chapter does not subscribe to the idea of a 'Constitution perfecting theory', nor does it believe in a process-perfecting theory, as advocated by Ely.[89] The constitutional framework I develop attempts to present some central issues that are often misconceived or misused. It attempts to argue that some basic mistakes can be avoided, by carefully defining each of these central issues. Moreover, the constitutional framework is open-ended. It is a vital space for contingent arrangements, which are an essential part of every constitutional practice.

The most important tenet of the constitutional framework, however, is that it makes a case for the superiority of constitutional law over moral and political philosophy, as far as the resolution of hard cases is concerned. The reason is that the constitutional framework allows for a decision in different stages. First, the tension is acknowledged. Second, the secondary reasons for opting for one choice over another are put forward. Third, the institutional question is raised. Fourth, a decision is taken. If it is perceived as a wrong decision, the institution will take responsibility for it.

A moral reading, on the contrary, only has one stage in the procedure. It asks one central question: are there good moral reasons for deciding that way? If the answer is yes, then the decision cannot be wrong. If the answer is no, then it resorts to secondary reasons such as coherence. It may be helpful to quote Dworkin on this point:

> We know that principles we accept independently sometimes conflict in the sense that we cannot satisfy both on some particular occasion. . . . Our model demands, as we shall see, that the resolution of this conflict itself be principled. . . . But we insist that whatever relative weighting of the two principles the solution assumes must flow throughout the scheme, and that other decisions, on other matters that involve the same two principles, respect that weighting as well.[90]

There are two points that must be stressed. First, the relative weighing of two principles in tension must be morally coherent; the weighing must originate from within the same scheme of justice. Second, once the relative weighing has been done, this constitutes a precedent for all other decisions and, from this point of view, requires institutional coherence.

The problem here is with the notion of coherence. Law and FLRs need not be intrinsically coherent. Of course, coherence is a value that should be pursued, but it does not represent a paramount concern. It is but one value in legal systems. Hence, there is little point in seeking a theory of interpretation that claims integrity all the way through, or a theory of adjudication that is concerned with

---

[88] James Fleming, 'Securing Deliberative Democracy', 72 Fordham L Rev 1435, 1459 (2004).
[89] John H Ely, *Democracy and Distrust: A theory of judicial review* (Cambridge, Mass: HUP, 1980).
[90] *Law's Empire* (n 7 above), 178.

that problem only. Equally, it is of little help to strive to construe a system of rights, where they all find a place next to each other: tensions are a constitutive element of the practice of FLRs.

Some scholars insist that the constitutional system can strive to maintain a reasonable level of coherence and an entrenched sense of the priority of a FLR. When FLRs conflict they need to be redefined in order to secure the priority of FLRs as a family (Rawls). Others insist that, in order to guarantee the rationality of the whole decision-making process, we have to rely on a procedure that would maximize the respect of FLRs (Alexy). What is interesting with Rawls, is that he distinguishes different stages at which value decisions are taken. However, he is not convincing when he focuses on the coherence of the Constitution as a whole.

Thus far, I have said many things that compromise constitutional guidance in matters of conflicts of FLRs. I want to suggest that if constitutional systems do come up with answers (more or less satisfactory), this is because they can appeal to rules. Of course, the fundamental rules are often rudimentary; that is part of the problem, and part of the answer. Rules can indeed be improved. The way the rules apply can only be elucidated within the wider constitutional framework.

But before moving on, let me just be clear on the notion of coherence that can be achieved through rules. We have already acknowledged that coherence is but one virtue in a constitutional system. At first, this might sound problematic as it questions the unity of the constitutional system. However, coherence is not simply a static property that is either present or not. It is a matter of degree. A constitutional system may constantly strive to achieve coherence without getting anywhere near attaining it. Furthermore, coherence within the broad constitutional framework can be understood in various ways. To start with, it can be understood as either vertical or horizontal. By vertical I mean coherence throughout the various constitutional stages that have been identified. On the other hand, horizontal coherence occurs within the same singular stage. Moreover, coherence can be tested by the dimension of time. In fact we can talk of coherence of present decisions in conjunction with past ones. Finally, there is a distinction between justice-seeking and not-only-justice-seeking types of coherence. The former presupposes the existence of one, and only one scheme of justice; this needs to be reflected by the constitutional system in every decision (Dworkin). The latter need not focus only on the best scheme of justice, but it tries to account for the way constitutional rules work.

The aim of law is to resolve conflicts. Conflicts of FLRs are no exception. Morality does not offer much assistance in dealing with genuine conflicts of FLRs entailing a strong form of incommensurability. Conflicts possess a double edged sword: on one hand, they allow us to sharpen our awareness of constitutional essentials, but on the other, they point out the limits of law as a practice. In order to overcome genuine conflicts of FLRs, law has to come up with sound decisions that seek societal acceptance. But what are the criteria that can assist in the making of such decisions? They cannot be substantive criteria if the issue raises a strong incommensurability problem. In these cases it is necessary to rely on second order considerations. A judge or a legislator may be forced to decide, according to their constitutive practices when they lack any other guidance, as to the decision of the issue. So, for instance, a judge will stress the role of coherence with past decisions or he will draw attention to a matter of institutional balance. The decision thus reached cannot be considered as written in stone. The outcome should be seen as a platform from which disagreement can start: consider *Roe v Wade* for example. And yet, it is clear that the legislator should take on responsibilities and come forth with a clear viewpoint.

Genuine conflicts of FLRs have to be examined with two concerns in mind. First, constitutional essentials have a hard core which needs refinement from time to time. Second, disagreement is likely to stem from whichever decision is taken on constitutional essentials. This should not be repressed as much as it should be welcomed.

The rules of conflict, as refined, constitute the ultimate rules of our systems. They open and close the system simultaneously. They open it by suggesting that constitutional essentials are there to be constantly refined. From this fixed position starts a healthy form of constitutional disagreement.[91] The rules close the legal system by suggesting certain solutions, which shape the identity of the entire legal system.

---

[91] Samantha Besson, *The Morality of Conflict* (Oxford: Hart, 2005).

PART II

THE PRACTICE OF CONFLICTS OF FUNDAMENTAL LEGAL RIGHTS

Introduction

> The thing that now suddenly struck Winston was that his mother's death, nearly thirty years ago, had been tragic and sorrowful in a way that was no longer possible. Tragedy, he perceived, belonged to the ancient time, to a time when there were still privacy, love, and friendship, and when the members of a family stood by one another without needing to know the reason.[1]

Part II examines the practice of conflicts of FLRs. By that expression, I do not mean that I will 'apply' the theoretical framework in order to come up with entirely new solutions. The following chapters are a continuation of the theoretical analysis. By focusing on two main illustrations, it attempts to shed light on the problem of FLRs' conflicts. At first, the conflict between the FLR to privacy and the FLR to expression will be examined. Then, I will focus on the conflict between the FLR to privacy and the FLR to life—in cases of physician assisted suicide.

The FLR to privacy is central to this enquiry. This deserves a couple of elucidations. First, the FLR to privacy is cherished by each of us as being something of very high importance. Yet its constitutional recognition is not always explicit.[2] From this point of view, therefore, I will try to understand what it means to have a FLR that is not always 'enumerated' within the constitution. To observe this FLR while it is in conflict with other FLRs will help in understanding its scope and its strength. Second, the FLR to privacy is interesting because it is perceived sometimes as being very strong, while at other times as being very weak. For example, it is weak when it is opposed to the FLR to free speech, at least as understood in the US.

There is little doubt that free speech, in the US, is an overwhelmingly important right, if not *primo inter pares*. When conflicting with an 'unenumerated right', few would argue that the FLR to free speech must give way to the FLR to privacy.[3] However, the FLR to privacy has been central in the most important decisions of the last 30 years concerning life and death jurisprudence. In many cases, both in Europe and in the US, the FLR to privacy has been presented as providing individuals with an impenetrable shield against the state's intrusion in one's fundamental

---

[1] George Orwell, *1984* (New York: Signet Classic, 1949) 28.

[2] There is no mention of it in the American Bill of Rights. Nor is the right to privacy mentioned in the French *Déclaration des Droits de l'Homme et du Citoyen* (1789) or in the 1946 Preamble. On the contrary, the European Convention of Human Rights, incorporated in the UK via the Human Rights Act 1998, does refer in Article 8 to the respect for one's private and family life, one's home and correspondence.

[3] This view has a strong appeal in England too where Hoffman LJ, for instance, did not hesitate in holding that free speech 'is a trump card that always wins'. In *R v Central Independent Television plc* [1994] Fam 192 at 203.

choices. Thus, for instance, the milestone case for the rights of women—*Roe v Wade*—was decided on the grounds of a woman's right to privacy.[4] Today, homosexual rights are grounded on their private choice in leading whichever sexual life better suits their preferences; the European Court of Human Rights pioneered this domain, with its decision *Dudgeon v United Kingdom*.[5] This considered an individual's sexual life as being 'a most intimate aspect' of his private life. The US Supreme Court recently followed this example, in what is already likely to be 'remembered as the *Brown v Board of Education* of gay and lesbian America'.[6]

To say that the Supreme Court has 'followed' the European reasoning is not sheer inaccuracy. Justice Kennedy, who wrote the leading opinion for the majority of the Supreme Court, expressly referred to European case law as a reason for overruling *Bowers v Hardwick*,[7] a case that upheld state legislation in making it a criminal offence to have sodomic sexual relations. Justice Kennedy held that:

> To the extent Bowers relied on values we share with a *wider civilization*, it should be noted that the reasoning and holding in Bowers have been rejected elsewhere. The European Court of Human Rights has followed not Bowers but its own decision in Dudgeon v United Kingdom.[8]

The implications of such an explicit reference are not clear. In particular, it is hard to understand what the normative consequences of such an approach are.[9] Beyond this question alone, it is important to note the growing interest in comparative constitutional law, both in academic and judicial fora. Note that this provides an appropriate opportunity to allude to the underlying methodological approach of this second part. It is meant to be a study of comparative constitutionalism. It tries to deal with the question of conflicts of FLRs by discussing the way in which France, the UK, and the US approach the issue. This does not make the thesis any less theoretical. On the contrary, in order to undertake meaningful comparative studies, one has to have a clear theoretical apparatus, which allows the developing of conceptual tools, and the furthering of the understanding of different experiences.

The structure of this second part is quite simple. As a preliminary enquiry in chapter 5, I will endeavour to understand what a FLR to privacy consists of. Then, in chapter 6 and chapter 7 I will present the central cases of conflicts: the FLR to privacy v the FLR to Free Speech, and the FLR to Privacy v the FLR to life.

---

[4] *Roe v Wade*, 410 US 113 (1973). Thus, Justice Blackmun holds: 'The Constitution does not explicitly mention any right of privacy. But the Court has recognized that a right of personal privacy, or guarantees of certain areas or zones of privacy, does exist under the Constitution'.

[5] *Dudgeon v UK* (1981) 4 EHRR 149.

[6] Laurence H Tribe, 'Lawrence v Texas: The "Fundamental Right" that Dare Not Speak its Name', 117 *Harv L Rev* 1893.   [7] *Bowers v Hardwick*, 478 US 186 (1986).

[8] Lawrence v Texas, 539 US 123 (2003) (emphasis added).

[9] William N Eskridge, Jr has tried to provide a tentative explanation, underlying the importance of comparative constitutional law. See 'United States: *Lawrence v Texas* and the imperative of comparative constitutionalism', International Journal of Constitutional Law 555 (2004).

5
The Fundamental Legal Right to Privacy

1. Privacy: An Ambiguous Concept

The search for a simple definition of privacy is never-ending. In this quest we can clearly identify two extremes. On one hand, there are those who look for a deeper value at the basis of privacy.[1] On the other, some scholars try to give an empirical overview of what is conventionally covered by the loose label of privacy.[2] In other words, there is a shared belief that the distinction between the private and public spheres can be neutrally described by simply observing conventional practices in the society.[3] I believe that for our purposes a more fruitful approach is to turn to the definition of a FLR to privacy, rather than to look at the notion of privacy *tout court*. Shaped in this way, this enquiry ties the issue of the foundation of privacy to its contingent recognition within legal systems. Thus, we avoid the philosophical conundrum of the unifying element of privacy by framing the question in the following way: what place does privacy have among FLRs?

However, before proceeding with that question it is necessary to give an overview of the difficulties related to the philosophical debate. I will name two: the difficulty in determining the desirability of privacy, and that of delineating the boundaries of the individual sphere as covered by the FLR to privacy.

The first question asks whether it is desirable to talk of a FLR to privacy as a fundamental aspect of everyone's life. This is far from being self-evident, because it lends itself to question the place and role of individuals within society. The relevant distinction here is that between liberals and communitarians. This is not the place to delve into such an intricate debate. Nonetheless a few observations are appropriate to understand the extent of problems. Societies, for the sake of a civilized cohabitation, have to establish the scope of the questions that are faced collectively. For the

---

[1] James Q Whitman, 'The Two Western Cultures of Privacy: Dignity versus Liberty', 113 Yale LJ 1151 (2004).

[2] Mark Tushnet, 'Legal Conventionalism in the U.S.—Constitutional Law of Privacy', in Ellen Frankel Paul, Fred D Miller, Jr, and Jeffrey Paul (eds), *The Right to Privacy* (Cambridge: CUP, 2000) 141.

[3] For a criticism of this position, see Frederick Schauer, 'Can Public Figures Have Private Lives?', in *The Right to Privacy*, ibid at 293–309. Schauer holds that 'public' and 'private' are ascriptive terms rather than descriptive. 'An ascriptive term', he adds, 'is one that, in the guise of description, is largely evaluative'.

remaining issues, it is advisable to allow each individual to decide how best to conduct his life in the face of widespread and unrelenting disagreement.[4] To put it in different terms, public reason stops at the gates of the private sphere. This is because it is impossible to settle fundamental disagreements without postulating the substantive premises of one's philosophical position. This point of view betrays 'an epistemic scepticism about the possibility of resolving controversies by sound rational argument without begging the question or engaging in an infinite regress.'[5]

The second difficulty with privacy is that it is deeply protean. It is hard to see a unifying element that ties together the different types of privacy as identified by privacy scholars. Four main types have been identified: physical, decisional, informational, and formational.[6] Physical privacy is a property concept. Decisional privacy concerns a person's decisions and choices about his private actions. Informational privacy refers to the control of information about oneself. Formational privacy refers to privacy as interiority.[7]

Lacking in a common ground, privacy is often explained by reference to a higher value, such as dignity or liberty.[8] An interesting, though debatable, way of understanding privacy has also been cast in terms of misrepresentation or incomplete understanding of an individual.[9] The latter argument runs as follows: in a world of short attention spans, an individual can be identified with the most ludicrous information about himself. This reduction can cause significant distress because the individual will feel misjudged on the basis of very partial information. A genuine problem arises when we mistake that partial information as a source of knowledge about others; that is, when we define others on the basis of very limited and marginal data about their habits and preferences. This spurious knowledge of others, which stems from a prurient interest of the public in demeaning news, must be opposed to the true knowledge of an individual, stemming from his ability of self-definition. Privacy is there to allow and protect that self-definition.

This argument is interesting, and certainly pinpoints an important social concern; though it does not amount to a correct definition of privacy. For the kind of misrepresentation to which it is referring can very easily occur in relation to public information about oneself. For instance, a very successful football player can be totally undermined because of a penalty he missed in an important match. Arguably, the information about him is correct and very public (it took place in front of millions of spectators). However the very negative representation of the

---

[4] For a very interesting discussion on this topic, see Thomas Nagel, *Concealment and Exposure & Other Essays* (Oxford: OUP, 2002).

[5] H Tristram Engelhardt, Jr, 'Privacy and Limited Democracy: The Moral Centrality of Persons' in Ellen Frankel Paul, Fred D Miller, Jr, and Jeffrey Paul (eds), *The Right to Privacy* (Cambridge: CUP, 2000) 120.

[6] Stefano Scoglio, *Transforming Privacy: A Transpersonal Philosophy of Rights* (Westport, CT: Praeger, 1998).

[7] Scott D Gerber, 'Privacy and Constitutional Theory' in *The Right to Privacy* 165.

[8] Robert Post, 'Three Concepts of Privacy', 89 Georgetown LJ (n 5 above), 2087 (2001).

[9] Jeffrey Rosen, *The Unwanted Gaze—The destruction of privacy in America* (New York: Vintage Books, 2000).

player because of this one act means that a single mistake could be paradigmatic of an entire existence.

The impression one gets from the discussion on privacy is that it is dependent on the views that one holds on three main themes. First, the extent to which an individual can self-define himself. Second, the reach of social norms in controlling the flow of information about individuals.[10] Third, the level of public interest in receiving information about others. These three themes are deeply interrelated and nearly impossible to fully separate. Frequently we hold a strong belief on at least one of these points. As a consequence the others are subordinated without further justification. In France, for example, dignity is deeply rooted in social norms. It is understood in bioethics as an absolute prohibition to use one's body parts.[11] No matter how sound this conception is, the consequence is that the individual's autonomy—and therefore his capacity of self-definition—is strongly limited on the grounds of dignity.

So where do we start to make sense of privacy, 'a value so complex, so entangled in competing and contradictory dimensions, so engorged with various and distinct meanings?'[12] Despite its irreducibility to one single concern, privacy as a FLR plays a crucial role in the allocation of decision-making roles.[13] My proposal is, therefore, to examine the structure and meaning of the FLR to privacy, rather than the concept of privacy. This will be the object of section 2. In section 3 I will compare the way in which the FLR to privacy is actually protected in France, the UK, and the US. Finally, in section 4 I will explain why it is important to analyse conflicts of FLRs.

2. The Structure of the FLR to Privacy

To seek a definition of the FLR to privacy is not a simple task either. But at least it can be broken down into different steps which can bring valuable information as to the construction of such a notion. There are three major steps. First, what is the most relevant theory in explaining FLRs? Second, what are the constitutional norms which ground the FLR to privacy? Third, what are the objects and the functions of a FLR to privacy?

A. Privacy and Theories of Rights

I will deal firstly with the implications of the underlying theories of fundamental rights. I believe the FLR to privacy is a good illustration of the limits of both

---

[10] Particular attention to the role of social norms is given by Thomas Nagel, James H Whitman and Jeffrey Rosen.
[11] Décision No 94-343-344 DC, Rec., p 100; GDCC No 47, 854. See also the decision of the Conseil d'Etat on the dwarf throwing exercise. [12] Robert Post (n 8 above), 2087.
[13] Laurence H Tribe, 'Lawrence v Texas: The "Fundamental Right" That Dare Not Speak its Name', 117 Haw L Rev 1893 (2004).

interest and will theories of rights in explaining FLRs. Roughly, the interest theory states that someone has a right when he can claim an important interest holding someone else under a duty to respect that interest. A FLR to privacy could only be seen as entrenching an important interest. However, we saw that it is most difficult to separate a clear interest which is protected by privacy. Moreover, it should also be stressed that sometimes the core of privacy lies in the autonomous capacity of the individual to make choices about his preferred way of living and behaving. Thus, from this point of view, it would seem that a choice theory would be better placed to explain the intricacies of the FLR to privacy. There are counter-arguments to this latter theory too. When someone simply claims to be let alone, say by the press, he is not claiming the possibility of reaching a meaningful choice, but simply asserting a fundamental interest in being undisturbed.

My opinion is that both interest and choice theories miss out on something fundamental. On one hand, the interest perspective cannot account for the importance of the individual in waiving, enforcing, and consenting to what is permissible to do with a FLR. Moreover, it seems too difficult to identify the central interest of the FLR to privacy. Is it the interest in preventing intrusions in the home? The interest in avoiding the disclosure of personal information? The interest in the protection of the intimacies of a marriage relationship? A broader interest in personal autonomy? On the other hand, the choice perspective fails to explain the situations in which the individual can exercise his autonomous will or those where this autonomous will is limited by someone else's interest. Can we really say that the core of the FLR to privacy is the control as exercised by the individual? How would this be any different from a general right to liberty?

The FLR to privacy, I want to suggest, can be seen as protecting an aspect of what I call the constitutional status of every individual.[14] It does not merely protect important interests, nor does it merely protect their choices. The FLR to privacy protects the way in which each individual decides to shape his 'secluded' life, in relation to his most important interests (but what those interests are depend on one's conception of life, private and public). In this way, it contributes to a horizontal distribution of liberty among individuals. But a FLR to privacy, just as any other FLR, also guarantees a vertical distribution of power between the state and individuals. Thus, a FLR to privacy allows the drawing of the boundaries of governmental power, as well as distributing that power within the branches of government. There exists an area which is withdrawn from the realm of politics. Within this area, the action of individuals can only be limited on the ground of someone else's liberty.

The methods of identification of FLRs vary in each legal system. However, I believe that the theory of constitutional status can represent a common ground from which to begin the articulation of FLRs.

---

[14] See ch 2 for my definition of constitutional status.

B. Privacy and Constitutional Norms

A FLR to privacy requires us to identify the constitutional norms that support it. Here, the disagreement is very strong, and, in a certain sense, it mirrors the disagreement at the conceptual level. Europe and the US seem to have an altogether different constitutional landscape. In the European Convention on Human Rights (ECHR), Article 8.1 clearly states: 'Everyone has the right to respect for his private and family life, his home and his correspondence'. The US Constitution does not mention a right to privacy, and some Supreme Court justices heavily underline this fact with comments like: 'I can find neither in the Bill of Rights nor in any other part of the Constitution a general right of privacy'.[15]

As already mentioned, *Lawrence v Texas* can be read as creating a bridge between Europe and the US. In that decision, Justice Kennedy mentioned a case decided by the European Court of Human Rights (ECtHR), which was decided on the basis of Article 8.1 of the ECHR. Also, he made it explicit that certain cases commanded the interpretation of 'values shared with a wider civilisation'.[16] However, the history of the constitutional protection of the FLR to privacy in the US does not start as late as 2003, but goes back to a seminal case concerning contraceptive techniques, *Griswold v Connecticut*.[17] Justice Douglas, writing for the majority, had attempted to distil a FLR to privacy from other constitutional norms. The case concerned a statute of the State of Connecticut that prohibited contraception as well as information about it. Two physicians were found guilty of counselling on contraceptive methods, and they challenged the constitutionality of the statute. The court found that Connecticut had violated the intimate relationship between physician and patient. To rectify this problem Justice Douglas argued that certain rights, even though not mentioned in the Constitution, are necessary for the respect of other rights that do appear in the constitutional text. Thus, the First Amendment had already been construed to include some peripheral rights that are in the '*penumbra*' of the main text. And here we have a case for distilling a right of privacy from other constitutional provisions such as the First, the Third, the Fourth, the Fifth and the Ninth Amendments.

The penumbra theory is still widely criticized. But since this time the FLR to privacy has met a growing recognition in the Supreme Court's case law. Laurence Tribe recently attempted to reconstruct the trajectory of this right 'that dare not speak its name'.[18] The story he tells us is, first and foremost, about the Fourteenth Amendment.[19] More precisely, Tribe talks about 'substantive due process', or what

---

[15] *Lawrence v Texas*, 539 US 123 (2003), *per* Justice Thomas.
[16] Ibid *per* Justice Kennedy.
[17] *Griswold v Connecticut*, 381 US 479 (1965).
[18] Laurence H Tribe (n13 above).
[19] For a brilliant discussion on the history and theory of the Fourteenth Amendment, see Michael J Perry, *We the People—The Fourteenth Amendment and the Supreme Court* (Oxford: OUP, 1999).

'that stubborn old oxymoron has meant in American life and law'.[20] Contrary to Justice Scalia's own definition of a FLR, revealing what is 'fundamental' does not amount to an exercise of naming protected activities, whose protection is deeply rooted in American history. Tribe believes *Lawrence* tells us that what is fundamental is the network of human relationships that are characterized by the idea of dignity and equal liberty.[21] In other words, individuating FLRs is not a mechanical exercise. It requires the mapping of 'patterns involving the allocation of decision-making'.[22] Tribe insists on the fact that *Bowers* demeaned homosexual relations, in the same way we would demean marriage by saying that it is only about marital sex. Demeaning gay and lesbian lifestyles has the potential to impact their lives and have them judged as inferior.

The core of Tribe's reconstruction is that fundamental rights are not about individual activities taken in an atomistic way. Fundamental rights are more about deeper relationships, and sometimes even tragic ones.[23] To fail to recognize this amounts to accepting that the state can intrude into everyone's life and decide on the acceptability of individual behaviour. Yet FLRs deny this, and they do not make it permissible for the state to micro-manage the relationships of individuals.[24] Thus, the FLR's structure is such that it prevents the intrusion of the state and is more concerned with 'the allocation of decision-making roles among individuals, associations, and other public and private entities'.[25]

I believe Tribe's account is both powerful and convincing. Yet it is not really any more about the FLR to privacy, than it is about the FLR to liberty as protected by the substantive due process clause in the Fourteenth Amendment. We cannot insist too much on this however, as the very definition of privacy given by Justice Kennedy amounts to: 'the liberty of the person both in its spatial and more transcendent dimensions'.[26] It is far from clear whether in Europe, and especially in continental Europe, we would interpret the FLR to privacy as being an instantiation of liberty.[27] A brief *tour de France* of their constitutional norms will hopefully shed light on this issue.

Dignity is often referred to as the cornerstone of the FLR to privacy.[28] But is this an accurate depiction of the French constitutional constellation? Constitutional norms do not link dignity to privacy. Moreover, they do not shed much light on the meaning of an extremely loose concept such as dignity. If we look at the decision of the Constitutional Council, we find that the FLR to privacy ('*le droit au respect de la vie privée*') is referred to in the constitutional norm

[20] Laurence H Tribe (n 13 above) 1897.   [21] Ibid, 1898.   [22] Ibid, 1899.
[23] Ibid, 1919.   [24] Ibid, 1922.   [25] Ibid, 1927 and 1931.
[26] *Lawrence v Texas* (n 13 above), *per* Justice Kennedy.
[27] James Q Whitman, 'The Two Western Cultures of Privacy: Dignity versus Liberty', 113 Yale LJ 1151 (2004).
[28] Etienne Picard, 'The Right to Privacy in French Law' in Basil Markesinis (ed), *Protecting Privacy* (Oxford: Clarendon Press, 1999), 49–104 at 72. See also James Q Whitman (n 27 above), who opposes France and Germany to the USA, indicating that the former legal cultures defend privacy on grounds of dignity whereas the latter does it on the ground of liberty.

(Article 66 of the Constitution) protecting individual liberty ('*liberté individuelle*').[29] Even the very meaning of individual liberty is widely debated, as it may be a synonym of FLRs in general ('*libertés individuelles*'), or it may be a specific FLR which is itself the foundation of all others.[30] Yet authors disagree as to whether the FLR to privacy could be considered as an independent head of constitutional review, or as an integral part of individual liberty.[31]

The upshot of that debate led the '*comité consultatif pour la révision de la Constitution*' to the provisional conclusion that the FLR to privacy should be inscribed in Article 66 of the Constitution. Later, the proposal suggested that dignity and the FLR to privacy should be inscribed in Article 1 of the Constitution. Even in the latter proposal, therefore, dignity and the FLR to privacy were kept separate.[32]

Later, the Constitutional Council reiterated its position as to the relation between the FLR to privacy and individual liberty.[33] However, in 1999 the textual reference on which the FLR to privacy is based is Article 2 of the Declaration of Human and Civic Rights: 'The aim of every association is the preservation of the natural and imprescriptible rights of Man. These rights are Liberty, Property, Safety and Resistance to oppression'.[34] Here, again, the reference is to liberty but not to individual liberty as in Article 66, which tied the protection of that right to the *juge judiciaire* (the ordinary judge as opposed to the administrative one). More recently, in 2004,[35] the Constitutional Council grounded the FLR to privacy on Article 2 and Article 4 of the Declaration. Article 4 states a definition of liberty as the ability to do anything that does not harm others (*tout ce qui ne nuit pas à autrui*), and the limits of liberty which lie in the existence of someone else's right. The border between the two must be drawn by the legislator. So where does the conviction that the FLR to privacy is grounded in dignity come from? There is a line of cases that suggests this,[36] and clearly some authors support it. Yet, the FLR to privacy does not seem to be grounded on dignity, any more than it is on liberty.

In the UK, the debate is much more recent. The Human Rights Act 1998 (HRA) reproduces in its full length Article 8 of the ECHR. Whether this means that the UK now has a FLR to privacy is an open question. After all there is no agreement on the status of the HRA. Does it create a fully fledged constitutional review, and therefore limit parliamentary sovereignty, or does it merely create a new heading of judicial review, which respects parliamentary sovereignty? The answer is not provided, and certainly the act itself eschews as much as possible, these vexed questions.

---

[29] Art 66 of the 1958 Constitution.   [30] Louis Favoreu and Loïc Philip, *GDCC*, 334.
[31] For the latter position, see Bruno Genevois, *La Jurisprudece du Conseil Constitutionnel* (Paris: STH, 1998) 214.
[32] This proposal for constitutional reform did not succeed in the end.
[33] Décision 352 DC, 18 January 1995.
[34] Translated from the French: 'Le but de toute association est la conservation des droits naturels et imprescriptibles de l'homme. Ces droits sont la liberté, la proprieté, la sûreté et la résistance à l'oppression'.   [35] Décision 492 DC, 2 March 2004, Journal Officiel, 10 March 2004, 4637.
[36] Starting from the decision 343–344 DC, 27 July 1994, on bioethics.

Thus, we can only observe that UK law presents a paradox. It is the only country, of the three examples, that explicitly mentions in a domestic text the right to privacy; and yet, it is very reluctant to acknowledge such a right. Some commentators urge courts not to go in the direction of formal recognition of a FLR to privacy—although they see its moral weight.[37] The moral case for a right to privacy is generally acknowledged, and the arguments can be listed under different headings. There are moral arguments that focus on intimacy,[38] those on the trust between two individuals in a relationship,[39] and those concerned with pure concealment of one's activities from an unwanted gaze.[40] Although those moral justifications are appealing, some authors make a case against the legal recognition of the moral right to privacy. The arguments against it are threefold. First, legal recognition would reduce the moral worth of the right, instead of strengthening it. Second, it is very difficult to balance privacy against competing rights, and in particular against free speech. Third, other rights and remedies already protect privacy in its essence.[41]

The first argument is hard to grasp. It relies on the superior strength of social norms over legal norms in protecting privacy. Yet, if the social trend shows a growing willingness to breach social norms in the name of despicable interests, then there is indeed a case for protecting social norms through legalization.[42] It is possible that the FLR to privacy is essentially a FLR against certain behaviours (both of government and other individuals). This does not tell much about the FLR itself, although, as we saw, the definition is inescapably protean.

The second argument is central to my argument. It is certainly true that the FLR to privacy will enter into conflict with other FLRs and in particular with the FLR to speech. It is also very true that deciding the outcome of the conflict is likely to be very difficult. But FLRs do not guarantee easy solutions to complex cases. The existence and acceptance of a conflict does not make a decision more difficult. The decision in hard cases will always be difficult. To be aware of conflict, however, forces the parties to produce more sophisticated arguments in defence of their position. This should be regarded as an advantage, rather than a weakness.

The third argument simply fails to see what a FLR to privacy stands for. If it is true that some aspects of privacy can be protected through the FLR to property or through the FLR to bodily integrity, those FLRs do not cover the entire range that the FLR to privacy does. How could a case such as *Roe v Wade* or *Lawrence v Texas* be decided without appealing to a general right to privacy? Bodily integrity and property do not protect the FLR of each party to self-definition and control over individual choices of lifestyle.

---

[37] Nick Barber, 'A right to privacy?' [2003] Public Law 602–10.
[38] James Rachels, 'Why privacy is important', Philosophy and Public Affairs 4 (1975) 323.
[39] Charles Fried, 'Privacy', 77 Yale LJ 421(1968).
[40] Jeffrey Rosen (n 9 above). See also, Ruth Gavison, 'Too Early for a Requiem: Warren and Brandeis Were Right on Privacy versus Free Speech' 43 Southern Calif L Rev 437 (1992).
[41] Nick Barber (n 37 above), 606.
[42] This was the crux of the argument adduced by Warren and Brandeis in their seminal article, 'The right to privacy', 4 Harv L Rev 193 (1890).

In the guise of conclusion, as far as constitutional norms are concerned, we can only say that the FLR to privacy does not appear explicitly in constitutional texts (USA and France). Even when it is entrenched (ECHR and HRA), it raises important debates (UK). However, its appeal does not seem to fade when certain aspects of private life can only be protected by the appeal to a FLR to privacy.

C. The Object and Functions of a FLR to Privacy

Can we really determine an object and a function of the FLR to privacy? I have already said that this question depends on the underlying theory of FLRs. The point of a constitutional status theory of FLRs is to identify the norms which are the ground of the constitutional status, and the extent to which they create a space for the autonomous decision-making of the individual. As such, it is impossible to isolate a singular aim of the FLR to privacy. As a matter of fact, the FLR to privacy covers a number of interests that are not all directly related to one another. A constitutional status has both a static and a dynamic element, and it is for this reason that it seems so difficult to identify a precise definition of the FLR to privacy. The static element concerns single activities shielded by the FLR to privacy (or by other overlapping FLRs). The dynamic aspect covers all the areas of individual freedom which a government is bound to gradually recognize.

The point of the FLR to privacy is, therefore, to encompass a spectrum of activities that go from the screening of private thoughts, beliefs, and convictions, to the actions that are taken on these grounds. To this extent, if social norms genuinely embraced pluralism and allowed the flourishing of those activities in the private (as well as in the public) sphere, then it would not be necessary to protect them via the FLR to privacy. But this is not the case because pluralism always inspires the anti-pluralism that goes hand in hand with the will of imposing certain lifestyles, in order to minimize individual discomfort.

Moreover, if we look at the development of the FLR to privacy, we can notice two, if not three, separate trends. One concerns informational privacy and imposes a heavy burden on the FLR to privacy due to the overwhelming presence of the FLR to speech. Another trend insists on decisional privacy that involves important choices at significant points in one's life: abortion, euthanasia, homosexuality, contraception. It is not clear to what extent these strands overlap or cross one another. Nor is it clear as to their consistency. And yet, it is really difficult to hold that we would do much better without a FLR to privacy.

3. The Legal Protection of the FLR to Privacy

The FLR to privacy is acknowledged in statutes and tort law, although its effective protection is not deemed very satisfactory. Leading scholars do not hesitate in stating that more and more privacy is stripped away,[43] or that privacy is being destroyed.[44] More than a century ago the eminent jurists Warren and Brandeis were bemoaning the fact that 'the press is overstepping in every direction the obvious bounds of propriety and of decency'.[45] In their article in defence of the right to privacy, they refer to both French and English Law. The latter is cited for its seminal case *Prince Albert v Strange*,[46] which created the tort of breach of confidence. French law is cited as the first example of statutory protection of the FLR to privacy.[47] Ironically, both French[48] and English[49] lawyers regard Warren and Brandeis as the 'founding fathers' of privacy tort. In outlining the legal protection of the FLR to privacy I will briefly sketch its evolution in the three sample legal systems and then evaluate its scope.

France seems an appropriate starting point because of its attachment to a strong understanding of honour, which is held to be a ground for privacy and dates back to the French Revolution.[50] However, French commentators locate the origins of the right to privacy back to the middle of the 19th century.[51] The development of the French law of privacy can be described as one taking place against two major interests: free expression and free market. This can be explained through a historical overview.

In the mid-19th century French law was developing the idea of a 'droit à l'image', a right to one's own image. The *Dumas'* case[52] is a good illustration of this phenomenon. A photographer took some pictures of Dumas in an improper 'habillage'. The photographer immediately asked for the right to property of these photos and obtained a copy-right. Dumas sued the photographer for breach of a right to his image. The court found in favour of Dumas, holding that the right to property must be qualified by the right to one's image. The argument for the primacy of the right to one's image is somehow vague: 'one's privacy, like one's honour, is not a market commodity'. Yet the resistance to commercialize non-patrimonial rights is clear.

When French law carved out a niche for privacy, it soon conflicted with free expression. Thus, the Constitution of 1790 mentions the right to a free press, while at the same time it stresses the role of honour. In 1868, *la loi sur la Presse* liberalized its regime, although that was also the first time that the right to privacy was explicitly mentioned in a statute. Finally, in 1881 the new statute related to the press eliminates the reference to the right to privacy. This brief overview of the

---

[43] Ellen Alderman and Caroline Kennedy, *The Right to Privacy* (New York: Vintage Books, 1997) xiii.
[44] Jeffrey Rosen, *The Unwanted Gaze—The destruction of privacy in America* (New York: Vintage Books, 2000). [45] Warren and Brandeis (n 42 above), 196.
[46] *Prince Albert v Strange*, 1 Mac & G 25 (1849).
[47] Loi relative à la Presse, 11 Mai 1868.
[48] André Bertrand, *Droit à la vie privée et droit à l'image* (Paris: Litec, 1999) 4 and 209.
[49] Nick Barber (n 37 above), 602. See also Sir Brian Neill, 'Privacy: A challenge for the next century' in Basil Markesinis, *Protecting Privacy*, (Oxford: Clarendon Press, 1999) 3.
[50] James Q Whitman (n 27 above), 1171.
[51] André Bertrand (n 48 above), 2.
[52] For a discussion of this case, see André Bertrand (n 48 above).

19th century shows how important it was to recognize a personal interest, in clear contrast to the interest of the press on one hand, and the interest of the free market on the other.

One century later, the French legislature made the right to privacy part of the civil code. The statute of 17th July 1970 introduces into the civil code a new Article 9 which states: everyone has a right to the respect of his private life.[53] The scope of the Article is still very much debated.[54] Article 9 focuses only on the non-patrimonial aspect of the right to privacy that makes it a defensive device, ie the right to be left alone.[55]

The right to be left alone is also at the core of the American right to privacy.[56] More precisely, the tort of privacy has been divided into four headings: intrusion into the plaintiff's private affairs, public disclosure of non-newsworthy facts, publicity placing the plaintiff in a false light, and appropriation of the plaintiff's name or likeness.[57] In contrast with French law, the American law of privacy did not develop in conflict with the free market or with free speech. The result seems to be that American law doesn't leave much room for the right to privacy, given that the interests of both free speech and the free market are always considered paramount. Some US commentators strongly disagree with the idea that European continental law offers a sounder ground for the FLR to privacy. They insist that the difference lies in the interpretation of pre-existing social norms regarding the extent and protection of private life. Therefore, American law would essentially be concerned with the sanctity of the home,[58] whereas continental approaches would insist on rights inherent to the individual. In the ultimate analysis, the continental culture of privacy would seem to be based on dignity, and the American on liberty. No hope of reconciliation seems foreseeable:

In truth, there is little reason to suppose that Americans will be persuaded to think of their world of values in a European way any time soon; American law simply does not endorse the general norm of personal dignity found in Europe. Nor is there any greater hope that Europeans will embrace the American ideal; the law of Europe does not recognize many of the antistatist concerns that American[s] seem to take for granted. Of course we are all free to plead for a different kind of law—in Europe or in the United States. But pleading for privacy as such is not the way to do it. There is no such thing as privacy as such. The battle, if it is to be fought, will have to be fought over more fundamental values than that.[59]

Overall, this position assumes that in order to understand and to better protect the values that are generally identified under the umbrella of the right to privacy,

---

[53] In French: 'Chacun a droit au respect de sa vie privée'.
[54] See on this point Bernard Beignier, *Le droit de la personnalité*, Paris: PUF/'Que sais-je', No 2703. [55] André Bertrand (n 48 above), 40.
[56] Samuel D Warren and Louis D Brandeis (n 42 above), 195.
[57] The systematization of the privacy tort is due to Prosser, 'Privacy', 48 Calif L Rev 383 (1960). For an alternative attempt to give a broader picture, see Ellen Alderman and Caroline Kennedy (n 43 above) passim. [58] James Q Whitman (n 27 above), 1211.
[59] Ibid, 1249.

we would have to overcome a battle at the level of more fundamental values such as dignity or liberty. As argued in section 1 there is little hope of reaching an agreement on the meaning of dignity, which is one of the most controversial concepts. An overview of the bulk of American doctrine shows that although Americans do cherish their privacy, there is virtually no legal protection which is strong enough to withstand a clash with other rights. The battle must be fought at a different level. The struggle consists of understanding what the FLR to privacy is about, and how strong it is, given that it is most of the time in conflict with other interests and other rights.

Equally important to an understanding of the legal right to privacy is an understanding of other interests that may override it. Whenever an invasion of privacy is claimed, there are usually competing values at stake. Privacy may seem paramount to a person who has lost it, but that right often clashes with other rights and responsibilities that we as a society deem important. Our right to be secure in our own homes often collides with a police officer's need to investigate a crime. A woman' right to terminate a pregnancy or refuse medical treatment often conflicts with the state interest in protecting life and potential life. Our right to keep facts about ourselves secret often clashes with a free press, an employer's right to run a business, and the free flow of information of us all. The trade-offs between privacy and competing social values or legal rights are different in each area.[60]

Probably, a more meaningful explanation of the difference between the American and the French approaches is the distinction between commercial and non-commercial values of privacy. Many commentators point to the disparity between the importance of the FLR to property and that of the FLR to privacy. 'The law thereby gives individuals a great deal of control over the use of their physical possessions and the products of their minds. It gives very little control over the use of their personal secrets.'[61]

When compared with property and copyright law, privacy law displays much less protection. After all, it could be argued that the control over what is commercially exploitable is the only thing that can really be measured (by financial considerations). It is not the case that there is no market for privacy: there is indeed, but its object is highly volatile and it loses its commercial value as soon as it is disclosed. This may well be an explanation as to why the rights of property and copyright are better protected. But it cannot amount to a justification for which we can happily breach the FLR to privacy whenever we like.

Unfortunately this is often the case. In the first instance, when privacy clashes with free speech it faces a heavy weight which is difficult to overcome. Second, courts do show a great amount of deference to the media's self-restraint. What is worse is that it is unlikely that this practice will change, because the attitude of courts is empirical and not normative. Essentially, the courts merely record the existing level of protection, and do not ask what ought to be done to improve it.

---

[60] Ellen Alderman and Caroline Kennedy (n 43 above) at xiv.
[61] David A Anderson, 'The Failure of American Privacy Law' in Basil Markesinis (n 49 above), 145.

Some authors find the protection of the FLR to privacy in America so desperate that they envisage, as a remedy, the emulation of the British way of expanding the tort of breach of confidence in order to strengthen the very weak tort of privacy. 'There seems to be some movement toward a broader concept of breach of confidence like that in England, where the law recognizes a duty of confidentiality not only in specific relationship like those discussed above, but wherever a relationship of confidence exists between the parties.'[62] This sounds ironic if we think that England has just adapted its test of the tort of breach of confidence to bring it more into line with American law.

English law is in the midst of an important debate on the appropriate test for the protection of the FLR to privacy as stated in Article 8 of the ECHR. In essence, as we have already noted, the debate concerns whether a new tort of privacy should be created. English law has traditionally dealt with problems related to the right to privacy through indirect devices. The central device is the tort of breach of confidence as created by the case of Queen Victoria's etchings, known as *Prince Albert v Strange*.[63] The test of breach of confidence evolved somehow in the last one hundred and fifty years. It includes three parts: (a) the information itself must have the necessary quality of confidence about it; (b) the information must have been imparted in circumstances importing an obligation of confidence; and (c) there must be an unauthorized use of that information to the detriment of the party communicating it.

In a recent case, *Campbell v MGN Limited*, the House of Lords returned to this issue. Lord Nicholls of Birkenhead made it clear that English law does not have a cause of action for invasion of privacy unlike the US.[64] However, he did add that protection of various aspects of privacy is a fast developing area of the law. Then, he engaged in a useful discussion of the evolution of breach of confidence. He distinguishes three stages of development. First, he says, breach of confidence was envisaged as a form of unconscionable conduct, akin to a breach of trust. In its original form it required that one person improperly used information disclosed to him by another person. The confidence, in this case, was arising out of a confidential relationship. Second, the tort of breach of confidence expanded beyond the bounds of the confidential relationship. This was in order to impose a duty of confidence whenever a person receives information he knows, or ought to know, is to be fairly and reasonably regarded as confidential. Lord Nicholls suggests that this second use is awkward because the information is not called confidential in ordinary language. Third, he states that the tort 'is better encapsulated now as misuse of private information'.[65]

Lord Hoffmann casts the second development in more straightforward human rights terms. First, he acknowledged that a confidential relationship is no longer

---

[62] Ibid, 166.
[63] The Queen cannot sue in her name: *Prince Albert v Strange*, 1 Mac & G 25 (1849).
[64] It is not clear how much more effective American law is.
[65] *Campbell v MGN* [2004] UKHL 22, § 14.

required.⁶⁶ Second, he insisted on the changes brought about by the HRA 1998. In particular, he stressed the fact that Article 8 of the ECHR has entailed 'the acceptance that privacy of personal information is something worthy of protection in its own right', ⁶⁷ and not because it is commercially valuable information. As a result, private information came to be considered something worth protecting as an aspect of human autonomy and dignity. It thereby shifted the centre of gravity in the action for breach of confidence. The latter becomes 'the right to control the dissemination of information about one's private life and the right to the esteem and respect of other people'.⁶⁸

If Lord Hoffmann's point on the shift of the centre of gravity was to be accepted, then we could clearly see a significant divergence from the American approach. Lord Hoffmann is one of the most committed judges to a human rights doctrine, although his overall approach has many ambiguities. Despite going further than anyone else in acknowledging the new foundations of the FLR to privacy, this is of little use in the present case as free speech often prevails. More generally, it is unclear as to the conditions under which Lord Hoffmann is prepared to make the FLR to privacy prevail over the FLR to free expression; it is hard to conceive an area where privacy could be stronger than free expression, as Hoffmann stated that the FLR to free expression 'is a trump card which always wins'.⁶⁹

In conclusion, the continental understanding heads in its own direction. American law, on the contrary, does not seem inclined to develop along the same lines yet this runs the risk of damaging that which the FLR to privacy stands for.

4. Conflicts and the FLR to Privacy

In the first section, I distinguished between different types of privacy: informational, decisional, formational, and physical. Taken together they cover a wide range of human activities. Yet, as pointed out, it is difficult to see the common core to all these forms of privacy. My argument in this chapter is that we should try to understand what the FLR to privacy amounts to. Also, we need to assess the kinds of arguments and reasons it provides when in conflict with other FLRs and other public or general interests.

Human life is in constant tension between exposure and concealment. It is not overly useful to state *a priori* what should belong to the private sphere and what should belong to the public sphere. This exercise would only be a disguised way of imposing one's own preferences as to how private or how public a life should be.⁷⁰

---

⁶⁶ *Attorney General v Guardian Newspapers Ltd* (No 2) [1990] 1 AC 90, *per* Lord Goff of Chievely.
⁶⁷ *Campbell v MGN* [2004] UKHL 22, § 46.   ⁶⁸ Ibid, § 51.
⁶⁹ *R v Central Independent Television plc* [1994] Fam 192 at 203. Hoffmann LJ rejects the possibility of balancing the FLR to free speech.
⁷⁰ Frederick Schauer, 'Can Public Figures Have Private Lives?' in Ellen Frankel Paul, Fred D Miller, Jr, and Jeffrey Paul (eds), *The Right to Privacy* (Cambridge: CUP, 2000) 293–309.

It is not very helpful either to state *a priori* that the FLR to free speech is the trump of trumps, or something along those lines. The values underpinning FLRs are all related in some way. Therefore, the ability to decide how to solve a conflict necessarily entails the ability to perceive the sacrifice involved in such a decision.

The only way to fully understand this is to engage in the practice of conflicts. We will first examine the conflict between the FLR to informational privacy and free speech. Then, focus on the conflict between decisional privacy and the FLR to life.

6

The Fundamental Legal Right to Informational Privacy v The Fundamental Legal Right to Free Press

1. Introduction

The free flow of information is fundamental to every democratic society, but the disclosure of private information may be harmful to individuals who wish to distance themselves from the unwanted gaze of the multitude. For example, take the case of a woman who has been kidnapped and raped: this event, as such, is already enough to plague her life; but there is more—photographs of her unclothed, while being rescued by authorities appear in a daily paper.[1] Is this permissible? This is just an example of the tension I am concerned with in this chapter. It is an instantiation of possible conflicts between FLRs, though it is quite a paradigmatic one, for several reasons.

At the outset, it deals with a conflict in which there is a 'superpower': the FLR to free speech. Its superior strength is underlined by several judicial decisions both in America and in Europe. Justice Cardozo, for instance, defined 'freedom of thought and speech' as 'the indispensable condition of nearly every other form of freedom'.[2] In an equal vein, Lord Steyn described freedom of expression as the primary right in a democracy.[3] The *Conseil Constitutionnel* recognizes that freedom of speech is a fundamental liberty that guarantees the respect of other rights and of national sovereignty.[4]

The FLR to privacy is very broad, as we have seen in the previous chapter. Therefore, the possibility of conflict with other FLRs is notably increased. Moreover, its strength is likely to be variable as it applies in many different settings. In this chapter it is possible to narrow its scope by concentrating on a FLR to informational privacy. This essentially amounts to the control of information

---

[1] *Cape Publications, Inc v Bridges* [1982] as quoted in Ellen Alderman and Caroline Kennedy, *The Right to Privacy* (New York: Vintage Books, 1997) 171.
[2] *Palko v Connecticut*, 302 US 319 (1937).
[3] *McCartan Turkington Breen v Times Newspaper* [2000] 3 WLR 1670 at 1686.
[4] Décision 84–181 DC, Entreprise de presse, *GDCC* no 36.

related to the identity of an individual. The relevant range of information covers an individual's sexual, moral, and commercial identity.

The present conflict of FLRs is horizontal. This means that both right holders are private parties, as opposed to a vertical conflict where one of the parties is the State. The debate about the horizontal effect of FLRs is a much disputed topic and I do not intend to discuss it in depth here. All I can say at this point is that it is difficult to understand where to draw a clear line between horizontal and vertical. After all, the state intervenes in order to guarantee the protection of a speaker when private individuals attempt to prevent him from doing so. Thus, it seems that the State, at least indirectly, provides FLRs with a horizontal protection. To this extent, the analysis of the conflict between the FLR to informational privacy and the FLR to free speech is also meant to shed some light on the vexing question of horizontality.

Both in theory and in practice conflicts of FLRs are acknowledged and then defined or explained away. Thus, a typical argument runs as follows: at the outset, there is a tension between two important values, but a closer look helps to assert one value over the other. In this case, I believe, there is no genuine conflict. The main question is simply evaded. There are different techniques in defining away a conflict. The most important includes the technique of balancing and that of categorizing. The former focuses on the strength of FLRs; the latter insists on the appropriate scope of FLRs. I suggest that both are misleading because they fail to explain where the tension lies.

The gist of this chapter consists of explaining the conditions which allow for the conflict of FLRs. Only then is it possible to suggest whether or not a solution is likely to be found. Moreover, increasing our knowledge about the way in which FLRs behave in conflict will enhance our knowledge of FLRs *tout court*. Indeed, the strength and scope of FLRs are better apprehended in circumstances of tensions, which can show their flexibility and adaptability.

The way in which I propose to structure this chapter is simple. First, I will endeavour to explain what exactly the conflict amounts to. Second, I will present the most common ways of responding to the conflicts. Third, after dismissing the conventional responses to that conflict I will outline my alternative proposal on resolution.

2. Situating the Conflict

Before delving into the specific conflict between informational privacy and free speech, let me recapitulate, very briefly, the conditions for identifying a genuine conflict. First, a necessary but not sufficient condition is the existence of a persistent disagreement on the issue of preference of one FLR to another. Second, there must be a reasonable agreement between the parties that the case is extremely difficult to solve. In other words, there is a 'deadlock'.[5] Notably, the agreement I am referring to here is minimal. It is an agreement to disagree. Nevertheless, it is very strong as it prevents the clear resolution of the case. The definition of genuine conflicts may be seen to overlap with a general definition of hard cases. This is not accidental. On the contrary I believe that conflicts of FLRs are the hardest of all cases.

A second preliminary point is that the FLR to freedom of speech/press and that of privacy are not always in tension. To the contrary, most of the time a system of rights is such that every element of that system contributes to the enhancement of all other rights. For instance, privacy would be meaningless without free speech/free press. Indeed, how could a breach of privacy be publicly denounced without the fundamental role of free speech? Equally, how could we be fully and meaningfully free to express our dissent if our behaviour was constantly scrutinized and eventually assessed? The point is to say that the conflict between free press and privacy is not inherent in these two rights. A genuine conflict arises only under particular conditions; the following is an attempt to draw out those conditions.

As we have already seen, a conflict amongst FLRs is a conflict of constitutional permissions, which leads to a normative inconsistency. Moreover, to better understand how constitutional permissions work, one must observe them in action. That is, one must consider the aspect of the constitutional status they protect.

The core of the conflict is quite clear—it is about the flow of information. The principle, no doubt, is the free flow. But as with anything that flows freely, the risk of overflow is high. Thus, the question is whether the FLR to privacy is able to build a dam around individuals and against the free flow of information encouraged by the FLR to free speech. To be more precise, free speech is not, by definition, limitless. In any country, some types of offensive speech or other non-protected-speech are not shielded by constitutional law. Nonetheless, it seems that when truth is at stake there are no barriers. If the information is true, then there are virtually no limits on its disclosure. Yet, it is against the disclosure of truthful information that the FLR to informational privacy is set.

The tension does not occur between two marginal instantiations of FLRs. The tension, and the fundamental opposition, is between two core articulations of the FLRs. On one side, the FLR to free speech permits the disclosure of all truthful information. On the other, the FLR to informational privacy forbids the disclosure of private information. There we have a normative inconsistency which makes the case so hard. Of course, someone may say that it suffices to define what 'private information' is, and protect only its very core. However, as Schauer correctly remarked, the public/private distinction is 'ascriptive'.[6] That is, it is an evaluative description, cast in descriptive terms. In other words, there is no such

---

[5] Hillel Steiner, 'Working Rights,' in M Kramer, N Simmonds and, H Steiner, *A Debate over Rights*, (Oxford: OUP, 2000).

[6] Frederick Schauer, 'Can Public Figures Have Private Lives?' in Ellen Frankel Paul, Fred D Miller, Jr, and Jeffrey Paul (eds), *The Right to Privacy* (Cambridge: CUP, 2000) 293–309.

thing that is 'by definition' private or public. We attribute the quality of private or public according to our social norms; and these, by definition, depend on our practices.

It seems clear, therefore, that we cannot avoid the genuine conflict by referring to the public/private distinction. This only creates a greater problem. Some other doctrines define the barrier in terms of newsworthiness, degree of offensiveness, and other tests. These will be dealt with later. For now it suffices to say that most of the solutions proposed do not capture the essence of a conflict of FLRs. The point is not to state which value is higher, or which party has the best case in a particular instance. The stakes are much higher, and they concern the shape of the fundamental rules by which we play. Also, a conflict concerns the necessity of making hard choices implicating trade-offs. All this is at stake, and we cannot satisfy ourselves with either a case by case approach, or an absolute trump approach.

(i) Lionized privacy

In the USA the First Amendment protects both freedom of speech and of the press. Little is needed in understanding that the First Amendment, and in particular the protection of free speech, is the golden rule of American Constitutional law. The FLR to free speech is generally regarded as the foundation of a free society, and there are numerous philosophical arguments supporting this.

There are three main arguments in favour of robust free speech. First, truth is always enhanced by the free exchange of arguments. Truth is regarded as a market place commodity and, as such, it is supposed to benefit from the widest possible unrestricted circulation. Second, free speech is supported by the argument from democracy. Free speech is particularly valuable when it concerns political issues. The entire political system benefits from robust free speech. This is because the only genuine way to test electoral candidates is to let them speak, and to exchange their views on the most heated of political issues. Third, free speech is also defended on the ground of autonomy. Every individual, it is argued, highly benefits from the possibility of airing his views and engaging in exchanges of arguments that will make him acquire a deeper understanding of the most important societal problems.

The point is to elucidate the way in which the conflict between free speech and privacy arises in the USA.[7] Hitherto, we have noted the basis for the FLR to free speech, as protected by the First Amendment of the Constitution. More specifically, we are concerned with the FLR to free press. This is undeniably rooted in the

---

[7] The literature on this issue is rich. See for instance, Thomas I Emerson, 'The Right of Privacy and Freedom of the Press', 14 Harv CR-C-L Rev 329 (1979). For a comparison with France, Jeanne M Haunch, 'Protecting private facts in France: The Warren & Brandeis Tort is alive and well and flourishing in Paris', 68 Tul L Rev 1219. Jeffrey Rosen, 'The purposes of privacy: A response', 89 Georgetown LJ 2117 (2001). Diane L Zimmerman, 'Requiem for a Heavyweight: A farewell to Warren and Brandeis' privacy tort', 68 Cornell L Rev 291 (1983). Peter B Edelman, 'Free Press v. Privacy: Haunted by the ghost of Justice Black', 68 Tex L Rev 1195 (1989–90).

first rationale for the protection of free speech. The press contributes to the enhancement of the marketplace of ideas. Privacy does not have as noble an origin as free speech. In the previous chapter I explained that the birth of privacy is doctrinal.[8]

In the 1960s Dean Prosser systematized the different torts of privacy.[9] There are four different torts of invasion of privacy, but only one is relevant for our conflict here. There is the tort of intrusion; it consists of penetrating into one's place of seclusion in a highly offensive manner. An example may be that of a person who is seriously ill and their photograph is taken in a hospital bed. There is the tort of publication of private facts; it prohibits the publication of highly offensive private information which is not of public concern. For instance, a businessman's adulterous relationship with his secretary is widely publicized in the local newspaper. The tort of false light; this prohibits publicizing a distorted picture of a person. For example, a picture of an innocent chemist is used in a campaign against illegal drugs. There is the tort of misappropriation of one's name or identity; this prohibits the use of one's name or likeness without his consent. An example may be the imitation of a famous person in advertising a product.

The relevant tort for the conflict we are dealing with is the second one listed; the publication of private facts. It is the most relevant one, as it provides protection against publication of truthful information too. This is the second leg of our conflict. We have therefore, on one hand, the First Amendment protecting free press, and a tort of privacy protecting individuals against highly offensive publication of private facts, on the other. For the FLR to free speech, truth is the engine and justification of the news published by the media. The press has to feed society with truthful, newsworthy information. Conversely, the tort of privacy gives the individual a protection against the all-intrusive curiosity of the media and the press.

A question immediately springs to mind: is the right to informational privacy a FLR? Privacy has no firm constitutional foundation. No article or amendment in the Constitution explicitly mentions such a right. To be sure, the Supreme Court has long recognized a FLR to privacy in *Griswold v Connecticut*, and that FLR seems now very well established, especially in light of *Lawrence v Texas*.[10] But can we extend the protection afforded by the FLR to decisional privacy to informational privacy? I would like to suggest that we can present the two instantiations of privacy as being related. Individual choices concerning certain intimate behaviour are strictly personal, and, as such, they are protected by the FLR to privacy.

Those choices concern, among other things: one's sexual preferences, whether to ask for abortion, or whether to use contraceptives. Since those choices are

---

[8] However, the *Boyd* case (*Boyd v United States*, 116 US 616 (1886)) is said to have anticipated Warren and Brandeis article on the right to privacy.

[9] Dean William Prosser, 'Privacy', 48 Calif L Rev 383 (1960).

[10] Arguably, the FLR to privacy as recognized in *Griswold*, 381 US 479 (1965) and subsequently in *Eisenstad v Baird*, 405 US 438 (1972); *Roe v Wade*, 410 US 113 (1973); *Planned Parenthood v Casey*, 505 US 833 (1992); and *Lawrence v Texas*, 539 US 558 (2003) is nowadays constitutional bedrock.

strictly personal and deserve protection, it is prohibited to criminalize them. Also, it must be prohibited to deliver them to the public as pieces of information. Otherwise, why would they be protected choices if they are subject to public scrutiny? Most of the information we don't want published belongs to the category of information concerning our own choices or behaviour which we don't want others to know as we don't want them to judge them. It may be argued that the tort of privacy came to be considered as constitutional bedrock and it can be grounded, to a certain extent, on the reading of the constitution as proposed by the Supreme Court.

(ii) Honour mon amour

In France, the place of informational privacy ('*vie privée*') has occupied an important role since the Revolution of 1789. Some authors regard the Constitution of 1791 as the first attempt to enhance privacy protection. The Constitution of 1791 attempted to draw a firm boundary between the freedom of the press and private life. Notwithstanding the recognition of the former, the latter saw its consecration in Article 17: 'Les calomnies et injures contre quelque personnes que ce soit relatives aux actions de leur vie privée, seront punies sur leur poursuite'. Leading French politicians and intellectuals of the time seem well aware of the possible dangers coming from a robust protection of the freedom of the press. Thus, Royer-Collard in a public oration declared that private life had to be walled off against the danger of 'calomnies' and 'injures'.[11]

The conflict between press and privacy has been an issue since then. As we saw, this conflict characterized part of the French Constitutional history. The 'loi de 1868' is the first statute to mention the right to privacy. The statute concerns the freedom of the press; privacy is explicitly mentioned as a basis for the limitation of the FLR to free press. The 'loi de 1881' confirms the freedom of the press but the right to privacy disappears from the statute. The 'loi du 17 juillet 1970' inserts Article 9 into the Civil Code, which structures the special tort of protection of privacy. In parliamentary debate, the issue of a conflict between privacy and freedom of expression was raised and widely discussed.[12] But the statute itself does not mention them. In any event, freedom of expression is not in danger.

Freedom of expression in France is very well protected. The Declaration of 1789, as well as the European Convention of Human Rights, states clearly that freedom of expression—and with it freedom of the press—are to be protected at the highest level. Thus, Article 11 of the *Declaration de 1789* states: 'The free communication of ideas and opinions is one of the most precious rights of man. Any citizens may therefore speak, write, and publish freely, except what is tantamount to the abuse of this

---

[11] Barante, *La vie politique de monsieur Royer-Collard, ses discourses et ses écrits* (Paris: Didier, 1863) 1: 474–475, as cited by James Q Whitman, 'The Two Western Cultures of Privacy: Dignity versus Liberty', 113 Yale LJ 1151 (2004) at 1171.
[12] André Bertrand, *Droit à la vie privée et droit à l'image* (Paris: Litec, 1999) 50.

liberty in cases determined by the Law.'[13] And Article 10 §1 of the European Convention on Human Rights (ECHR) states: 'Everyone has the right to freedom of expression. This right shall include freedom to hold opinions and to receive and impart information and ideas without interference by public authority and regardless of frontiers.'[14]

The conflict between privacy and free expression is acknowledged by most commentators: 'The right to privacy, as well as the right to one's image, arises from the conflict between the exercise of two liberties, equally fundamental, the liberty to communicate and individual liberty'.[15] Generally, the FLR to privacy as protected by the Constitution, the ECHR and as instantiated by Article 9 of the Civil Code, can be limited on grounds of newsworthy information (nécéssité de l'information du publique sur un avenement d'actualité).[16] This requirement comes from American law and is accepted also by the European Court of Human Rights (ECtHR). French law, however, starts from the opposite premise to American law, although of late it seems to be moving closer to the American approach.[17]

Recent case law has also recognized the existence of the conflict. The general trend seems to give free press a primary position.[18] Thus, it is possible for the press to publish images of a public assembly,[19] to give details about the life and death of a public figure,[20] to publish images of public catastrophe and so on.[21] However, the Mitterand case reopens the debate as to the position of French judges with regard to the conflict. In that case, a magazine published a photograph of Mitterand on his deathbed. At the end of a long legal battle which reached the *Cour de Cassation*, the FLR to privacy was glaringly victorious over the FLR to free press. The motivation of the *Cour de Cassation* is not exemplary though.[22]

Interestingly, the *Cour de Cassation* holds a ban against the pictures of persons on their deathbed. The court does not question whether the FLR to free press can

---

[13] 'La libre communication des pensées et des opinions est un des droits les plus précieux de l'Homme : tout Citoyen peut donc parler, écrire, imprimer librement, sauf à répondre à l'abus de cette liberté dans les cas déterminés par la Loi'.

[14] 'Toute personne a droit à la liberté d'expression. Ce droit comprend la liberté d'opinion et la liberté de recevoir ou de communiquer des informations ou des idées, sans qu'il puisse y avoir ingérence d'autorités publiques et sans considération de frontière'.

[15] 'Le droit au respect de la vie privée, comme le droit à l'image, se situe au conflit entre l'exercice de deux libertés, également fondamentales, la liberté de communiquer et la liberté individuelle'. J-P Ancel, *Protection de la personne: image et vie privée*, Gaz Pal 2 Sept 1994, 13.

[16] André Bertrand (n 12 above), 52.

[17] M Guerrin, 'Droit à l'image, droit à l'information', *Le Monde*, 19 Juin 1999, 18.

[18] TGI Paris 1ère ch., 4 Juill 1984: *D*. 1970, J 466, concl. Cabannes et, note HM.

[19] TGI Paris 1ère ch., 4 Juill 1984: *D*. 1985, 14, note Lindon.

[20] CA Paris 1ère ch., 13 Mars 1986, *Ici Paris c/ Noah*: *D*. 1986, somm. 445, note Lindon.

[21] TGI Paris 1ère ch., 20 Oct 1987: *D*. 1988 somm. 197, note Lindon.

[22] 'Si l'article 10 de la convention européenne des droits de l'homme reconnaît à toute personne la liberté de communiquer des informations au public, ce texte prévoit en son seconde paragraphe que l'exercice de cette liberté peut être soumis à certaines conditions, restrictions ou sanctions prévues par la loi qui constituent des mesures nécessaires dans une société démocratique, notamment pour la protection des droits d'autrui: tel est l'objet des dispositions des articles 226–1 et 226–2 du Code pénal, relatives à l'intimité de la vie privée'. Cass Crim, 20 Oct 1998: *D*. 1999, J 106, note Beigner.

justify the taking of such photos in certain circumstances. To the contrary, it asserts authoritatively that the FLR to free press must be limited in this case. This decision shows the limits of the protection of free speech, at least by the ordinary jurisdictions. Moreover, it shows the limits of the style of judicial decisions in France. There is no hint of a clear motivation and there is no apparent exchange of arguments. An absolute ban on the FLR to free press is stated in the most authoritative terms. The judge has to decide, in complete isolation, whether a piece of information is newsworthy or not. And he does that without giving motivations.

(iii) Caught in between Scylla and Caribdis

The situation of English law is currently the most dynamic. There is a very lively debate as to the question of the conflict between free press and privacy.[23] England is a good case study for our purposes. On one hand, it shares some of the presuppositions which made free speech so powerful in America[24]; on the other, it is sensitive to the pressure exercised by the ECtHR, which may have an obviously continental approach.[25]

Our aim here is to present the conflict as it arises under English law. We have already seen that the Human Rights Act 1998 (HRA 1998) has incorporated within domestic law the ECHR. Therefore, the case of free press is easily presented. Article 10 § 1 of the ECHR, as already cited, strongly protects freedom of expression and freedom of the press. Freedom of the press can be split into two discrete rights: the right to impart information, and the right to receive information. A flux of information is flawless when the offer fully meets the demands. However, that is not necessarily the desirable state of affairs since the quality of information in this case may heavily depend on the prurient taste for gossip in the public. The right to impart information must not be subservient to the public's right to know. By this I mean that the quality of information must not be entirely dependent on the tastes of the public. In order to have a virtuous circle of information, the producer must always challenge the public's settled ideas and the public must be able to cope with that.

In England, there is no right to privacy.[26] However, the impact of the HRA 1998, coupled with the growing interest in the conflict between press and privacy, has altered the general overview very quickly. But we should not rush to hasty conclusions. The most familiar cause of action to protect aspects of privacy is breach of confidence. This tort has certainly seen a considerable development

---

[23] Joshua Rozenberg, *Privacy and the Press* (Oxford: OUP, 2004). Gavin Philipson, 'Transforming Breach of Confidence? Towards a common law right of privacy under the Human Rights Act', (2003) 66 MLR 726. Lord Phillips of Worth Matravers, 'Private Life and Public Interest', 56 CLP (2003) 153. *Campbell v MGN limited* [2004] UKHL 22. Richard Clayton and Hugh Tomlinson, *Privacy and Freedom of Expression* (Oxford: OUP, 2001).

[24] Ian Loveland, *Importing the First Amendment—Freedom of Speech and Expression in Britain, Europe and the USA* (Oxford: Hart Publishing, 1998).

[25] *Peck v the United Kingdom* (Application No 44647/98), 28 January 2003.

[26] *Wainwright v Home Office* [2003] 3 WLR 1137.

throughout the last two centuries. The point of this tort was to protect confidential relationships. If one party of the relationship used some information acquired through that relationship, then that party must be held liable for any harm suffered by the other party. Later, confidence was stretched to encompass a more general duty of confidence. Whoever received information of a confidential nature could reasonably expect that its disclosure would be harmful. Nowadays, it might be argued that the point of breach of confidence has fundamentally shifted towards the nature of the information, rather than the nature of the relationship. Thus, Lord Nicholls says that breach of confidence is really concerned with misuse of private information.[27]

The pressure exercised by the ECtHR on this issue is undeniable. In a recent decision, *Peck v United Kingdom*[28], the Strasbourg Court reviewed the whole of English law on the protection of privacy. It studied the institutions which evaluate, in a non-judicial way, different issues related to privacy. These institutions are: the Press Complaint Commission (PCC), The Independent Television Commission (ITC), and the Broadcasting Standards Commission (BSC). Subsequently, it focused on English law in order to present all the torts available for the protection of privacy. It identified six main torts, plus some other minor causes of actions. Breach of confidence, defamation, malicious falsehood, tort of nuisance, tort of harassment, and tort of trespass, are the fabulous six. You can add to this the possibility of suing on the grounds of copyright, breach of contract, or inducing breach of contract.

All this may induce commentators to think that a FLR to (informational) privacy is but a luxury.[29] But this is the subject of controversy. So, for example, Sedley LJ was prepared to acknowledge that there is a qualified right to privacy in English law.[30] And this seems to be the conclusion of the Strasbourg Court. Of course, the ECtHR doesn't venture into the perilous domain of definition of privacy:

Private life is a broad term not susceptible to exhaustive definition. The Court has already held that elements such as gender identification, name, sexual orientation and sexual life are important elements of the personal sphere protected by Article 8. That Article also protects a right to identity and personal development, and the right to establish and develop relationships with other human beings and the outside world and it may include activities of a professional or business nature. There is, therefore, a zone of interaction of a person with others, even in a public context, which may fall within the scope of private life.[31]

However, the court is willing to acknowledge that beyond the classical areas protected by privacy or its equivalents, the FLR to privacy as protected by Article 8 also protects the 'zone of interaction of a person with others, even in a public context'. Therefore, privacy is not to be located exclusively within the sacrosanct

---

[27] *Campbell v MGN Limited* [2004] 2 AC 457 § 14.
[28] *Peck v United Kingdom* [2003] ECHR 44.
[29] Nick Barber, 'A right to privacy?' [2003] Public Law 602–10.
[30] *Douglas v Hello! Ltd* [2001] 1 WLR 992.
[31] *PG and JH v The United Kingdom*, No 44787/98, § 56, ECHR 2001–IX.

precinct of one's home but also in certain external activities. This is the last attack in time to the fortress of breach of confidence, as expanded by the common law. The question is whether the tort of breach of confidence can be stretched to a point which encompasses the protection of certain parts of life, taken part of in public, but deemed to be shielded by privacy.

The response was offered by a recent case of the House of Lords, *Campbell v MGN*.[32] The overall point is that where common law already provides a remedy for the redress of harm, then the court is willing to strike a balance between the competing FLRs in Article 8, and Article 10. If such a remedy does not exist, then the court cannot create it. In short, common law cannot come up with a general right to privacy, but it can stretch a breach of confidence almost at pleasure. The HRA, which requires the judges to come clean as to the balance that they strike between free press and privacy, gives ample room for manoeuvre to do this.

The core of the conflict is captured by Lord Nicholls:

> The present case concerns one aspect of invasion of privacy: wrongful disclosure of private information. The case involves the familiar competition between freedom of expression and respect for an individual's privacy. Both are vitally important rights. Neither has precedence over the other. The importance of freedom of expression has been stressed often eloquently, the importance of privacy less so. But it, too, lies at the heart of liberty in a modern state. A proper degree of privacy is essential for the well-being and development of an individual. And restraints imposed on government to pry into the lives of the citizen go to the essence of a democratic state: see LA Forest J in R v Dymont [1988] 2 SCR 417, 426.[33]

We are now in a position to say that American, French and English law do acknowledge the existence of a conflict between the FLR to free press and the FLR to privacy. Thus far, we also attempted to put the finger on the underlying tension which characterizes the conflict. It is submitted that that tension is not merely a superficial semantic problem, but that it penetrates into the roots of each FLR, as understood in their legal contexts. This is to say that the conflict is genuine and that its contours can be more precisely drawn (here we have only begun to trace those contours). To understand this point is very important and central to this thesis. It is not sufficient to loosely say that two rights are in tension, and therefore the decision will be difficult. The understanding of what that tension amounts to, helps in refining our understanding of what a conflict actually is. The immediate implications are very important. If a conflict is merely apparent, then it suffices to explain why this is so and then the solution of that problem will be less problematic. However, if the conflict is genuine, then there is no fast way to solve it or to define it away.

A. Conflicts of FLRs in judicial discourse

Courts do acknowledge the problem of conflicts, but most of the time it is just a preamble to the introduction of their favourite technique in deciding hard cases.

---

[32] *Campbell v MGN Limited* [2004] 2 AC 457.   [33] Ibid, *per* Lord Nicholls § 12.

Thus, some judges prefer balancing, others prefer categorization and so on. I do not want to deal with the methods of solving conflicts of FLRs as of yet. Rather, I will try to understand the way judges and justices approach the issue of conflict. The methodology is the following: I outline a case for each system where the issue of privacy versus press is particularly important.

(i) Learning the practice of rights

England offers a multitude of good examples of press/privacy conflicts. The House of Lords has recently expressed its view on the matter in the case *Campbell v MGN*. The facts of the case are relatively simple, although the problems raised are most complex. The court faced the issues of the horizontal effect of rights, and of their conflict. To be sure, the latter issue depends on a positive answer to the former. This was accepted without much discussion, so the central issue seems to be that of the actual conflict.

What happened? Naomi Campbell was caught by a reporter for 'The Mirror' newspaper outside of a Narcotics Anonymous meeting venue, after attending a meeting. Images of her there were published, and her history of addiction was recounted. If the story stopped here, all the justices agreed, there would be no problem. Privacy on a topic such as healing from drug addiction is widely acknowledged. The trouble is, however, that Naomi Campbell publicly denied her addiction on several occasions. Therefore, in this case, the press is regarded as merely straightening the record. Indeed, Naomi Campbell accepted that her story was worth publishing; but she contends that the press went too far in the publication of details. To be more precise, Naomi's barrister dressed a list of five categories of information, and pointed out where the threshold was passed. The categories are the following:

(1) the fact of Miss Campbell's drug addiction; (2) the fact that she was receiving treatment; (3) the fact that she was receiving treatment at Narcotics Anonymous; (4) the details of the treatment—how long she had been attending meetings, how often she went, how she was treated within the sessions themselves, the extent of her commitment, and the nature of her entrance on the specific occasion; and (5) the visual portrayal of her leaving a specific meeting with other addicts.[34]

The first two categories of information were accepted as publishable in light of her lie as to her addiction. In short, her reasonable expectations of being let alone with her problem considerably shrunk after her public statements. Thus, the case is about the protection of categories (3), (4), and (5).

We already have a fair amount of information about the judicial treatment of the conflict. First, the conflict at (1) and (2) is *ex officio* won by the FLR to free press. The rationale for this depends on the falsity of the information provided by Naomi concerning her true status as a drug addict. From this point of view, we

---

[34] *Campbell v MGN limited* [2004] 2 AC 457 at 466–67.

could depict the press/privacy conflict as a battle for the truth. If the truth is clearly on one side, it triumphs. I would like to express a concern at this point. What was Naomi supposed to do when a journalist asked a question on her addiction? To tell the truth, keep silent, or tell a lie? I think that the only decent thing to do, if pressed, was to deny it.[35] How else can someone protect his/her own private life otherwise? My point is that the law should not make truth an absolute trump. Otherwise, the FLR to privacy would *always* lose against free speech because there is an intrinsic asymmetry between free speech and privacy. For, if a conflict arises, the only way for the privacy side to win is to disclose more information. But this is in itself a defeat.

A second point concerning the conflict at (1) and (2) is that if Naomi was 'immaculate' (ie if she hadn't lied), then the conflict would have been won. This means that the information itself is regarded as having an essentially private nature. Why? Lord Hoffman states for instance: 'The facts are unusual because the plaintiff is a public figure who had made very public false statements about a matter in respect of which even a public figure would ordinarily be entitled to privacy, namely her use of drugs'.[36] The last part of the passage is suspect. To hold that the use of drugs falls within the category of private information requires explanation. For it is the subject of serious controversy as to whether drug-taking should be decriminalized.[37] After all, in England 'the possession and use of illegal drugs is a criminal offence and a matter of serious public concern'.[38]

However Lord Hoffmann does not provide any explanation. This is problematic. The labelling of information as private or public should not fall into the realm of personal belief. It should be carefully explained and justified. Otherwise, it is always up to the judge to draw lines in a totally arbitrary way. The consequence is that conflict loses whatever sense it may have. If the conflict between disclosure and concealment of private facts merely amounts to know what is private, then the conflict is disposed of by the mere attribution/lack of attribution of the label 'private'. But, there is no such thing as clearly private information. If there is a genuine conflict, it means that each party has a reasonable claim against the other party. If that claim could be easily dismissed then there would be no conflict.

This less than satisfactory approach is more than reiterated by Lord Hope of Craighead. At different points he says: 'the test [to the question whether the information is public or private] is not needed where the information can easily be identified as private'.[39] And also: 'If the information is obviously private, the situation will be one where the person to whom it related can reasonably expect

---

[35] Compare it with Thomas Nagel, 'The Shredding of Public Privacy' in Thomas Nagel, *Concealment and Exposure and Other Essays* (Oxford: OUP, 2002).
[36] *Per* Lord Hoffman, § 36.
[37] For a good argument in favour of decriminalisation, see David AJ Richards, *Sex, Drugs, Death, and the Law—An essay on Human Rights and Overcriminalization* (Totowa, NJ: Rowman and Littlefield, 1982). [38] *Per* Baroness Hale, § 151.
[39] *Per* Lord Hope, § 94.

his privacy to be respected'.[40] Or, to put it differently: an easy case is not difficult to decide. Unfortunately, a genuine case of conflict involves a situation in which information that the individual is trying to keep for himself could theoretically fall within the realm of newsworthiness.

Points (3), (4), and (5) raise different questions. The minority (Hoffmann and Nicholls) hold that these details are just complementary to the main information. Therefore, they are protected as elements of the main story. The majority (Hope, Hale, and Carswell) hold that those details are severable from the main story. Baroness Hale, for instance, argues that information at (3) and (4) is of a clinical nature. Hence, it should be protected by increased confidentiality, as acknowledged in *Z v Finland* by the ECtHR.[41] However, the clinical nature is controversial (the Court of Appeal dismissed this point). Even if (3) and (4) were classified as clinical information, this does not make them severable from the main clinical information, namely the fact that Naomi was being treated for drug addiction. You can compare it to the situation of a person being treated for cancer. Once you have permissibly disclosed the fact that the person is treated, why would it be impermissible to disclose the name of the clinic and the nature of the treatment that he is going through?

The relevance for the question of conflict is similar to the point made before. The press/privacy conflict is explained away by artificially fencing some of the information. How could the press draw such a line whilst in the act of buttressing the case for the article? This way the court is shifting the burden of solving the conflict on the judgement of the press. But the press cannot be the arbiter of its own morality—it cannot decide to publish news, and at the same time narrow down the story. The only relevant question that the press can ask, in a very restricted amount of time, is whether to publish or not. If they decide to publish, then they must provide the full range of details because that is the only way to assess whether they have a good case or not.

In conclusion, Naomi was lucky. Her case seems to have been decided in order to please Strasbourg's recent decision in *Peck* that made it clear that England should raise its privacy protection. The decision reached is the result of an unclear compromise based on a dubious ontology of private information. The guardians of that ontology are the judges, but the main actor is the press which is required to do something impossible: provide the public with information while keeping an eye on the morality of information. In the contest between press and privacy, the only winner is the public's right to know enough gossip, but not too much.

(ii) Florida Star *and the American obsession with free speech*

The US Supreme Court has pondered the issue of press disclosure of private information in four major cases: *Cox Broadcasting Corp v Cohn*,[42] *Oklahoma Publishing*

---

[40] *Per* Lord Hope, § 96. [41] *Z v Finland* (Application No 22009/93) (1997).
[42] *Cox Broadcasting Corp v Cohn*, 420 US 469 (1975).

Co v District Court,[43] *Smith v Daily Mail Publishing Co*,[44] and *Florida Star v BJF*.[45] In *Cox*, a television channel disclosed the name of a rape victim, which was learned in a public trial. In *Oklahoma Publishing*, a newspaper disclosed the name of a juvenile murderer, which it also learned in a public trial. In *Daily Mail*, a newspaper disclosed the name and photograph of a juvenile murderer as acquired from different sources: the police radio, witnesses to the shooting, and prosecutors. In this trilogy, free speech systematically trumped informational privacy.

In *Florida Star*[46] the result is unsurprising: the free press wins. However, I would like to analyse this case a little further in order to show that the way in which the court construes the conflict is relevant in determining the outcome. The facts are easily summarized. BJF is raped at knifepoint. The police record the incident and place the report in the press room without hiding the victim's name as required by Florida law. A journalist copied and then published the entire report including the name of the victim—despite the signs posted on the wall outlining the law against the publication of rape victims' names.

At first, I will deal with the definition of interests. The conflict is often presented as a clash of interest. The most common presentation is the private interest in privacy, as against the public interest in knowing the information. This is often misleading. The FLR is said only to protect the interest of the private party. Conversely, the FLR to free press is meant to protect the interest of the press, but also the interest of the public in receiving the information. Framed this way, it is hard to argue that the FLR to privacy should be preferred at times. However, the FLR to privacy protects other aspects of an individual's well-being. Moreover, if what was really in conflict was the right of the public to know and the individual right of the person to his privacy, it may well be argued that the former has little strength.[47] Likewise, this confusion might be increased if we start confusing the 'public right to know', with 'public interest'. The 'public right to know' is only the right of each individual to receive information.

An uncontrolled discussion of interests does not help clarify. I maintain that the only meaningful way of constructing a conflict is by individuating the right holders that are parties to the process. There may be other interests at stake, but they must not be accounted for in the presentation of the conflict of FLR. In *Florida Star*, the parties to the case are the newspaper and BJF, the victim of the rape. Moreover, the FLRs at stake are the FLR to free press on one side, and the FLR to informational privacy on the other. As noted by Justice Marshall writing for the majority:

The tension between the right which the First Amendment accords to a free press, on the one hand, and the protections which various statutes and common-law doctrines accord to

[43] *Oklahoma Publishing Co v District Court*, 430 US 308 (1977).
[44] *Smith v Daily Mail Publishing Co*, 443 US 97 (1979).
[45] *Florida Star v BJF*, 109 S Ct 2603 (1989).
[46] For a longer commentary see, Peter B Edelman, 'Free Press v. Privacy: Haunted by the ghost of Justice Black', 68 Tex L Rev 1195 (1989–90).
[47] Frederick Schauer, 'Can Public Figures Have Private Lives?' in Ellen Frankel Paul, Fred D Miller, Jr, and Jeffrey Paul (eds), *The Right to Privacy* (Cambridge: CUP, 2000) 293–309.

personal privacy against the publication of truthful information, on the other, is a subject we have addressed several times in recent years. Our decisions in cases involving government attempts to sanction the accurate dissemination of information as invasive of privacy, **have not, however, exhaustively considered this conflict.** On the contrary, although our decisions have without exception upheld the press' right to publish, we have emphasized each time that we were resolving this conflict only as it arose in a discrete factual context.[48]

The difficulty is again constituted by the fact that we are concerned with the disclosure of truthful information. The role of truth is overstated in these cases. It is so because we attribute to it a public function, no matter what kind of information we are talking about. Of course, a newspaper will not publish the truthful fact of a hen laying six eggs. But it is prepared to publish the details of a personal tragedy because this would in no doubt be newsworthy. Since it protects the 'truth', the FLR to free press becomes over-extensive. Through the truth we bring back the interest of the public at large in the conflict between the press and the individual, thereby withdrawing the responsibility of the press to act in a careful manner.

The important point that Justice Marshall is making is that the Supreme Court decided several similar cases involving a conflict, but never in a principled manner. The court, on the contrary, analysed the conflict stressing the discrete factual context. Unfortunately, this tells us more about the inability of the court to discuss the conflict *per se*, than about the real incomparability of the case with other cases. The whole discourse on discrete factual context is geared at preventing the framing of rules of solution for future cases. However, the immediate result is that the law on this point (on the conflict, in this situation) is uncharted and ultimately unclear.

Florida Star and the trilogy of cases concerned the issue of whether truthful information can be restricted. However, the Court has always avoided an open answer to that question. Instead, it has focused on side issues. In *Florida Star*, for example, the court creates a mini test for the press to pass in order to be exempted from responsibility. The test consists in showing that the information has been 'lawfully obtained'. If this is the case, then the disclosure will not be sanctioned. But even this requirement oversees the point of the FLR to privacy.

In *Florida Star*, that test has an unpleasant consequence. It discharges the responsibility of the actors who have the control in the disclosure and diffusion of the information. The state has a clear policy as to the names of rape victims: they should not be disclosed. In this case, an error made disclosure to the press possible. Yet, the press clearly knew about the state prohibition of naming the victims. So what we can gather is that 'lawfully obtained', protects any form of acquisition of information provided it is not a criminal offence. This is an extraordinarily broad blanket, and it is deeply unsatisfactory because it turns the issue of the disclosure of truthful information into a permission to publish any information that falls into the hands of the press.

[48] *Florida Star v BJF*, 491 US 524 (1989) at 530 (emphasis added).

The harm to the victim is very real when her name is published. However, the press cannot be held responsible. Nor can the state, even if an error has been committed. Justice Marshall's conclusion is worth quoting:

> Our holding today is limited. We do not hold that truthful publication is automatically constitutionally protected, or that there is no zone of personal privacy within which the State may protect the individual from intrusion by the press, or even that a State may never punish publication of the name of a victim of a sexual offence. We hold only that where a newspaper publishes truthful information which it has lawfully obtained, punishment may lawfully be imposed, if at all, only when narrowly tailored to a state interest of the highest order, and that no such interest is satisfactorily served by imposing liability under § 794.03 to appellant under the facts of this case.[49]

In order to prohibit publication under the 'lawfully obtained' doctrine, a private person should show that there is a state interest of the highest order which prevents the press from publishing. In my view, it fails to see the weight of the FLR to privacy in the equation. So the conflict is framed in the following way: a state interest in disclosure of truthful information versus a state interest against that very disclosure. Put that way, the individual interest in privacy does not overly matter.

(iii) France framing the question

France presents a reverse mirror image to the American position. The FLR to free press is systematically trumped by the FLR to informational privacy.[50] In order to understand the difference in approach I would like to focus here on what we have hitherto identified as the core of the conflict. Can truthful information be concealed on the basis of the respect of privacy? In France, the answer to this question is affirmative.

In a seminal case in 1975,[51] the *Cour de Cassation*, in its criminal formation, is faced with the status of truth when information is disclosed. The procedure is a little complex, but the overall point is central to our concern. The plaintiff is a notary (notaire) who has been called 'escrow' in the newspaper, the *'l'express-méditerranée'*. He sued the newspaper for defamation on the basis of the Press Law 1881. Meanwhile, the notary was being tried for the actual crime of which the newspaper accused him. Hence, the court of appeal which was deciding the defamation case, suspended the proceedings until the determination of the notary's culpability. The notary argued that the court of appeal was in no position to decide on the suspension and that the court simply had to decide the defamation case.

The *Cour de Cassation* made a very important point concerning defamation and privacy. It argued that in the case of defamation, the court of appeal is entitled to suspend the process if it estimates that evidence of the truth of the accusation can be brought. Conversely, if privacy was at stake, the court could not suspend

---

[49] Ibid, at 541.   [50] André Bertrand (n 12 above), 68.
[51] Cass Crim, 18 Nov 1975, no 74–91103.

the process because in any event the evidence of truthful information could not justify the intrusion of privacy.[52]

An interesting interpretation of the relationship between truth and privacy is offered in the famous Mitterand cases.[53] President Mitterand lied to Frenchmen for over 14 years about his health. He did this notwithstanding an obligation he undertook to disclose a weekly health report. One of his physicians, Dr G, published a book about the great secret (so the book was called); the book was seized, and its circulation prevented.[54]

Of even greater interest to our discussion is the second case concerning Mitterand. Shortly after his death, photographs of his deathbed were taken and subsequently published in a newspaper. Mitterand's wife sued the newspaper for invasion of privacy. The court of first instance argued that the FLR to privacy does not stop at the end of one's life. Therefore, the president's image is protected. The idea that dead people have a private life is a fascinating, albeit undefendable, position. To avoid the problem, the *Cour de Cassation* framed the point in a different way. It argued that the right to one's image remains in the control of the heirs of the dead person.

The most important point, however, concerns the framing of the press/privacy conflict in light of the ECHR. The *Cour de Cassation* acknowledges the protection of free expression as stated in Article 10 ECHR. But it immediately went on to say that exceptions to that principle are acceptable under Article 10 §2. Instead of arguing for the substantive reasons which justify the curtailment of free expression, the court merely stated that the FLR to privacy is one of the rights that justifies the limitation of expression.

The conflict is not taken seriously. The court asks none of the relevant questions that may help in deciding the case. Questions such as: is the information provided valuable? Is the harm which occurred substantive? Is the sacrifice of free expression justifiable? Instead, the court prefers to create an absolute ban asserting the existence of a protected category of information.

The way the conflict is framed by the *Cour de Cassation* does not meet the free expression requirements of Strasbourg case law. This is probably the reason why the *Cour de Cassation* drastically changed its opinion on a recent case concerning the publication of an image of a dead body. *La Dépêche du Midi*, a newspaper from the south of France, published the story of a man found dead in his garage, his body burnt and stabbed. A photograph was taken and published. The article named the man, his profession, and held that he suffered from depression. The

---

[52] Ibid, the Cassation Court holds: 'Qu' a l' appui de sa decision l'arret enonce que cette information "peut apporter la preuve de la verité du fait imputé ou de sa fausseté" et contribuer ainsi a "éclairer la religion de la cour"; attendu qu'il resulte de l'article incriminé que les faits reputés diffamatoires imputés au notaire V ne concernaient pas la vie privée; que des lors la preuve de la verité desdits faits était legalement recevable'.

[53] For a summary of the Mitterand saga, see *Case of Edition Plon v France*, 18 May 2004 (Application No 58148/00).   [54] However, the book is available on the internet.

wife, on behalf of the family, sued the newspaper and sought damages for the violation of their privacy.

At the outset, the *Cour de Cassation* made clear that the FLR to privacy ceases its protection on the death of a person. Then, it presented the conflict in a more interesting way than it did in Mitterand 2. Despite the fact that the argumentation remains too sketchy, the court made an effort to take the two FLRs together and to ask relevant questions as to the extent of the conflict. Thus, it asks whether the FLR to privacy of the family had been infringed. The answer was negative, because no information on the other family members was disclosed. However, the information concerning the dead man fell in the newsworthy category, and therefore justified publication. It may be argued that this solution is not satisfactory; indeed I do not think it is. But we still have to know whether there is any meaningful way of solving genuine conflicts of rights.

3. Solving the Conflict?

Sometimes the disclosure of truthful information harms individuals. The disclosure might be protected by a FLR to free expression, while private information may be protected by a FLR to informational privacy. How do we solve that conflict? The way a conflict is construed directly influences the way a conflict is solved. Sometimes, authors claim that the only relevant question is 'how do we solve conflicts of rights?' instead of 'what are conflicts of rights?'[55] I disagree. I think that the latter question must come first as it helps in elucidating the terms of other questions.

There are four broad approaches in response to a situation of conflict. A theory may try to accommodate the conflicting elements; it may try to explain away the conflict; it may ride roughshod; or, eventually, it may even lose credibility. The last two options are of less value, although one is more appealing than the other. Both, however, face the spectre of counterintuitive information. A theory that rides roughshod will attempt to dismiss counter intuitions using theoretical power. Other theories will simply acknowledge the impossibility of making sense of an extremely intricate issue.

The preferred approaches of both lawyers and philosophers consist of accommodation, or reductive explanation. By reductive explanation I mean, in this context, the task of showing that there are no genuine conflicts. This is supposedly achieved by dispelling false assumptions. By accommodation, I mean the task of redefining the elements in conflict so that theory can accommodate new cases. The aim of this process is to constantly refine rational arguments as to constitutional essentials. Therefore, the problem can be resolved by expanding the scope of theory.

[55] Carl Wellman, *Real Rights* (New York: OUP, 1995).

What are the major problems with these approaches? Reductive explanation tends to be unable to give a full account of the subtleties of conflicts. Accommodation tends to increase theoretical complexity, which in turn may result in a loss of the ability to solve concrete problems. In what follows I will try to flesh out these two broad positions, in relation to the press/privacy conflict.

B. Explaining Away

Constitutional discourse offers two, apparently opposed, ways of dispelling conflicts of FLRs. On the one hand, balancing; categorization on the other. Simply put, balancing is about individuating and weighing opposite interests. Categorization is about individuating and excluding opposite interests. Balancing offers a very loose understanding of FLRs: simple interests or even state interests can sometimes pass the test of FLRs and tip the balance in a certain way. Categorization, on the contrary, runs the risk of reifying interests, turning FLRs into meaningless absolutes.[56]

Balancing is by far the most successful strategy in recent times.[57] Yet, I will attempt to explain why balancing and categorization are the two sides of the same coin. This will be more closely studied in our domestic contexts. However, to anticipate the point, it suffices to say that free press can trump privacy systematically, by using either balancing or categorization. I believe that both methods do not take FLR conflicts seriously, and I will attempt to show this in our comparative study.

(i) USA: the reality is not Black or White

One thing is clear: freedom of speech wins. The rest is confused. For example, it is difficult to understand what the difference between balancing and categorization is when they yield the same result repeatedly. It does not matter whether we consider the First Amendment as an absolute or not. In the balance, it has never lost against privacy.

Balancing and categorization attract different stereotypes. Balancing is seen as deferential, whereas categorization is seen as activist. But the opposite can be equally true. For, an absolute right can still be accompanied by absolute exceptions. And, balancing can present rights embedding interests which are far superior to state interests.

Privacy has no leverage when in competition with free speech (understood as an absolute right). But, it has little chance in a balancing process too. For, on the side of free speech there are at least three different interests. The interest of the press in speaking freely, the interest of the public in receiving news, and the interest of the

---

[56] For this fear, see James E Fleming, 'Securing Deliberative Democracy', 72 Fordham L Rev 1435 (2004). See also Thomas M Scanlon, 'Adjusting Rights and Balancing Values', 72 Fordham L Rev 1477 (2004).
[57] Alexander Aleinikoff, 'Constitutional Law in the Age of Balancing', 96 Yale LJ 943 (1987).

state in securing a strong protection of the value of free speech. On the other side, judges attach to privacy only individual interest.

If we go back to the case of *Florida Star*, what we notice is that the Justices make clear their preference for free speech. But they do not say that the interest protected by free speech outweighs the interest of privacy, namely preventing a newspaper from publishing the name of a rape victim. The court simply says that the information has been found lawfully.

In that case, Justice White dissented. He thought that the privacy of the victim should have won against free press. Moreover, he was the only Justice who invoked the need for balancing.

> Of course, the right to privacy is not absolute. Even the article widely relied upon in cases vindicating privacy rights, [Warren & Brandeis, The Right to Privacy, 4 Harv.L.Rev. 193 (1890),] recognized that this right inevitably conflicts with the public's right to know about matters of general concern—and that sometimes, the latter must trump the former. *Id.*, at 214–215. Resolving this conflict is a difficult matter, and I fault the Court not for attempting to strike an appropriate balance between the two, but rather, fault it for according too little weight to B.J.F.'s side of equation, and too much on the other.

But surprisingly enough, he does not fault the decision for a lack of balancing. He faults it for according insufficient weight to privacy.

The majority in *Florida v BJF* held that the press lawfully obtained the information. As a consequence, the plaintiff has to show that the protection of his privacy meets 'a need to further a state interest of the highest order'. Needless to say, to prove that is extremely difficult, if not impossible.

Justice Black would have welcomed that. Many attribute to him an absolutist interpretation of free speech. In fact, that characterization is misleading. And it is interesting that in a famous dissent Justice Black held that free speech is very strong when it comes to public expression. Hence, there is a room to interpret free speech differently when it comes to private information:

> I have always believed that the First Amendment is the keystone of our Government, that the freedoms it guarantees provide the best insurance against destruction of all freedom. At least as to speech in the **realm of public matters**, I believe that the 'clear and present danger' test does not 'mark the furthermost constitutional boundaries of protected expression' but does 'no more than recognize a minimum compulsion of the Bill of Rights.[58]

Justices White and Black are apparently at opposite ends of the constitutional spectrum. In a Press/Privacy conflict, Justice White would come down on the side of privacy. Justice Black would come down on the side of free press. They seem apparently opposed, also as to the methods. Justice White would prefer balancing; while categorization would be Justice Black's preferred way of solving cases.

But the impression is that the methodology here is completely irrelevant. It is not difficult to make free speech win every time a balance is striken. It suffices to

---

[58] *Dennis v US*, 341 US 494 (1951) at 580–81 (emphasis added).

select only strong interests to put on that side of the balance. The same applies to those who want to protect privacy through a categorization approach. The idea is to try to define an area of privacy that cannot be invaded by anyone. The difference between Justice Black and Justice White does not seem to lie in their methodology. But then where does this difference lie?

The answer is: in their realm of values. Justice Black believes in a society which is much better off with strong and energetic free speech. Sometimes, this may harm individuals or groups, but this is the price one has to pay for enhancing the most important good of the society. Justice White believes instead that a society is better off when each individual can protect himself from outside intrusion, and can flourish independently from anyone else's views. This represents an important societal value, and it must be protected from the press.

Both of them have already undertaken balancing in the realm of values. They have worked out *in abstracto* the advantages of certain priorities and designed their ideal society accordingly. FLRs do not work in the same way as values do.[59] The balancing that is allowed at this stage cannot be infused in constitutional practice.

FLRs—understood as constitutional norms grounding a constitutional status—conflict in a different, more complex, way. When we are focussing on that issue, we are begging the question of institutional competence, constitutional interpretation, and constitutional adjudication. All this must be done with an eye to the evolution of the constitutional system and to the intentions as expressed by the constitutional text.

There is little point in either imposing one's own balancing of values (Black), or in candidly pretending to go on balancing during the stage of decision (White). FLRs, when in genuine conflict, do not trump one another, nor can they be balanced. FLRs must be regulated within a constitutional framework. A constitutional framework can help us in achieving four important tasks. First, a clear conception of FLRs is to be sought in order to help us in distinguishing values from rights. Second, a theory of interpretation should be developed. Third, a method for articulating FLRs' requirements should be offered. Fourth, legal reasoning should be adapted to the difficult problems related to rights adjudication.

Justice Black and Justice White have a loose understanding of FLRs. A balancer like White, or like Frankfurter, is prepared to count unqualified interests in order to tip the balance in one way or another. An absolutist like Black is unprepared to see the dark side of a bright star like the First Amendment. Is the news relevant or material? Instead of a pragmatic balancing or an absolutist categorization, the courts would better come clean and favour a rule based solution. This would guarantee both the predictability of solutions, and the possibility of developing a coherent body of exceptions. I will develop this idea at the end of this section.

---

[59] Thomas Scanlon (n 50 above), 1478–79.

(ii) France: suspicious pragmatism

The FLR to privacy is held as paramount in France. Truthful private information is regularly protected by the screen of the FLR to privacy. The FLR to expression is largely understood as a benefit to the public. The right to know of the public is the core of the FLR to expression. Undoubtedly, genuine conflicts of FLRs are not easily solvable. But the courts must not be the only master in these conflicts. Courts cannot have the monopoly over defining conflicts. The Constitutional Council seems to enjoy the opportunity to shape conflicts at will. Its attitude has been characterized as pragmatic and voluntarist.[60] It is pragmatic, in the sense that there is no settled method or rule to solve conflicts. The council itself shapes its method of solving conflicts case by case. It is voluntarist in the sense that the council construes certain cases as conflicts in order to be in a position of control.

The key to every conflict is the general interest, *l'interet general*. Thus, the press/privacy conflict is framed in terms of the right of the public to know. For the Constitutional Council, it suffices to measure the general interest in order to reach a solution that sounds satisfactory. The Constitutional Council tries to reconcile conflicting FLRs. By that, I mean that there is a solution that can make everyone happy. Of course, it is not the case.

The Cassation Court, on the other hand, is very concerned with privacy. Paradoxically, it decides cases on the opposite grounds: as seen in the Mitterand case, individual rights are important and not the public interest.

The Constitutional Court and the Cassation Court have opposing conceptions of FLRs. The former bases FLRs on the general interest.[61] The latter exclusively grounds fundamental rights on private interests.[62] The Cassation Court explains away conflicts. The Constitutional Council attempts to accommodate them under the general interest umbrella. As to the methods, the Cassation Court uses an absolutist approach, the Constitutional Council a balancing one.

The Constitutional Council sketches two rules as to the resolution of conflict. The first is formal: the legislature is competent in principle to reconcile FLRs among themselves. The second is substantive: the decision of the legislature should not be manifestly unbalanced.

Thus, the very recent decision just quoted concerns the reconciliation of the FLR to privacy and the FLR to intellectual property. The two are in conflict, since the legislature proposes to allow companies to collect private information about individuals who are in breach of intellectual property law. The Constitutional Council acknowledges the conflict, but holds that reconciliation can be reached in the name of the general interest.[63]

---

[60] Nicolas Molfessis *Le Conseil Constitutionnel et le Droit Prive* (Paris: LGDJ, 1997), 34–47.
[61] Ibid.   [62] André Bertrand (n 12 above).
[63] 'L'autre dossier concerne la création de fichiers privés par les entreprises, associations et collectivités locales. Il s'agit, comme l'ont écrit dans *Le Monde*, d'anciens membres de la Commission, de *"casiers judiciaires parallèles"* ou de *"listes noires"* contre des fraudeurs ou des mauvais payeurs, réels ou

The general interest cannot be the only meter of satisfaction of FLRs, as the Constitutional Council seems to suggest (with the approval of the *Conseil d'Etat*). By using a very loose definition of general interest, the Constitutional Council controls, at its own desire, the decisions of the legislature.

Therefore, it would be easy for the Constitutional Council to hold that freedom of expression, as used by the press, has pride of place as it protects the general interest, as opposed to the FLR to privacy. This would be misleading, and it is surprising to hear criticism of the Cassation Court on the grounds that it prefers the FLR to privacy in a misleading way which does not take account of the general interest.[64] In conclusion, in France, balancing and absolutism are presented as a way of solving conflicts, but both are open to criticism.

(iii) FLRs and confusion

Lord Hoffmann is the most articulate human rights judge in the UK. Yet, he does not seem to have a fully coherent position when it comes to freedom of expression. Sometimes, he seems to have an absolutist position.[65] While other times, he acknowledges that freedom of expression should be balanced.[66] To me that confusion is not all that surprising. Hitherto, I have tried to show how the two positions are only apparently different.

The deeper confusion lies in the idea that values and FLRs can be equated. Hoffmann certainly believes in the paramount position of free speech in his ideal society. In that sense, he considers free speech an absolute. But as an officer of Her Majesty the Queen, he is under a number of constraints and he acknowledges that even his heavyweight should manage a place to other rights.

I shall first consider the relationship between the freedom of the press and the common law right of the individual to protect personal information. Both reflect important civilized values, but, as often happens, neither can be given effect in full measure without restricting the other. How are they to be reconciled in a particular case? There is in my view no question of automatic priority. Nor is there a presumption in favour of one rather than the other. The question is rather the extent to which it is necessary to qualify the one right in

---

supposés, mis en place par des personnes morales se jugeant victimes d'infractions. Le Conseil constitutionnel a limité cette prérogative aux sociétés de perception et de gestion des droits d'auteur, afin de lutter contre le téléchargement illégal de films ou de chansons sur Internet. Il s'agit, pour les dix sages, de *"répondre à l'intérêt général"* tout en assurant *"le respect de la vie privée"*. En l'absence d'une législation suffisamment précise, cette mesure ne pourra en revanche être étendue aux autres secteurs d'activité'. Le Monde,' 1 August 2004.

[64] André Bertrand (n 12 above), 68.

[65] *R v Central Independent television plc* [1994] Fam 192, 203. 'It cannot be too strongly emphasised that outside the established exceptions, or any new ones which Parliament may enact in accordance with its obligation under the Convention, there is **no question of balancing** freedom of speech against other interests. It is a trump card which always wins'.

[66] *Campbell v MGN* [2004] UKHL 22, para 36: 'But the importance of this case lies in the statements of general principle on the way in which the law should strike a **balance** between the right to privacy and the right to freedom of expression, on which the House is unanimous'.

order to protect the underlying value which is protected by the other. And the extent of the qualification must be proportionate to the need.⁶⁷

The previous citation encapsulates the main elements of Lord Hoffmann's theory of rights. First, he believes in a deep entanglement between values and FLRs. Second, he believes in equality of values (no automatic priority; no presumption). Third, he believes in the qualification of rights through proportionality (balancing).

Having set his own framework, he goes on to say that often there is no real conflict. When there is a public interest in the disclosure of information, free expression wins. When there is no public interest in the disclosure, then privacy shall be protected.⁶⁸ As a result, Hoffmann reserves for the court a very broad power. There is no effort in the definition of public interest. As we know, this can be used and manipulated at will. The second important conclusion that he reaches is that the press, and more generally the media, have room for discretion as to the levels of detail they publish.

In conclusion, balancing and absolutism are two methods of resolution of conflicts that beg more questions than they solve. Often, they are there just to conceal the lack of a coherent theory of FLRs and to cloak subjective value preferences with apparently objective legal reasoning in terms of proportionality. These two approaches fall within the category of reductive explanation of FLRs' conflicts. That is, conflicts are said to be merely apparent, and therefore, they are solved by applying one of the preferred methods.

C. Accomodating Conflicts

Can we really expand constitutional theories in order to fit hard cases, such as the conflict between press and privacy? Many scholars believe that this is possible. Nonetheless, a sharp distinction must be drawn between those who believe in constitution-perfecting theories,⁶⁹ and those who develop accurate constitutional theories.⁷⁰ The difference lies in the fact that constitution-perfecting theories work to provide happy endings to any hard case; accurate theories, on the other hand, are left with a sense of tragedy in certain hard cases.

In the ultimate analysis, a constitution-perfecting theory can only subscribe to spurious conflicts of FLRs. For, if there were genuine conflicts, there would always be a moral residue which prevents striving toward a 'perfected constitution'. But this fails to grasp the tragic aspect of hard cases. In what follows, I will explore the press/privacy conflict, from the point of view of constitution-perfecting theories. Then I will put forward my preferred, rule-based, alternative of conflicts accommodation.

---

⁶⁷ Ibid, para 55. ⁶⁸ Ibid, para 56.
⁶⁹ James E Fleming, 'Constitutional Tragedy in Dying: Or Whose Tragedy Is It, Anyway?' in William Eskridge, Jr and Sanford Levinson (eds), *Constitutional Stupidities Constitutional Tragedies* (New York: NYUP, 1998).
⁷⁰ Larry Alexander, 'Constitutional Tragedies and Giving Refuge to the Devil' in William Eskridge, Jr and Sanford Levinson (eds), ibid at 115.

(i) Constitution-perfecting, conflict-solving, theories

How would a constitution-perfecting theory resolve a conflict concerning the disclosure of truthful private information? That heavily depends on the background constitutional theory to which one subscribes. In the USA, there is extensive literature on this topic. In France, and in England, it is much less discussed. Therefore, we will mainly concentrate on the American debates.

This is not the place to map the intricate theories of American constitutional law. As a result, we are forced to select one main strand of the literature and treat it as representative. It is quite safe to hold that Rawls's political philosophy has had a great impact on many constitutionalists. The last generation of Rawlsian constitution scholars grew up with the teaching of a *Theory of Justice*, as amended by *Political Liberalism*. In the latter, Rawls presents his theory as a desirable brand of liberalism as applied to political affairs, as opposed to a comprehensive theory in search of good for the society.

A growing number of scholars argue that Rawls's liberalism can provide a sound framework for the resolution of conflicts among basic liberties.[71] The key concepts that are relevant for such an endeavour are: the priority of the family of liberties; the constitution as a whole; and the distinction between regulating and restricting liberties. When basic liberties conflict they must be mutually adjusted, Rawls holds. Not balanced; not taken as absolute trumps. In order to do that, we have to accept that basic liberties may be regulated, but not restricted. Their central range of protection must always be secured. Regulation appeals to time, manner, and space types of rules. Thus, someone who wants to speak must be allowed to do so, but when, how, and where are up for the authorities to review.

Basic liberties form a family of constitutional essentials. They take priority over other interests as a family, and not individually. Hence, regulation is always aimed at enhancing the whole system of basic liberties, not just liberties individually. Moreover, regulation is not arbitrary and it should be carried out 'in order to guarantee the fair value of the equal political liberties'.[72] Rawls's political constructivism is the starting point of a constitutional constructivism which expands a framework for the resolution of difficult questions. Constitutional constructivism borrows from its political counterparts the two fundamental themes: deliberative democracy and deliberative autonomy.

These two themes are relevant for our enquiry, because privacy is at the core of deliberative autonomy. And free press, as an instantiation of free speech, is at the core of deliberative democracy. How would the framework help us in deciding our core case of conflict? To be fair, we have to acknowledge that the framework does not aim to give any legal answer to the specific question. It depends on a

---

[71] A notable example is James Fleming who organized a symposium on 'Rawls and the law', held in Fordham Law School on 7–8 November 2003.

[72] James E Fleming, 'Securing Deliberative Democracy', 72 Fordham L Rev 1435, 1459 (2004).

division of labour between law and philosophy, which Thomas Scanlon explains as follows:

> First, it [Rawls' framework] can distinguish clearly between rights and the values with reference to which they are to be justified and interpreted. Second, it may specify more fully how this process of interpretation (or definition and adjustment) is to proceed. Specifically, it may offer a particular view of how the values relevant to the justification of certain rights are to be understood. Finally, since such claims about values are bound to be a matter of controversy, the framework may provide a larger theoretical rationale for giving these particular values this special place in our thinking. Rawls' framework does all three of these things.[73]

Rawls' framework helps to clear the ground of constitutional essentials, although it makes no claim as to the details. Constitution-perfecting theories are meant to carry on Rawls' project, at the level of constitutional law, thereby tackling actual constitutional cases.

But does that help in the resolution of our conflict? Deliberative autonomy and deliberative democracy are presented as co-original and of equal weight. Thus, at the general level there is no guide as to whether we should prefer privacy or free press. We know that neither should be preferred to the other, on the grounds of principle alone. Hence, we may want to suggest that a regulation, as opposed to a restriction, can help in solving the dilemma of disclosure of private information. Free speech should not have absolute priority, nor should privacy.

How do you maintain the central range of both basic liberties while regulating it in such a way that helps reach one decision? Is the test of lawfully obtained information a good regulation? It does seem a regulation as to the manner in which we acquire information. But is it a good regulation? This can be legitimately doubted, since it is the exclusive responsibility of the government to screen certain information. However, if the government is negligent, then the press cannot be held responsible.

Is the newsworthy test a regulation that secures the fair value of both privacy and free press? I think that we can hardly make sense of privacy if we stick to the newsworthy test. A personal tragedy may well be considered newsworthy. Yet the central range of privacy should be there to protect precisely that piece of information.

Is the reasonable expectation of privacy test able to enhance the fair values of both privacy and free press? Even in that case, I do not think that is the case. A reasonable expectation is grounded on what the society commonly perceives as being harmful and intrusive. That is not necessarily in line with what a reasonable conception of privacy should allow protection of. Can there be a regulation that allows us to shield truthful information about individuals without restricting free speech? Conversely, can there be a regulation that allows the disclosure of private information, whilst preserving informational privacy?

---

[73] Thomas Scanlon, 'Adjusting Rights and Balancing Values', 72 Fordham L Rev 1477 at 1478–79.

The problem is that if we acknowledge the existence of genuine conflicts of FLRs we cannot hope to achieve a coherent 'happy' family of all basic liberties. In some cases, it is impossible to secure the central range of both FLRs as the conflict concerns the clash of the requirements falling within that central range of protection. We can only develop a framework that allows us to take decisions that explain sacrifices. In other words, the family of basic liberties cannot possibly be perfectly harmonious. To be sure, there are a lot of good intentions in striving to make the family as harmonious as possible. But, we cannot turn a blind eye to the possibility of genuine conflicts.

(ii) Accommodating FLRs

Free press and privacy belong to the same family. There is room for their mutual adjustment in different cases. Sometimes, for instance, certain aspects of politicians' private lives could be brought to light in order to provide more information to voters. Nonetheless, I do not think that politicians' private lives should be fully exposed. First, some of that information is plainly not relevant.[74] Second, other people, who are not politicians, can be caught in the disclosure of private information. Also, one may wonder why private tragedies should be publishable at all. Rape, kidnapping, thefts: why should victims be publicly named if they do not want to make news? Of course, what happened to them is news, but why should we disclose their identities in this unfortunate situation?

Despite my privacy concerns, I would now like to argue that free press should be recognized as having qualified priority. Moreover, the press should be allowed to have a margin of manoeuvre when deciding what, when, and how to publish. I make these points in anticipation of the outcome I reach by application of my framework. In the remaining part of this section, I attempt to explain how the framework works, and why the solution that it reaches is supported by the best constitutional interpretation of FLRs.

The framework I favour is not rooted in a particular constitutional history. From a certain point of view, it can be considered a meta-framework because it aims to be applied to all constitutional frameworks. It is an attempt to theorize the way in which FLRs affect the decision-making process in different countries.

Bills, charters, and declarations of rights contain very similar lists of FLRs' norms. They are nowadays part of every domestic legal system. A system of enforcement of FLRs is often available, albeit it can vary considerably. Often, FLRs have been distinguished in different waves or generations. This was an attempt to provide a typology of FLRs with regard to its content. I would like to suggest that theories of FLRs are running short of arguments, when it comes to the decision of genuine conflicts of FLRs. What I propose is a second generation of FLRs' systems. I think that new rules as to the functioning of these systems

---

[74] See Fred Schauer on this point, 'Can Public Figures Have Private Lives?' (n 42 above) 293–309.

should be thought of in order to make hard case decisions more transparent, so as to properly allocate the burdens of the decision process. When applied to our press/privacy conflict, that means that we have to come up with rules which regulate the behaviour of FLRs taken together and could eventually allow sacrifices in certain cases.

There are two broad types of rules that can achieve that purpose. First, there are substantive rules of priority. These rules are twofold. They can be internal to the FLRs' systems, or external to them. Internal rules of priority concern the relationship between different rights. For instance, when we seek for a rule of priority concerning free press and privacy, we can start by laying down a spectrum of four broad possibilities: absolute priority for free press; absolute priority for privacy; qualified priority for free press; or qualified priority for privacy. Most of our systems of FLRs support one of these broad options. I think that it is particularly important to come up with a clear rule. That does not mean that the FLR that has priority would never be qualified. On the contrary, when we start with a clear priority, then we can elaborate sophisticated arguments in favour of the overrule of that priority. That qualified priority rule also has the advantage of avoiding the balancing and absolutism rhetoric which plague FLRs' systems.

The second rule of substantive priority concerns the system of FLRs as a whole. Equally, that system has a qualified priority over any other type of considerations, interests and other countervailing reasons. Often, state interests or public interests are erected to the status of FLRs, in order to provoke a conflict which state interests are meant to win. Recently, that technique has been preferred if we think about the state interest in security, which often is used to curtail FLRs. This device is not acceptable without strong reasons for its support. FLRs, as a family, have qualified priority over any other types of interests.

Beyond substantive rules of priority, we have procedural rules. These concern the distribution of powers when it comes to hard cases. First, they concern the distribution of power between different branches of government. Second, they concern the repartition of that power between the State and individuals. Free press versus privacy is a horizontal conflict. In the next chapter, we will examine a vertical conflict. The plaintiff is an individual, and the defender is the State. What is at stake is the decisional privacy of the individual in questions of life and death.

7
Mortal Conflicts of Fundamental Legal Rights—The Fundamental Legal Right to Life v The Fundamental Legal Right to Decisional Privacy

1. Introduction

Can we provoke the death of someone else in 'his best interest'? Can the state prevent us from doing that in order to preserve 'life'? This chapter asks these two questions, although their relation may not be immediately clear. From the constitutional perspective, the question may be put as follows: who decides the issue, and on what grounds? There are two major problems: first, representative institutions shy away from their responsibility of enacting well reasoned public policies in relation to death; second, legal prohibition of intentionally killing is a blanket ban, but that is not always an accurate depiction of the protection afforded by the FLR to life. For instance, even if we all have a great respect for life, we may still feel compassion and a deep respect for individual autonomy, in particular when a terminally ill patient asks to be spared a painful death.

Mortal issues probably should not be dealt with by courts, yet they are. In many jurisdictions, an impressive body of cases concern questions at the edges of life. Courts decide whether it is permissible to withdraw the treatment of patients in a persistent vegetative state (PVS).[1] They also decide whether to impose the separation of conjoined twins.[2] They decide whether to let a seriously ill patient die.[3] And above all, they have to decide whether killing is different from removing a feeding tube or respirator and letting someone die.[4]

It is difficult to classify these issues and very hard to disentangle the ethical, medical, social, and political dimensions. But then, it is hard to understand how judges can be competent to solve these questions. However, legislators seldom

---

[1] *Airedale NHS Trust v Bland* [1993] AC 789.
[2] *Re A (Children) (Conjoined Twins: Medical Treatment) (No 1)* [2000] HRLR 721.
[3] *Cruzan v Director, Missouri Department of Health*, 110 S Ct 2841(1990).
[4] *Washington v Glucksberg*, 521 US 702 (1997); *Dennis Vacco v Quill*, 521 US 793; *R (Pretty) v DPP* [2002] 1AC 800; *Rodriguez v British Columbia (Attorney-General)* 107 DLR (4th) 342 (1994).

provide a framework. Moreover, physicians specifically appeal to courts in order to see their informed opinions cloaked by the legitimacy of law. Ethicists, to be sure, express highly informed opinions. But, in the end what matters is what the courts say.

It takes a considerable leap of faith to believe that courts speak for everyone in a clear, non controversial, way. The issues we are concerned with here are the most controversial. Can death outweigh life? In order to know that, we enter a *terra incognita* which requires us to think of troublesome questions, such as what is the meaning, or the value, of life? Even if this may appear a vain exercise, most of those who engage in such debates put forward, implicitly or explicitly, their own interpretation of life, and of its value.

A widespread strategy is to insist on the principle of sanctity of life. Thus, for instance, Ronald Dworkin insists that since life is protected by the principle of sanctity of life, different conceptions of what that principle means should all be protected by the religious freedoms enshrined in the First Amendment.[5] Other authors, whose views are informed by their religious convictions, insist that only God has the ultimate word on matters of life and death. Therefore, we should make sure that our institutional arrangements do not conflict with precise religious convictions. In other words, regardless of religion, when it comes to death we should abide by the views of the religious leaders as to how we should die.[6]

I think that courts ought not to dwell on the meaning of life because it is beyond their reach. Instead, they can safely rely upon the distinction between a FLR to life and the value of life. Roughly, a FLR to life consists of the permission for the right-holder to lead his life as he pleases, and in the prohibition *erga omnes* against the intentional deprivation of one's life. The value of life is deeply controversial, and its meaning will depend on comprehensive philosophical and/or religious views.

The definition of the FLR to life I put forward does not help in solving these moral dilemmas. However, it helps in avoiding convoluted discussions about the meaning of life in judicial fora. In this chapter I would like to discuss a case of intentional killing in the interest of the victim: the case of physician-assisted suicide (PAS). To understand this issue better, some preliminary distinctions are in order. Euthanasia and PAS are two ways of intending the death of someone. The patient asks for, and the physicians provide, help in terminating his life. The difference between euthanasia and PAS is that in the former case, the physician carries out the ultimate act, whereas in the latter, it is the patient that performs the act terminating his life.

I have decided to focus on PAS because the issue of decisional privacy is clearer. The patient decides to die and performs the act which achieves that aim. There is no solution of continuity between one's personal beliefs about the value of life,

---

[5] Ronald Dworkin, *Life's Dominion* (NY: Haper Collins, 1993).
[6] Ironically, this is not true when it comes to the death penalty in the USA.

and one's action informed by these beliefs. To the contrary, in the case of euthanasia it is much easier to hold that the patient's fate ultimately depends on the judgement of the physician. This is not strictly accurate because the physician could not decide on his own initiative to terminate a life. But admittedly, the fact that the patient's life is dependent upon the physician's act makes it easier to believe that it all depends on the physician's evaluation of the value of life.

Indeed, the soundest argument of those who oppose any form of intentional killing is the slippery slope argument (SS).[7] The SS holds that the distinction between PAS and voluntary euthanasia is very thin. This is because, most of the time, physicians will intervene if something goes wrong in an assisted suicide. Moreover, the real problems arise, they say, when we slip from voluntary to non-voluntary euthanasia (that is euthanasia performed on incompetent patients—NVAE), and eventually to involuntary (euthanasia against one's will—IVAE). The SS argument has strong appeal: it underlines the importance of the prohibition set by the FLR to life. Physicians and the general public are prohibited from intentionally terminating someone else's life. However, I can also see the merits of the FLR to decisional privacy which allows each individual to act on the grounds of his/her innermost beliefs.

In other words, I see a conflict between the FLR to life and the FLR to decisional privacy. Few people agree with this view. Many think that the only conflict is between the interest in self-determination of the individual, and the state interest in the protection of life. Framing the question that way is deeply problematic, especially if we hold a strong conception of FLRs, as it equates a FLR to decisional privacy to a simple interest. Then, it opposes the state interest in the protection of life to the simple interest aforementioned. This characterization of the conflict debases the importance of FLRs in constitutional adjudication. This is because the interest embedded in the FLR does not seem to have any specific priority in relation to the interest protected by the State.

Others do not see any conflict at all. Sometimes they argue that a FLR to life is not such if it cannot be waived. Other times, they deny the existence of a FLR to decisional privacy. To the former, I would reply that FLRs can be waived except when waiving amounts to alienating. Think, for instance, about the FLR not to be enslaved. Even if willing, individuals would not be able to become slaves. To the latter point, I would reply that in many countries there is a body of evidence which shows how decisional privacy is increasingly recognized.

Moreover, I am not prepared to lower the pull of either FLR. The prohibition against intentional killing, as set by the FLR to life is a strong prohibition, and rightly so. PAS cannot be accepted on the grounds of individual consent alone. That is merely a precondition. For instance, suffering from depression would not justify the request of assisted suicide. The only really meaningful cases are those of

---

[7] For a very good discussion of the slippery slope argument, see John Keown, *Euthanasia, Ethics and Public policy—An argument against legalization* (Cambridge: CUP, 2002) 70.

terminally ill patients. For those, the real choice is between a slow and painful death, and a quicker and less painful one. Even in these cases, however, the physician ought not to have a blank check for killing.

This chapter presents the conflict of the FLR to life versus the FLR to privacy in PAS cases. It does so by focusing on the way legal reasoning frames this conflict of FLRs. To be sure, moral theorists may frame the problem in a totally different way. My point will be that there is a fundamental difference between moral and legal reasoning. For instance, one may reasonably argue that it is morally permissible to intentionally kill in certain cases. This, however, does not guarantee a conclusion that it is wise to legalize certain forms of intentional killing. Moral reasoning often treats these issues on a case by case basis. Legal reasoning must avoid coming up with bad rules which fit one case, but prejudice others. As I said at the beginning, it may not be a favourable thing that courts decide on mortal issues. But, often they must face this task. To frame the issue as a conflict of FLRs has some clear advantages. We are forced to consider the strongest case on each side. As a consequence we are invited to review, very closely, all the reasonings which stand for both FLRs at stake. Any decision will be reached with the awareness that a FLR is sacrificed. But in order to do this, we need clear rules which help us select the lesser of two evils.

In the second section, I present the issue of PAS in general. Then, I present the anatomy of a FLRs conflict focusing on the meaning of both FLRs. In section 4 I compare moral and legal perspectives on the conflict. Section 5 briefly expands on the role of the parties in the conflict. Finally, in sections 6 and 7 I address the vexing question of finding a solution to the conflict; my point will be that we need clearer rules, as opposed to loose adjudicative principles, such as balancing. Section 7 concludes that a strong conception of FLRs requires the state to accept some individual tragedies, instead of imposing its own controversial view.

2. Physician-assisted Suicide Around the World

When talking about PAS and euthanasia, the most famous example is Holland's. In 1984, the Dutch Supreme Court decriminalized certain cases of PAS and euthanasia. Dutch criminal law made it criminal to kill another person at his request or to assist someone's suicide. In the first instance, the doctor (Dr Schoonheim) had been convicted. However, the Dutch Supreme Court held that, in certain cases, doctors could invoke the defence of necessity. In particular, this is the case when a doctor is faced with a conflict of duties. On one hand, he is under the duty not to intentionally kill, or to assist in suicide, as stated by the criminal code. On the other hand, he is under a duty to relieve his patient's suffering.

This covers the conflict of duties as seen from the doctor's point of view. But, if we turn to the patient's viewpoint, we can safely say that if the doctor is under these duties, this is because the patient has certain rights. And, if these duties genuinely conflict, there is a case for saying that the patient's rights conflict. What is the patient's FLR then?[8] The requirements set by Dutch criminal law no doubt instantiate the FLR to life of the individual. Hence, on one hand we have a FLR to life stating the prohibition of intentional killing. On the other, the physician's duty to relieve one's sufferings corresponds to a less well defined FLR on the part of the individual. I believe this corresponds to the FLR to decisional privacy. For, it is only in the event of the patient asking for the ultimate relief of his pain that the doctor is meant to act.

My reinterpretation of the Dutch case as a conflict of FLRs is, I admit, purely hypothetical. It assumes that the judges had assessed the issue in terms of FLRs, even if no such concept was available to them in 1984. However, I maintain that my hypothetical reinterpretation of the Dutch case in these terms is useful in understanding why cases of PAS (and of euthanasia) raise issues of conflicts.

We will now look at America. In June 1997, America said no to PAS in two landmark decisions: *Washington v Glucksberg*[9] and *Vacco v Quill*.[10] The question concerned the unconstitutionality of Washington's and New York's statutes prohibiting assisted suicide. In *Glucksberg*, the Court of Appeals of the ninth circuit, found a liberty interest in the Fourteenth Amendment which protected the individual's choice as to the time and manner of death. In *Quill*, the Court of Appeals of the second circuit found that the statute against assisted suicide breached the equal protection clause of the Fourteenth Amendment. This was because terminally ill patients on life-support systems were allowed to ask for the withdrawal of those systems, thereby hastening their death. While on the contrary, all other terminally ill patients would not be able to hasten their death.

Here we have two strands of arguments: one is based on liberty, the other one on equality. Chief Justice Rehnquist, writing for the majority, argued against both arguments. In *Glucksberg*, Chief Justice Rehnquist explained that seven centuries of history weighed against the liberty interest found by the Court of Appeals of the ninth circuit. In *Quill*, he argued that the Court of Appeals of the second circuit failed to see a fundamental distinction between refusing an intrusive treatment, and asking for assistance in a suicide. In the first case, the patient dies because of his disease; in the second, he dies because of the physician's intervention. And of course, he added, intending the death of someone is a long-standing prohibition of the common law tradition.

That said, Chief Justice Rehnquist went on to hold that in order to pass constitutional review the law against suicide should protect important state interests. He found that the protection of vulnerable people and the risk of a slippery slope were sufficiently important state interests to call for statutory protection. Two points can be made. First, it is quite incredible that Justice Rehnquist is unable to see an

---

[8] A possible reason why the court did not frame the issue in terms of FLRs is that Holland only recently adopted a domestic bill of rights.   [9] *Washington v Glucksberg*, 521 US 702.
[10] *Vacco v Quill*, 521 US 793.

important interest on the part of the terminally ill patients. Second, it is not surprising that a state interest in support of the statutes can be found in the myriad of state interests. As a consequence, an issue which is of utmost importance to individual well-being is presented as a matter where the state can decide as it desires. For this reason I think that tackling the issue in terms of FLRs' conflict can prove much more profitable.

The concurring opinions of Justice O'Connor and Justice Stevens show more concern for the individual, although they are unable to conclude in favour of PAS. O'Connor argues that the interests of terminally ill, mentally competent patients should be balanced against the state's interests in protecting those who might seek to end life mistakenly or under pressure.[11] To be sure, she can see a tension of some kind; however, the framing of the tension is hard to grasp. This is because Justice O'Connor randomly identifies a state interest, which may well be re-characterized as an individual interest in being left alone when making an important decision on one's own death.

Much more subtle and well argued is Justice Steven's argument. He concurs in the decision insofar as he does not see a constitutional right to commit suicide.[12] However, he holds that this does not preclude the possibility of finding some cases of prohibition of PAS unconstitutional. The most interesting part of his reasoning lies in the discussion of the interests at stake. On the part of the individual, he clearly sees a liberty interest. This interest, though, does not support the idea of being able to choose whatever one likes. Instead, it suggests that the individual may sometimes be able to choose a preferred method of dying. On the other side, he starts by acknowledging a state interest in the preservation of human life. Interestingly, however, he goes on saying that: 'Properly viewed, however, this interest is not a collective interest that should always outweigh the interests of a person who because of pain, incapacity, or sedation finds her life intolerable, but rather, an aspect of individual freedom.'[13] I see this as an implicit recognition of a FLRs' conflict.

In Europe, an English case recently dealt with the issue. Mrs Pretty, a 43 year old woman, was diagnosed with motor neurone disease. By the time of her request for assisted suicide she was already in a terminal stage. Soon after the decision of the court rejecting her request she died. What she was asking for was the waiver of her husband's responsibility in assisting her death by the Director of Public Prosecutions (DPP). She attacked the refusal on the grounds that she had a right to be assisted in her suicide. Mrs Pretty relied on a number of arguments from the rights protected by the European Convention for Human Rights (ECHR), and incorporated into domestic law by the Human Rights Act 1998 (HRA). The main arguments concerned her FLR to life (as protected by Article 2 of the ECHR) and her FLR to privacy (as protected by Article 8 of the ECHR). The Strasbourg

---

[11] Ibid, 890.   [12] He should add to PAS.
[13] *Washington v Glucksberg*, 521 US 702 at 746.

Court held that the FLR to life was based on the principle of sanctity of life, and that it could not be interpreted as having a negative side. That means that it could only be invoked for the protection of life, and as a basis for the prohibition of taking life intentionally. That said, the Court argued that Article 8.1 confers upon the individual a FLR to privacy. The Court actually argued that preventing an individual from exercising his right to decisional privacy amounts to an interference of the State. However, the Court goes on in justifying the interference on the grounds of Article 8.2, which allows proportional interferences. The gist of the Court's reasoning follows here:

> The very essence of the Convention is respect for human dignity and human freedom. Without in any way negating the principle of sanctity of life protected under the Convention, the Court considers that it is under Article 8 that notions of the quality of life take on significance. In an era of growing medical sophistication combined with longer life expectancies, many people are concerned that they should not be forced to linger on in old age or in states of advanced physical or mental decrepitude which conflict with strongly held ideas of self and personal identity.[14]

In a rather awkward way the court points to a conflict between the principle of sanctity of life, and that of quality of life. If the principle of sanctity of life means that no one can intend his death, then to accept that one can do so on grounds of quality of life precisely amounts to a negation of sanctity of life.[15] Thus, to conclude, the court sees a tension, but it frames it in the wrong way. It presents it firstly in terms of values instead of in terms of FLRs. Furthermore, it frames the conflict of values in a rather inconsistent way, as has just been seen.

3. The Anatomy of a FLRs Conflict

PAS cases involve a conflict between the FLR to life and the FLR to decisional privacy. An examination of the approach of the USA, France, and England displays a considerable divergence at the constitutional level. In the US, what I called a FLR to life and a FLR to decisional privacy, are both 'unenumerated' rights. That is, they are not mentioned in the Bill of Rights. On the contrary, both in England and in France they are explicitly mentioned and they occupy a central position. The clearest text is the ECHR.

Article 2 of the ECHR (right to life) states:

1 'Everyone's right to life shall be protected by law. No one shall be deprived of his life *intentionally* save in the execution of a sentence of a court following his conviction of a crime for which the penalty is provided by law.'

---

[14] Case of *Pretty v UK*, Application 2346/02, para 65.
[15] John Keown, 'European Court of Human Rights: Death in Strasbourg—assisted suicide, the *Pretty* case, and the European Convention on Human Rights', International Journal of Constitutional Law (2003) 722–30(9).

2 'Deprivation of life shall not be regarded as inflicted in contravention of this article when it results from the use of force which is no more than absolutely necessary:
   a) in defence of any person from unlawful violence;
   b) in order to effectuate a lawful arrest or to prevent the escape of a person lawfully detained;
   c) in action lawfully taken for the purpose of quelling a riot or insurrection.'

Article 8 of the ECHR (right to respect for private and family life) states:

1 'Everyone has the right to respect for his private and family life, his home and his correspondence.'
2 'There shall be no interference by a public authority with the exercise of this right except such as is in accordance with the law and is necessary in a democratic society in the interests of national security, public safety or the economic well-being of the country, for the prevention of disorder or crime, for the protection of health or morals, or for the protection of the rights and freedom of others.'

The American Constitution makes only a very laconic reference to those rights in the famous due process clause: 'Nor shall any State deprive any person of life, liberty, or property, without due process of law.'

These textual differences should not prevent us from examining the issue in depth. First, I will attempt to understand what information we can gather from the texts, in relation to the PAS issue. Then, we will focus on the central conflict between those rights.

A. The FLR to Life

What is it that the FLR to life really protects? Offhand, there is no agreement on the meaning of life, as already pointed out. This should not prevent us from searching for one nonetheless. But I do not think that much can be achieved by advancing a definition of 'life'. Legal texts offer a different platform from which to start. For example, I think that Article 2 of the ECHR is clear. The FLR to life protects everyone from being intentionally killed. I think that this is the core of the provision, and it determines the central range of the FLR. The FLR to life is a negative right, insofar as it requires others, or the state, to refrain from attempting to intentionally kill an individual. To be sure, it is the intentional aspect that should be stressed. What is really prohibited is to act with the intention of causing the death of someone else. If your act has no intentional significance, then killing may even be justified. For instance, a medical doctor who prescribes painkillers may not intend the death of his patient at all. Yet, painkillers may sometimes cause death.

What is the difference between the criminal law prohibition of killing, and the FLR to life? The FLR to life creates a constitutional status which protects individuals against the modification of all prohibitions of intentional killing. Criminal law is dependent on the good will of the state to secure life in an equal manner. To illustrate this point we can take the British legal system as an example. Before the incorporation of the ECHR, only criminal law would protect the right not to be killed. That was a simple right, and could theoretically be withdrawn by parliament. Now, with the incorporation of the ECHR into domestic law, every individual's life is protected independently from the will of parliament. Hence, if parliament was to arbitrarily decide that certain people (eg terrorists) can be intentionally killed without justification, then this would be against the FLR to life.

What is the scope of the FLR to life? Some argue that for a FLR to be meaningful, the right-holder must be able to waive it. Hence, a right-holder should be able to die, if he deems it reasonable to do so. I think that this argument presents a twofold confusion. The most basic one lies in the distinction between waiving and alienating. The second confusion hinges on the duties that a FLR can create on other people. The former distinction is relevant to understanding the permissible exercises of a FLR. I believe that waiving is, in principle, permissible unless it coincides with alienating. To understand that point, we could draw a parallel with the prohibitions against slavery and forced labour. An individual cannot be made a slave, even if he consented to it. He simply cannot waive his protection against slavery, because that waiver would amount to the perennial loss of control over his status, and that is not permissible. The latter issue (the kind of duties created by FLRs) is even more relevant for us. It is not because we all have a negative duty *erga omnes* not to be killed that we can claim a positive duty *erga omnes* to be killed, at our own will by someone else. Those are two different types of duties and the FLR to life guarantees us only a negative duty not to be killed.

The best cases to understand the role of the FLR to life are those at the edges of life, when it is necessary to decide whether killing someone is permissible. I will now examine a number of cases from America, France, and the UK in order to evaluate the problem.

Common law sets a strong prohibition on killing in the 19th century. In the famous landmark case *R v Dudley and Stephens*, the Queen's Bench division of the High Court of Justice found that the captain and the crew of the boat were guilty of murder.[16] This is because there is no defence (short of cases of self-defence) of necessity against intentional killing. The court explained that in cases such as this, the highest duty is to die, and not to live at the expense of the weakest. In two notable contexts—war and shipwreck—the duty to die of some members of the crew outweighs the duty to preserve their own life. In a shipwreck, the captain of the ship has this duty towards his crew, and the crew towards the passengers. Given this hierarchy, it was more honourable for the captain to die, rather than to kill the cabin boy, for the sake of saving the rest of the crew. Interestingly, this case seems to be grounded on a conception of honour, rather than on a conception of life. The reason we cannot kill in order to survive, is that one's social position and duties do not allow that option, according to the court.

---

[16] *R v Dudley and Stephens* (1884) 14 QBD 273. For a discussion of this case, see ch 3.

Compare the former case with that of the conjoined twins Jodie and Mary.[17] Physicians held that the only way to save Jodie was to kill Mary. However, the parents refused to accept the death of one to save the other on religious grounds. Thus the court had to step in to solve the dilemma. The court concluded that Mary ought to be killed in order to save Jodie. The reasoning of the court presents some interesting features. I will try to break it down into eight points, following Walker LJ. First, Marie has a right to life. Second, Jodie has a right to life. Third, their right to life implies bodily integrity and autonomy. Fourth, due to a tragedy, Mary and Jodie have been deprived of their bodily integrity and autonomy, which is their natural right. Fifth, the purpose of an operation is to give Jodie a normal life. The purpose is not to kill Mary although this would be the natural consequence. Mary, however, would have her natural right to bodily integrity restored, even if in death. Sixth, continued life for Mary would mean pain and discomfort. Seventh, the operation is in the best interest of both children. Eighth, the operation would not be unlawful; it is intended to save Jodie's life but not intended to provoke Mary's death. Death is merely foreseen as a consequence.

The conclusion was that Jodie had a (quasi) right to self-defence which arose out of necessity.[18] The gist of the problem lies in the reasoning. Most of the judges insisted that they were not evaluating the quality of life of either child. I insist that they were evaluating the quality of life of both, by stressing the abnormality and unnaturalness of conjoined twins. Their position is only the blatant statement of our ignorance on issues of conjoined twins.[19] The implicit preamble of that decision is: having a conjoined twin does not fall within our parameters and it is therefore abnormal. Then there is the problem with the definition of life. No clear definition is sought. Instead, life is defined through its 'normal standards': bodily integrity and autonomy. The most ridiculous aspect of all is that Marie is said to eventually regain her bodily integrity, even if it is bodily integrity in death.

My criticism does not point to a better solution. It underlies, however, the assumptions that guide a decision that aims to single out the best interests of either child, and to weigh them one against another with the aim of coming up with a fair decision. That is overly simplistic. The FLR to life can only be understood as being separate from the FLR to bodily integrity and the FLR to decisional privacy. As said before, the FLR to life can be defined in terms of a prohibition of being intentionally killed. That is quite a clear and strong requirement. Of course, it is not the whole story; rightly so, I would say, because the rest of the story is told by the other FLR (to decisional privacy).

---

[17] *Re A (Children) (Conjoined Twins: Medical Treatment) No 1* [2000] HRLR 721.

[18] *Per* Ward LJ at 775. Ironically, the right to life was more strongly protected in *Dudley*, when there was no bill of rights. But this is not the issue, since in hard cases, a FLR to life cannot be considered as an absolute in any case.

[19] Alice Domurat Dreger, *One of us: Conjoined Twins and the Future of Normal* (Cambridge, Mass: HUP, 2004).

In the USA, the disagreement about the meaning of life was triggered by abortion issues. Here, I only want to hint at that debate. Most of the pro-life partisans are so for religious reasons. And, even a liberal thinker such as Dworkin believes that the idea of the sanctity of life has a very strong pull.[20] That may be sociologically correct in America, but I do not believe that it can be easily generalized. Nor do I buy Dworkin's argument that individual choice should be protected on the grounds of the free exercise (of religion) clause, as stated in the First Amendment. I do not have problems in acknowledging that life is inviolable, but that can be stated independently from my (or someone else's) religious beliefs.

The debate in the USA turned to the question as to whether the foetus is a right-holder or not. This question is considered essential. I do not agree. Would the right of the foetus (if he had one), clearly trump the right of the mother? Most people seem to believe so. That is, they believe that the right to life of the foetus would clearly trump the right to the decisional privacy of the mother. I disagree. First, I think that reasons must still support one position or the other. Second, independent from the question as to whether the foetus is a right-holder or not, there is the question of what the FLR to life actually means. I insist that it merely amounts to a prohibition of intentionally killing someone. That prohibition, however, is not absolute and must be adjudicated in the context of a conflict with other rights.

In France, the FLR to life is often related to dignity. But dignity is not easy to handle either. The French Constitution does not mention a right to life, but of course the ECHR applies in France too. Here, the question is whether France protects in its own way the right to life, either directly or indirectly. In 1994, the parliament voted on two statutes concerning medically assisted procreation; respect for the human body, and permitted uses of the human body. The core issue was the beginning of life. These statutes were reviewed by the Constitutional Council in a decision that became famous for the affirmation of the principle of dignity.[21]

In that decision, dignity is considered a principle of constitutional value. It is explicitly stated to be in conflict with individual liberty, the right to a family, and the right to health. Dignity, as a legal principle, should be put in relation to other rights, and may eventually be outweighed (if only it were possible to know which right was the 'heavier'). Dignity, as applied to the edges of life, is deeply controversial. Pro-life advocates may use dignity as an objective standard which affords high protection to whatever form of life. Pro-choice advocates, on the contrary, may associate it with concepts like death and pretend that each of us would have a 'dignified death', meaning by that a death that does not involve too high a threshold of suffering.

Dignity is used by the Constitutional Council as a proxy for the respect of human life. Thus, for instance, a recent case concerning the extension of the

---

[20] He does gives a 'lay' definition of sanctity of life, but it is hard to understand how that definition can be accurate.   [21] Decision 343–344 DC, *Bioéthique*.

available period of abortion from 10 to 12 weeks states that the legislature did not upset the balance between safeguarding human dignity against any form of deterioration and the freedom of women under Article 2 of the Declaration of Human and Civic Rights.[22] Here, the conflict is not presented as pro-life v pro-choice, but as one between dignity and freedom. However, the two are clearly comparable and the difference in presentation merely refers to a different level of specification of the rights at stake.

We can safely conclude that human dignity stands, in fact, for the respect for human life. And, that respect for human life, in FLRs terms, amounts to a prohibition of intentionally killing. Thus, the strongest case for the FLR to life is one that insists against the intentionality of any killing. That is a strong FLR. However, it sometimes conflicts with the FLR to decisional privacy.

B. The FLR to Decisional Privacy

The decision to ask for assistance in suicide must be informed, personal, and persistent. The physician must inform the patient of all alternative routes. The patient must take the decision on his own, placing aside the pressure coming from others or society. Finally, the patient must reiterate his willingness in order to avoid a decision taken during a particularly hard moment. If those conditions are met—others can be added—then how could we intentionally disregard the private decision of a terminally ill person?

The Archbishop of Wales, on behalf of the Catholic Bishops' conference of England and Wales, submitted a lengthy document both to the ECtHR and the House of Lords arguing against the legalisation of PAS. He held that: 'the ending of life is not a private matter, but it is a legitimate concern of public authorities whose duty is to protect the lives of citizens within their jurisdiction'.[23] The Archbishop also added that:

> Article 8 does not encompass a right to self-determination *as such*. Rather, Article 8 relates to the right to private and family life in respect of the manner in which a person conducts his life. Where rights under article 8 are engaged, it is to protect the physical, moral and/or psychological integrity of the individual . . . Such rights may—indeed, sometimes do—include right over the individual's own body. However, the alleged right claimed by Mrs Pretty would ineluctably and necessarily extinguish the very benefit on which it was purportedly based, namely respect for her private life.[24]

I disagree. I really wonder what a private matter actually is, if it is not the ending of one's life. Regardless of public authorities' efforts to protect lives, in the end, we all die. And that moment, I want to suggest, is a private issue. Moreover, in the case of

---

[22] Decision 2001–446 DC, 27 June 2001, para 5. You can find the decision in English on the website of the Constitutional Council: <http://www.conseil-constitutionnel.fr/langues/anglais/a2001446dc.pdf>. [23] Cited by John Keown (n 15 above), 729.
[24] Ibid, 729.

a terminally ill patient, the decision is not between life and death. It is between death and pain, or death without pain. Thus, the decision of Mrs Pretty does not amount to extinguishing life. On the contrary, it is aimed to extinguish death. But what the Archbishop is trying to achieve is the limitation of Article 8 which grounds the FLR to decisional privacy. He says: no self-determination, but only a mild possibility to choose one's lifestyle within a framework of objective values that protect life. This is a very partial understanding of individual liberty. The FLR to decisional privacy, as it has emerged in the last thirty years, goes far beyond the narrow boundaries set out by conventional religious doctrine. Now, I will briefly illustrate the situations in the UK, in the USA, and in France.

We have already observed the trajectory of the right that 'dare not speak its name'[25]: the right to privacy in the US.[26] Since *Griswold*, American citizens can freely determine for themselves, whether or not to use contraception[27]; to abort[28]; to engage in sexual activity with the partner of one's choice.[29] That is obviously possible against the opposition of religious (and other) associations. However, the US Supreme Court has denied, for the moment, the existence of a right to assisted suicide.[30]

In *Glucksberg*, Justice Stevens draws a distinction between physical and decisional privacy. He says that it is permissible to refuse life-sustaining treatment on the grounds of physical privacy, which is the limitation of bodily intrusion against one's consent. However, it is not permissible to give a blank check to every individual asking for assisted suicide, on the grounds of decisional privacy. But, he is ready to acknowledge that preservation of life 'does not have the same force for a terminally ill patient faced not with the choice of whether to live, only of how to die'.[31] Hence, it seems safe to say that decisional privacy does not cover all possible choices in between life or death, but it covers at least mortal choices of the type: which kind of death?

Decisional privacy in the PAS context has a special meaning, because it involves a tragic relationship *a trois:* the physician, the patient, and the family. The US Supreme Court insists that decisional privacy must be conciliated with the interests of the other parties in the relationship. I wonder. I can see that the situation is tragic. If your only choice is death with pain or death *tout court*, then there is a case for tragedy. But, I wonder whether in such issues, the scope of decisional privacy can really be determined by the fact that such a decision can affect other people around us. Even if others have a strong interest in our survival, their interest is very small when our survival is very painful.

In Europe, as pointed out, the ECHR gives at least a textual reference of the FLR to decisional privacy. Hitherto, however, Article 8 has been interpreted, in a loose way, as a right to individual autonomy. To frame it that way has the risk of

---

[25] Laurence Tribe, 'Lawrence v. Texas: The "Fundamental Right" that Dare Not Speak its Name', 117 Harv L Rev 1893 (2004).   [26] See ch 5.
[27] *Griswold*, cf above.   [28] *Roe v Wade*, cf above.   [29] *Lawrence v Texas*, cf above.
[30] *Washington v Glucksberg*, cf above.   [31] Ibid, 746.

blurring the already too fragile boundary between private and public life. I prefer the decisional privacy formulation. Notwithstanding the semantic difficulty, there is a substantive recognition of the importance of Article 8 in issues of PAS. In the Pretty case, the European Court of Human Rights (ECtHR) has acknowledged that, in domestic law, a person may exercise 'a choice to die' by refusing life-prolonging treatment.[32]

The House of Lords sharply opposes that view. Lord Bingham, who wrote the leading opinion, asserted that if Mrs Pretty had a right to decide when to die, then the court could not logically exclude a right to voluntary euthanasia. John Keown argues that the court could have gone even further by asking why people who are neither dying nor disabled would not be entitled to a right to decide when to die.[33] I think that that is a double mistake. First, it is a mistake on the level of specification of the FLR to decisional privacy. A new right, which is the upshot of a broader right, is defined and treated in absolute terms. Here, in order to dismiss completely the possibility of PAS we target a ridiculous misinterpretation of the right, which supports certain cases of PAS. The point is that decisional privacy does not support a general right to decide when to die. But, it only supports a limited instantiation because of the nature of the choice at stake (death with pain or death without pain). Second, it is a failure to see the existence of a conflict. Even if we were to recognize a fairly general right to decide when to die, then that would not entail that that right prevails every time over the prohibition of intentional killing, as protected by the FLR to life.

France, of late, has given an example of the existence of confusion as to these issues. So much so, that even the right to refuse treatment seems in jeopardy.[34] In a recent case, *Senanayake*,[35] the State Council strikes a contestable balance between the will of the patient, and his right to life, despite major legislative evidence on the strengthening of decisional privacy.[36] The case is a simple one, and it concerns a Jehovah's Witness' refusal of a blood transfusion.

The gist of the problem lies in the conceptions of dignity, which are used inconsistently. On one hand, dignity is considered as an eminently liberal concept, which supports individual liberty. On the other, dignity is interpreted as a communitarian principle, which enforces conventional views of the society, and is more frequently dubbed as human dignity (as opposed to the dignity of the individual); as such, it is considered as a universal principle, which transcends individual will and protects life (at least a particular conception of life).

What is of interest for our purposes is to notice the considerable regression in bio-medical-ethical principles, which can be enforced on the basis of human

---

[32] *Pretty v UK* (n 14 above). [33] John Keown (n 15 above), 728.
[34] Jocelyn Clerckx, 'Une liberté en péril? Le droit au refus de soins', RDP 139 (2004).
[35] CE Ass, Senanayake, 26 October 2001, *RFDA*, 2002 n 1, p 150.
[36] Charter of the hospitalized patient (6 May 1995). Code of medical deontology (6 September 1995). At the European level, there is a European Convention on Human Rights and Bio-Medicine. Again in France, Art L 1111-4 Code of Public Health. Incorporated by the Statute n 2002–303, 4 March 2002 concerning the rights of patients and the quality of the health system.

dignity. Today it is widely accepted that a patient can decide, at any moment, to suspend a life-sustaining treatment. By analogy, the patient should be able to refuse intrusion into his body. This is the position of legislative and international instruments, which underlie a growing importance of consent and, as a consequence, of decisional privacy. Hence, the State Council's decision and the principle of human dignity, on which the decision is based, are open to criticism. These may lead us to reinforce the idea of the FLR to decisional privacy as a form of respect for a decision that is not of public concern.

4. Moral and Legal Conflicts

Moral philosophers can be friends of the court (*amici curiae*). But they should be aware of the limits of their reasoning, for the purposes of adjudicating hard legal cases. Here I am concerned with the arguments filed by six moral philosophers in a brief to the US Supreme Court, in order to plead in favour of the legalisation of PAS. The argument of the brief is illuminating insofar as it dispels some mistaken distinctions embedded in common language. However, it does not point to a practicable route to follow, because it overlooks some important legal constraints.

The brief [37]: six moral philosophers (hereafter MP6), joined their efforts to support the case for legalisation of PAS in American Constitutional Law. Their starting point is *Cruzan*, a precedent case of the US Supreme Court, where an individual was granted a right to refuse life-sustaining treatment. They conclude that letting someone die can be equated to killing, holding that both should be permissible when the patient consents.

The brief's argument is mainly negative: it criticizes a common sense distinction drawn by the court. The distinction is that between act and omission. The court says that while an omission is not problematic, an act is morally problematic. MP6 disagree, because they think that the real distinction is between act/omission which cause death, and act/omission which do not cause death. The argument for PAS follows as a logical consequence from *Cruzan*: if it is acceptable to respect the will of a patient by letting him die, it is also acceptable to respect the will of a patient by assisting his suicide.

If the distinction between act and omission is not relevant, the distinction between killing and letting someone die is.[38] The former distinction is not relevant because it is already widely accepted that a medical act not intending, but foreseeing death is permissible. For example, a physician is permitted to prescribe morphine intending to lessen the pain and simply foreseeing a hastened death.

---

[37] Available at <http://www.nybooks.com/articles/1237>: John Rawls, Judith Jarvis Thomson, Robert Nozick, Ronald Dworkin, T M Scanlon, and Thomas Nagel, Assisted Suicide: The Philosophers' Brief.

[38] Frances M Kamm, 'A right to choose death?', <http://bostonreview.mit.edu/BR22.3/Kamm.html>.

The latter is not compelling. Imagine a patient who does not want to die, but needs a heart transplant in order to survive. A physician may let him die if the only heart available is needed by another patient that requested it before. Imagine now another patient not willing to die. His heart would be needed by other patients, but its transplant would cause the death of the patient. The physician is not permitted to kill the patient. The difference between these two cases is precisely supported by the distinction between killing and letting die.

The distinction is also valid in cases where a patient is willing to die in order to determine the scope of permissible refusal of treatment, as opposed to the scope of permissible assistance in suicide. MP6 think that the scope of the permissions should be the same. I disagree. On one hand, a person may refuse treatment, even if this is against his best interest. The wrong of bodily intrusion cannot be outweighed by our interest in the patient's well-being. Conversely, a person may not ask for assistance in suicide, if it is not in his best interest to be killed. The explanation of that difference can be found in the analysis of alternatives. In the former case, the choice is between letting him die and imposing a treatment. In the latter case, the choice is between assisting suicide and leaving the person alone. On one hand, the wrong of forcing treatment justifies the alternative, letting him die. On the other, the alternative to assisting a suicide is not as repugnant as forcing a treatment, and as such it can be more easily accepted.

The previous discussion should not be misinterpreted to say that letting an individual die is always permissible, and that killing is always impermissible. My point, for the moment, is that the scope of permissibility is different. Hence, the argument offered by the brief is not necessarily compelling philosophically. Moreover, the brief does not take seriously enough the practical legal argument: the slippery slope argument.

The slippery slope (SS): the best version of the SS argument is offered by John Keown.[39] Keown introduces a very helpful distinction between empirical and logical SS. The empirical SS argument runs as follows: even if a line could be drawn in between VAE and NVAE, this line could not be policed effectively. There are two problems. First, how could we know whether the patient's will is really free? The doctor may lack psychological skills in understanding this. Furthermore, even if he has these skills, he may lack in time or resources to enquire properly as to the patient's state of mind.

Second, how can we make sure that the doctor accurately evaluates the terminal state of the illness? A doctor may misdiagnose the patient. He may think that an illness is terminal when it isn't. Furthermore, a doctor may also lack knowledge as to the prognosis: the illness is terminal, but there are some innovative cures available.

Even more impressive for Keown is the logical SS: the argument in favour of VAE is equally in favour of NVAE. I will try to briefly unpack this argument. The central point in favour of VAE is the argument for autonomy: a patient duly

[39] John Keown (n 15 above), 70.

expresses his will and a physician ought to comply with it. However, in the case of an incompetent patient, his choice will have to be reconstructed; and that allows, what Keown calls, a 'substituted judgement'. Also, it seems hard to distinguish between patients that have illnesses that are supposed to cause unbearable sufferings, and patients whose illness is debilitating, but the pain bearable.

Keown insists that what really counts is the judgment of the doctor, that the request is justified as death would benefit the patient. Hence, the practice of VAE will eventually uphold the conviction of a physician, as opposed to the autonomy of the patient. I think that Keown's argument is very clear, and the distinction he draws between empirical and logical SS is illuminating. However, I believe that it is not entirely compelling. In order to understand this we can use Keown's very distinction, albeit from a different point of view: the type of judgement required by the doctor. The judgement of the doctor may concern the genuine nature of the will of the patient, or it may concern the benefit that death carries with it.

What really worries Keown is the second judgement. Keown does not want physicians to become the oracles on the value of life. This is a fair concern, but it can be dispelled by insisting on the role of the will of the patient which must take priority. For instance, there may be a case where a physician thinks that the patient's life is not worth living. However, if the patient, or whoever represents the patient, holds that the patient's will is opposed to VAE, then the physician must simply respect that will. To be sure, the physician will always express his judgement, thereby influencing the opinions of other people. To that, I respond that we ought to have a measure of trust in a person who has been trained and has a long-standing experience.

The second problem with Keown's argument is that he drops the distinction between VAE and PAS. The SS works better when applied to VAE. For VAE requires an ultimate act of the physician, whereas PAS requires the patient to perform the last act. No doubt the boundary may be blurred at times, but the distinction is more illuminating than distorting, and it should be kept. Nowhere does Keown explicitly hold that the distinction is not helpful at all. Therefore, keeping in mind that distinction, it is possible to hold that PAS is the strongest case for the argument from decisional privacy. Keown's argument seems to work fine when it concerns the move from VAE to NVAE. However it is not fully convincing when applied to the slope from PAS to VAE.

Even if I disagree on the general applicability of the SS argument, it remains an important argument which has hitherto convinced both North American and European courts. Keown's enquiry is interesting because he frames his question in the following way: 'Even if VAE were morally acceptable to relieve a patient from unbearable sufferings at the patient's free and informed request, relaxation of the law to cater for such admittedly difficult cases would, sooner or later, result in its extension by law to patients who are incompetent and who are not suffering unbearably'.[40] Supreme Courts have sided with Keown's position, rather than

---

[40] John Keown (n 15 above).

with MP6's. I think that various reasons explain the reluctance of high courts to authorize PAS, but I would like to insist on the difference between moral and legal reasoning.

A. Reasoning with Law

Judicial reasoning does not have the luxury of being able to draw sophisticated distinctions on a case by case basis. Lack of resources and predictability are good enough reasons. The brief fails to provide us with a sound argument for euthanasia, because it only asks whether there is a moral difference between killing and letting someone die; and it concludes that there is not. This is far from being clear, as we saw. But more importantly, even if killing was sometimes morally permissible, it doesn't follow that it should be legalized, because of the risk of the slippery slope. The underlying problem is the following: can something be morally permissible and legally prohibited? I think so. The reason is that moral permissibility is only one element to be taken into account in the final shaping of public policy.

It is possible to have a situation where an act/omission is morally permissible, and legally impermissible. Moral reasoning can always refine its resolution of cases, by distinguishing subtleties that only expert philosophers can fully grasp. Law must pay its due to clarity and predictability. Judges, for instance, do not have the resources that philosophers have. Mainly, they lack time. Also, they lack expertise. But, to be sure, they are concerned with shaping rules that are going to be applicable in future cases.[41]

As a matter of fact, most of the countries around the world are sticking to their criminal statutes. I think that we generally see the tragedies of *Pretty*, *Glucksberg*, or *Rodriguez*. But there is a tendency to think that the law cannot permit PAS in these cases without going down the slippery slope. PAS advocates claim that the law is inconsistent in many respects. There are five arguments to this effect.

First, the law is held to be ineffective. This is mainly because the prohibitions against VAE and PAS are not respected in practice. Many physicians do help their patients to die already, but this is a very difficult thing to prove with accuracy. It is because surveys are not frequent, and the questions they raise are likely to be misinterpreted. Take, for instance, the important distinctions between active and passive euthanasia, or those between VAE, NVAE, or IVAE. These are definitions on which there is no agreement. Therefore, it is very difficult to come up with an accurate survey without interviewing a very large number of physicians. The problem, moreover, is that it is impossible to expect honesty from personal interviews; physicians know that in disclosing certain information they run unnecessary risks.

Second, some argue that it is difficult to grasp why palliative care is allowed, but not euthanasia. The explanation, however, is not too problematic. Palliative care is

---

[41] For an extremely clear example of this concern on the part of the judges, see *Evans v UK* (Application No 6339/05), 7 March 2006.

administered with no intention to kill, whereas euthanasia is, by its very definition. Moreover, palliative care is a duty of the physician: he must seek to relieve one's pain. I do not think that euthanasia has ever been conceived as a duty in itself. Finally, strong palliative care, say the administration of morphine, may lead to a person's death. But, when death is merely foreseen and not intended, then palliative care is widely accepted.

Third, it is held that the de-criminalization of suicide should also entail de-criminalization of assisted-suicide. However, the de-criminalization of suicide did not create a right to suicide. It is one thing to say that an act is not punished by law, and it is another to say that law holds another person under a duty to aid one's suicide.

Fourth, the distinction between letting die and killing is contested. Some authors reject it,[42] although others heavily insist on it.[43] Courts generally stick to that distinction as it is a plausible strategy.

Fifth, patients in a persistent vegetative state are compared to terminally ill competent patients. The problem is that the former cannot express their will, while the latter insist precisely on the respect of their will. Therefore, we are confronted with two different types of euthanasia. The former is a case of passive euthanasia, whereas the latter is a form of VAE.

Moral permissibility does not entail legal permissibility. To start with, MP6's thesis is not shared by all moral philosophers[44]; and, more importantly, the two types of reasoning differ in many ways. In the first instance, values bear only a very loose relation to FLRs. In addition, rules must be able to illuminate a series of cases, and not only one. Furthermore, rules are framed in a loaded context: legislation and precedents cannot be overruled too easily. Finally, lack of time and resources make it more difficult to place the discussion in a broader framework.

5. Whose Tragedy Is It?

PAS seems to me to be a good example of a constitutional tragedy insofar as it presents the decision-maker with an extremely hard choice which results in a loss, in either case. Some other constitutional theorists see tragedy also in the rigidity of a constitution requiring an evil choice (in the case of PAS, its refusal for terminally ill and consenting patient). Also, they see a tragedy when an incorrect interpretation leading to a wrong is preferred to the right interpretation leading to a happy ending.[45]

---

[42] The MP6, for example.   [43] John Keown (n 15 above).
[44] See Frances Kamm (n 38 above).
[45] James E Fleming, 'Constitutional Tragedies in Dying: Or Whose Tragedy is it, Anyway?' in William N Eskridge and Sanford Levinson, *Constitutional Stupidities—Constitutional Tragedies* (New York: NYUP, 2001) 163.

I believe that it is not possible to reconcile the idea of constitutional tragedies with that of happy endings. Rigidity has certain advantages. For instance, it is good to have a rigid prohibition against torture. But of course, rigidity has its own price; sometimes a prohibition may offend certain categories of people (eg terminally-ill, consenting people). However, there may be a case for electing the lesser of two evils (prohibition against PAS versus generalization of NVAE).

The question is to know how much a constitution protects decisional privacy and how much it protects persons from intentional killing. The conflict of FLRs is 'vertical', at least in the sense that it involves a conflict between the state interpretation of FLRs, and the individual interpretation. Some constitutional scholars claim that the constitution can always be improved (constitution-perfecting theories). Generally, an improvement consists of an elimination of arbitrary intervention by the state. Others think the constitution ought not to be betrayed (originalists). A betrayal is generally perceived as the disrespect of a moral convention. Constitution-perfecting theories attempt to look for happy ending, which they take to be the ending required by the best moral philosophy available. At the other end of the spectrum, we find originalists who insist that the constitution protects only those activities that have a 'legal pedigree' by virtue of their historical record of legal protection.

Neither interpretation fully grasps the conflict of FLRs. James Fleming, a representative of a constitution-perfecting theory, puts forward that the tragedy is exclusively on the part of the individual:

The noble protagonists in this constitutional tragedy are citizens who have the courage to use their own deliberative reason and to take responsibility for their own lives and for their own judgments about how to respect the sanctity of life. The tragic flaw of these protagonists—the characteristic that is both their greatness and their downfall—is their autonomy, their daring to live autonomously rather than as mere creatures of the state or of God.[46]

I think that the former remark misses the point on the role of the state. The state exists to police the respect for life, which is a very laudable aim. As far as respect for life is concerned, autonomy is to be limited; so that no one can kill on the grounds of this. We can only conceive of the tragedy if we have a strong sense of the respect for life, to the point of seriously questioning an individual's autonomy in asking for assistance in suicide. Originalists would say instead that the tragedy is only on the part of the state. Justice Renhquist together with Justice Scalia would comment that 700 years of prohibition against suicide, and assisted suicide, cannot be wiped away.[47]

It is clear that we ought to be able to see the tragedy from different points of view. We have to be able to distance ourselves from our own moral convictions, and to try to understand the argument from the other perspective. To understand the reasons of all parties is crucial in order to be able to accept tragedy. Tragedy will

---

[46] Ibid, 165.   [47] *Washington v Glucksberg*, 521 US 702 (1997) at 710–11.

not disappear—it is an essential part of life—but at least it should not involve a never-ending struggle between two opposite factions.[48]

6. Present Solutions: How do Courts Solve the Conflict?

It is often held that FLRs further individual benefits. The individual, however, cannot abuse these benefits. First, he cannot impose the burdens of his benefits onto unwilling individuals. Second, he cannot arbitrarily force upon the state his principles with the aim of changing the rules by which the society plays.

The conflict between the FLR to life and the FLR to decisional privacy concerns the second problem aforementioned. On one hand, the individual asks that his decision on how to die is respected by his family and his physician. On the other, the individual asks for the rewriting of the rules which protect the inviolability of life. But these rules are not simply statutory rules; they are themselves entrenched in the constitution by virtue of the FLR to life. In fact, the individual himself benefited from them throughout his life.

Hence, to solve the conflict cannot simply amount to establishing which of the FLRs should apply in that case. The relevant question is, I think, how much room for manoeuvre can be granted to the individual, without upsetting the regulative power of the state? The point is that FLRs do not merely concern the attribution of liberty to individuals. They also concern the distribution of (normative) power between branches of government, and between the state and the individuals.[49]

A. Deference

Constitutional texts are not clear as to who should decide mortal issues. It is not even clear whether judicial institutions are supposed to enter into the domain. However, as was said at the beginning, courts are questioned on these issues. Once we take the step of asking a court, it is already too late, as the rejection of a case amounts to giving a negative answer to the plaintiff.

Viewed from that perspective, the question of deference is most awkward. The task courts are best prepared to perform is to interpret legal texts and precedents, and to then adjudicate the case by applying the legal materials they have analysed. In PAS cases, however, parliament has always avoided taking a stance[50]; thus, in most of the cases, judicial institutions are left with no specific guidance. Courts can only interpret pre-existing criminal laws on the prohibition of intentional killing. These statutes happen to be very strict. To invalidate part of those statutes,

---

[48] For a similar perspective, see Laurence H Tribe, *Abortion—The Clashes of Absolutes* (New York: WW Norton, 1992) 7.   [49] See ch 3.
[50] If we except the Dutch Parliament, the State of Oregon, the Parliament of the Northern territory in Australia, and the Belgian Parliament.

in order to include permission for PAS is risky for two reasons. First, criminal statutes may lose clarity in the process. Second, courts may not be in the best position to carve out a well-defined exception to the prohibition of intentional killing.

There are different types of deference. The first type of deference is about initiative. Who has the power to initiate a discussion on controversial moral issues that have never been dealt with before in a comprehensive way? The second type is about technical knowledge. Is there a group of people whose specific skills may improve the decision process? The third type of deference is about authority. Who has the final word about a certain issue/case? The fourth is about liberty. To what extent can an individual decide questions about his life without giving reasons for his acts?

The answer to the problem raised by initiative-deference is clear, although difficult to enforce. Representative institutions ought to take the initiative, and issue guidance as to mortal issues. I am not saying that they should settle every possible case; that is not feasible. However, they should produce an independent piece of legislation that sets out the principles and the assumptions behind the rules we play by. If parliament does not take that responsibility, then I do not believe that judicial institutions are allowed to issue a comprehensive framework, on how to deal with a controversial moral issue. This is what the US Supreme Court did in *Roe v Wade*. Notwithstanding the immediate improvement in women's position within society, the decision polarized the debate in a detrimental way.

Ethically charged issues are often deferred to ethical committees. Generally speaking, the position of ethical committees is taken into account only if it does not say anything innovative. Basically, the committee entrenches the status quo. If the point of view of the ethical committee risks becoming politically unpopular, then it is simply put aside. I do not think that clear guidance on those issues can ever be popular. Therefore, deference to ethical committees is seldom to be recommended.

Judicial institutions nowadays suffer from Hercules' syndrome.[51] They believe they can be right in most of the issues they adjudicate. Most of all, they let individuals believe that they exercise their authority in a way that can only further justice. Thus, parties often decide to defer the decision of their own moral dilemmas to courts. But they are mistaken. Courts cannot resolve, in any comprehensive way, moral controversies which have not as yet been dealt with in that way. In fact, courts can only attempt to draw a line between individuals and the state. What a court can police, is the extent to which PAS's decisions are left to the individual. And, as a consequence, the extent to which parliament can regulate the way we die. To draw a line, however, does not mean to provide a comprehensive framework, according to which the entire society should decide. It simply means that sometimes, under specified conditions, society cannot have its word on the decision of an individual.

What really matters, in the end, is deference to individuals (the fourth type of deference). I think that an individual should be able to decide by which means he

---

[51] Ronald Dworkin, *Law's Empire* (Oxford: Hart's Publishing, 1998 re-edition).

wants to die, without being condemned by society. The problem, however, does not end there. For, if an individual can make up his mind on his own about the way he intends to die it does not follow that he has a right to be assisted whenever he decides so.

B. Balancing

Can we really weigh the FLR to life against the FLR to decisional privacy? It is really hard to make sense of that all-encompassing metaphor, without using platitudes or developing a fully fledged theory of values. I have already expressed my doubts about it in previous chapters. Here, I would like to briefly examine how supreme courts actually justify their rejection of PAS.

The US Supreme Court insists on the century old criminal prohibition of suicide and assisted suicide. This doubts the existence of a liberty interest on the part of the individual to ask for assistance in dying. In the words of Chief Justice Rehnquist:

> by establishing a threshold requirement—that a challenged state action implicate a fundamental right—before requiring more than a reasonable relation to a legitimate state interest to justify the action, it avoids the need for complex balancing of competing interests in every case.[52]

In other words, there is a clear and constant legislation against suicide, on one hand; while, on the other, there is an unclear and hard to define liberty interest, on the part of the individual. Justice Rehnquist's conclusion is that criminal legislation should not be revised for the sake of accommodating uncertainty as to how much freedom the individual has.

The previous reasoning shows an incredible unwillingness to think about hard questions anew. To treat a medical question as if it were an instantiation of criminal law is simply mindless. It would be like trying to resolve the question of intellectual property abuse on the Internet by means of the age old law of property. It does not work; it is simply unsuited for this purpose. The same applies to the effort of defining FLRs simply by appeal to the idea of 'historically protected activities ("so rooted in the traditions and conscience of our people as to be ranked as fundamental")'.[53] FLRs ought to favour a pluralistic understanding of life and cannot therefore be reduced to historically protected activities.[54]

FLRs are similar to dormant clauses. They may have never been used to protect a given activity, but when they are activated they then afford a strong level of protection. That is the case in decisional privacy. The US Supreme Court itself recognized this in *Lawrence v Texas*. In *Lawrence*, the liberty interest of the

---

[52] *Washington v Glucksberg*, 521 US 702 at 722.   [53] Ibid, 721.
[54] I think that the historical understanding of FLRs is a dead-end. It would work if our societies were homogenous and value-monist. It does not precisely because European and American societies are not anymore (or never have been) homogenous and value-monist.

individual consisted of a free choice in one's sexual partner, and it made the Texas statute against sodomy invalid.

In PAS cases decisional privacy is certainly crucial, but it has to confront the FLR to life. Generally, the liberty of the individual to decide whether or not to die is valued in common law countries by the decriminalization of suicide. That does not mean that there is a right to suicide. It simply means that if an individual wishes to do so, he cannot be prosecuted and he does not have to explain his act, because that is a matter of his private judgment. What is protected is therefore his decision, but no support is given to the enforcement of his intent.

I do not think that support should be given as a matter of principle. If one's decision is clear enough as to their will to die, then it is of individual responsibility to find the means to carry out that decision. But there are extreme cases. Some people may not be able to move because their illness has paralysed them: they may be unable to walk or use their arms. Sometimes they can barely speak. Yet they can understand perfectly well and they can express themselves. They do understand, in particular, that they are going to die soon. This was the case with Mrs Pretty, for instance. It is true that there are different types of terminally ill patients, some can linger for a long time with the help of medicine, others will endure a more painful death. I think that these are important distinctions, and the court failed to raise them.

Of course a risk of SS is always present. But I am talking about cases where the individuals can freely make up their mind, and yet they cannot carry out any of their projects. These people should be helped. The possibility of such a case is left open by Justice Stevens: 'Although as a general matter the State's interest in the contributions each person may make to society outweighs the person's interest in ending her life, this interest does not have the same force for a terminally ill patient faced not with the choice of whether to live, only of how to die.'[55]

And then concludes: 'Although, as the Court concludes today, these potential harms are sufficient to support the State's general public policy against assisted suicide, they will not always outweigh the individual liberty interest of a particular patient'.[56]

In Europe, the most important decision that has so far been delivered by the ECtHR is *Pretty*. We have already examined that decision, but here we can concentrate on the reasoning that led the Court to reject the request for criminal exemption for Mrs Pretty's husband. At the outset, let me say that the case was a weak one. Mrs Pretty was not asking for a PAS strictly speaking, but a suicide assisted by her husband. I think that there is a distinction to draw there, and not a minor one. PAS, in my mind, could be sometimes justified because the physician is required to take on the responsibility of the state to protect life. To exempt a family member from the requirement of criminal prosecution is a wholly different matter that can reasonably be abused in certain cases.

---

[55] *Washington v Glucksberg*, 521 US 702 at 746.   [56] Ibid, 749.

That said, I think that if Mrs Pretty had asked for a PAS, the court ought to have accepted it. The conditions of her case made it such that it could be distinguished from many more controversial ones. But what matters here is the reasoning of the court. The ECtHR accepted that the FLR to privacy had been breached, but it justified the breach by balancing the interference with the legitimate purpose of the state.

An interference with the exercise of an Article 8 right will not be compatible with Article 8 § 2 unless it is "in accordance with the law", has an aim or aims that is or are legitimate under that paragraph and is "necessary in a democratic society" for the aforesaid aim or aims.[57]

Generally, the ban on assisted suicide is justified on protective grounds, as the House of Lords Select Committee points out:

We are also concerned that vulnerable people—the elderly, lonely, sick or distressed—would feel pressure, whether real or imagined, to request early death. We accept that, for the most part, requests resulting from such pressure or from remediable depressive illness would be identified as such by doctors and managed appropriately. Nevertheless we believe that the message which society sends to vulnerable and disadvantaged people should not, however obliquely, encourage them to seek death, but should assure them of our care and support in life.[58]

The ECtHR briefly acknowledges that the UK government is incapable of justifying the refusal against Mrs Pretty on grounds of her vulnerability. But, eventually, the Court held that on balance the state is entitled 'to regulate through the operation of the general criminal law activities which are detrimental to the life and safety of other individuals'.[59] This last remark is highly deceptive. There is no explanation of why the state is permitted to interfere with Mrs Pretty's well-informed decision to terminate her life. The impression is that the Court was prepared to accept the argument of the plaintiff, but did not dare to breach the margin of appreciation left to national states. The conflict has not yet been seriously dealt with.

7. Accepting or Imposing Sacrifices

The prohibition of intentional killing must face the case of the prohibition of intentionally inflicting pain. I hope that by now the existence of a conflict is plain. Also, I think that the tragedy underpinning the conflict of FLRs should be clear too. For, whichever decision the patient takes, a sacrifice is faced. The test for deciding such a conflict, provided that we accept a judicial solution, is to understand which one of the two evils is the lesser. Even if I think that the FLR to life takes priority, that priority is not absolute. It is qualified. That means that we

---

[57] See *Dudgeon v UK* (1982) 4 EHRR 149.
[58] *Pretty v UK* (n 14 above) § 72.   [59] Ibid, §74.

ought to be able to see the strength of certain narrow exceptions without fearing the slippery slope argument. After all, why would our fear of a slippery slope always outweigh the informed consent of a terminally ill patient whose only request is to abandon his dead body?

I argued that generally speaking, the prohibition of intentional killing is a central principle in our legal systems. It normally imposes few costs. Possibly, it constitutes a pre-condition to everyone's enjoyment of life. However, permitting PAS amounts to the permission of a form of intentional killing when the individual consents to it. The cost of that permission may be very high in cases where the will of the person is not free. It is equally the case if the consent is vitiated by misinformation (eg a misdiagnosis). Therefore, the permission ought not to be generalized. However, to impose a blanket prohibition may amount to imposing unreasonable sacrifices to certain categories of terminally ill patients. For instance, patients with motor neurone disease like Mrs Pretty.

In that case, we are imposing a sacrifice on the person for the sake of preserving a fig leaf around mortal issues. Terminally ill patients, with no capacity to move, are instead asking us to accept their sacrifice, on the grounds of the respect for their decisional privacy. The problem is that whatever they decide (privately), it may well be impossible for them to carry out the acts consistently with their innermost beliefs.

When a conflict of FLRs arises and has such a disruptive effect, we ought to pause and think what the lesser evil is. Is it the imposition of a painful death to a certain category of terminally ill patients or the acceptance that our society cannot fully control and police the edges of life? I think that the qualified priority of the FLR to life can accommodate the narrowly tailored exception of mentally capable, but physically incapable, terminally ill patients. Ultimately, I think the problem lies with society. It does not want to accept the existence of conflicts of FLRs. It does not want to accept the existence of tragedies. It does not want to accept the existence of sacrifices. It only wants to impose them. That is not consistent with a strong conception of FLRs.

8
Conclusion[1]

Justice is conflict[2]

Two main points have been articulated in this book. First, genuine conflicts of FLRs are unavoidable. In other words, they cannot be eliminated or defined away. Whichever way we decide, we are opting for a sacrifice on the part of a right-holder or the society. There are two broad types of conflict. On one hand, we have horizontal conflicts of FLRs; these are the cases in which two right-holders claim they should win on the ground of a FLR that protects their act. This has been illustrated through the example of the FLR to informational privacy v the FLR to free press. On the other, we have vertical conflicts where the state claims that a FLR bars a certain permission, which the right-holder claims is granted by another FLR. This was illustrated with the example of the FLR to life v the FLR to decisional privacy in cases of physician-assisted suicide.

Second, conflicts of FLRs cannot be settled once and for all. But then, how do we deal with these conflicts? My position partly depends on the conflict we are facing. Moreover, it is of vital importance that the constitutional framework functions smoothly. Horizontal conflicts, I have suggested, can be better dealt with by establishing a system of rebuttable presumptions. The contest between free speech and privacy is routinely decided *a priori*. Many judges hold strong preferences for free speech and regard privacy as a mere obstacle. My suggestion is to 'come clean' over the assumption concerning the contextualized ranking of the two rights. It is possible, I think, to establish a rebuttable presumption in favour of free speech, for example. Some may argue that this position favours free speech unduly; the truth, however, is that free speech is often favoured implicitly. As a result, we accept extensive breaches of privacy. Privacy is declared as important, but never important enough to win the actual competition with free speech.

Vertical conflicts of FLRs should be dealt with differently. Where possible the state should extend the autonomy of individuals instead of limiting it. But, of course, even this cannot be limitless. One of the tests that I try to advance is based on the distinction between imposing and accepting sacrifices. The state should

---

[1] Here, I limit myself to very cursory remarks. The main arguments have been articulated in the book and I think they should not be replicated in this short conclusion.

[2] Heraclitus, Fragment 80.

strive to find a compromise that brings together the different parties to the conflict in order to allow communication and mutual understanding as to the sacrifices implied by the choice. The bottom line is that we have to respect individual choices regarding personal tragedies. When our only choice left, as in the PAS of a terminally ill paraplegic patient, is to die with pain or without pain, then the individual should be allowed to elect his own preferred option.

In this book, I have distinguished four different stages at which constitutional decisions, relevant for conflicts of FLRs, are taken. It is important to distinguish these stages because they each involve a different type of decision. First, we are faced with the problem of identification and selection of sources that play a role in the conflict in question. Second, we encounter the problem of interpretation of those materials, which are very often crafted in very broad terms, and are, subsequently, very difficult to interpret. Third, substantive decisions are postponed, or bypassed, through the device of deference. However, a negative decision as to one's competence does not avoid the substantive issue; on the contrary, it solves it by denying the claim at stake. Fourth, it is sometimes held that balancing is the ultimate procedure for the 'correct' resolution of conflicts of FLRs. This cannot be the case as balancing, as we saw, is not likely to provide a solution for each case of conflict. As a result, balancing must be taken for what it is, ie a helpful tool for the resolution of a well-defined number of cases, which do not include genuine conflicts of FLRs.[3]

FLRs concern the fair distribution of competences and powers. They regulate their distribution between different branches of government, between the state and the individuals, and between the individuals themselves. A proper theory of FLRs should strive to spell out the guidelines according to which decisions are taken or deferred. Courts themselves have little interest in embarking upon difficult decisions necessary in extremely hard cases. FLRs have no doubt made the fortune of courts in terms of heightened legitimacy. However, hasty decisions on issues of conflicts of FLRs may have the opposite effect. Moreover, certain hard cases call for the scrutiny of a representative body. It still remains a difficult task to provide a framework for the decisions of such questions, but representative bodies must accept their responsibilities.

Bills of rights need to be reviewed and modified if we want a more satisfactory system of FLRs. A better system can best be achieved by spelling out more clearly how decisions on the grounds of FLRs really function. Moreover, conflicts should be explicitly referred to, and guidelines as to their treatment should be included. Such conflicts cannot be prevented; however, procedural and substantive rules can be made more transparent. First, procedural rules should be more explicit on the question of conflicts. This means that procedural rules should invite parties and the adjudicator to construe the best case on each side and to begin from that

---

[3] Of course, spurious conflicts and *lato sensu* conflicts of FLRs are routinely dealt with by balancing various requirements.

perspective. In other words, procedural rules should insist on the importance of accepting the strength of the opposite position. Also, procedural rules should formalize the repartition of competences and powers.

Second, although substantive rules cannot achieve too much, there is still something to be said about them. When FLRs are duly defined and circumscribed, then a rebuttable presumption can be established between the instantiations of the conflicting FLRs at stake. A rebuttable presumption will depend on the legal culture, and the social practices, of the context in which the conflict occurs. Its entrenchment in a norm will call for the definition of the conditions under which the presumption can be reversed. I think it is possible to establish a qualified, and contextualized, priority. It is qualified in the sense that one FLR takes priority but allows of a number of well-defined exceptions. It is contextualized in the sense that the qualified priority only applies in a discrete area where the two FLRs conflict.

An ideal society would not allow for the proliferation of conflicts. In other words, the overall objective of the constitution of any society, as much as the constitution of the human body, is to find harmony between all of its constitutive parts. In an ideal situation, we could perhaps eventually all agree on what we take to be a harmonious society. However, in a liberal, pluralistic society, the challenge of any given conception of harmony is regarded as a necessary feature of any evolving community. And that is probably the very core of liberty, and its paradox.

Bibliography

Adler, MD, 'Rights against Rules: The Moral Structure of American Constitutional Law', 97 *Mich L Rev* 1 (1998)
—— 'Rights, Rules and the structure of Constitutional Adjudication: A Response to Professor Fallon', 113 Harv L Rev 1321 (2000)
—— 'Personal Rights and Rule-Dependence: Can the two Coexist?', Legal Theory 6 (2000) 337–89
—— and Dorf, MC, 'Rights and Rules: An Overview', Legal Theory 6 (2000) 241–51
Aleinikoff, A, 'Constitutional Law in the age of balancing', 96 Yale LJ 943 (1986)
Alexander, L, 'Constitutional Tragedies and Giving Refuge to the Devil' in WN Eskridge, Jr, S Levinson (eds), *Constitutional tragedies, Constitutional Stupidities* (New York: NYUP, 1998)
—— 'Rules, Rigths, Options, and Time', Legal Theory 6 (2000) 391–404
—— (ed), *Constitutionalism; Philosophical Foundations* (Cambridge; CUP, 1998) (2001 paperback)
Alexy, R, *A Theory of Constitutional Rights* (Oxford: OUP, 2002)
—— 'Basic Rights and democracy in Jurgen Habermas' Procedural Paradigm of the law', *Ratio Juris* 7 (1994) 227–38
—— 'Constitutional Rights, Balancing, and Rationality', Ratio Juris 16 (2003) 131–40
—— 'On Balancing and Subsumption. A structural Comparison', Ratio Juris 16 (2003)
—— 'Discourse Theory and Human Rights', *Ratio Juris* 9 (1996) 209–35
—— 'Rights, Legal Reasoning, and Rational Discourse', Ratio Juris 5 (1992), 143–51
—— *Theorie der Grundrechte* (Baden-Baden: Nomos Verlagsgesellschaft, 1985)
Alderman, E, and C Kennedy, *The Right to Privacy* (New York: Vintage Books, 1997)
Allan, T, 'Human Rights and Judicial Review: A Critique of "Due Deference" ' CLJ 65(3) (2006) 671–95
Ancel, J-P, *Protection de la personne: image et vie privée*, Gaz. Pal. 2 Sept 1994, 13
Atienza, M, and JR Manero, 'Permissions, Principles and Rigths. A Paper on Statements Expressing Constitutional Liberties', Ratio Juris 9 (1996) 236–47
Bamforth, N, 'Parliamentary Sovereignty and H.R.A 1998,' in [1998] Public Law 572
Barante, *La vie politique de monsieur Royer-Collard, ses discources et ses écrits* (Paris: Didier, 1863)
Barber, N, 'A right to privacy?' [2003] Public Law 602–10
Beatty, D, *The Ultimate Rule of Law—A Study of Balancing* (Oxford: OUP, 2004)
Berlin, I, *Four Essays on Liberty* (Oxford: OUP, 1969)
—— *Liberty* (Oxford: OUP, 2002)
Bertrand, A, *Droit à la vie privée et droit à l'image* (Paris: Litec, 1999)
Besson, S, *The Morality of Conflict—Reasonable Disagreement and the Law* (Oxford: Hart, 2005)
Bobbio, N, *L'età dei diritti* (Torino: Einaudi, 1990)
Bork, R, *The Last Tempting of America—The Political Seduction of the Law* (New York, Free Press, 1990)

Brudner, A, *Constitutional Goods* (Oxford: OUP, 2004)
Campbell, T, *Rights: A Critical Introduction* (Oxford: Routledge, 2006)
Celano, B, 'Defeasibility e Bilanciamento. Sulla Possibilità di revisioni stabili', Ragion Pratica 10 (2002) 223–39
—— 'I diritti nella jurisprudence anglassone contemporanea. Da Hart a Raz' in Paolo Camanducci e Riccardo Guastini, *Analisi e diritto* (2001)
—— 'Norm Conflicts: Kelsen's view and a rejoinder' in Stanely and Bonnie Paulson, *Normativity and Norms* (Oxford: Clarendon Press, 1998)
Champeil-Desplats, V, 'La notion de droit "fondamental" et le droit constitutionnel français' (Paris: Dalloz, 1996) chron., 328–36
—— 'Raisonnement juridique et pluralité des valeurs: Les conflits axio-téléologiques de normes', *Analisi e Diritto 2001, Giappichelli Editore, Torino,* 58–60
—— *Les Principes Fondamentaux reconnus par les lois de la République* (Aix-Marseilles: PUAM, 1998)
Choudry, S, and H Fenwick, 'Taking the Rights of Parents and Children Seriously: Confronting the Welfare Principle under the Human Rights Act' (2005) 25 OJLS 453
Clayton, R, and H Tomlinson, *Privacy and Freedom of Expression* (Oxford: OUP, 2001)
Clerckx, J, 'Une liberté en péril? Le droit au refus de soins', RDP 139 (2004)
Cole, D, 'Uncle Sam is Watching You', *New York Review of Books*, Vol 51, No 18, 18 November 2004
Coleman, J, and S Shapiro, *The Oxford Handbook of Jurisprudence and Philosophy of Law* (Oxford: OUP, 2002)
Craig, P, 'The Courts, The Human Rights Act and Judicial Review', LQR (2001) 117, 589–603
Dershowitz, A, *Rights from Wrongs—A Secular Theory of the Origins of Rights* (New York: Basic Books, 2004)
Dicey, AV, *The Law of the Constitution* (Boston: Adamant Media Corp, 2000)
Domurat, D, *One of us: Conjoined twins and the Future of Normal* (Cambridge, Mass: HUP, 2004)
Dorf, M, and L Tribe, *On Reading the Constitution* (Cambridge, Mass: HUP, 1991)
Dorf, MC, 'The Heterogeneity of Rights', *Legal Theory* 6 (2000) 269–97
Drago, G, 'La conciliation entre principes constitutionnels', *Recueil Dalloz-Sirey*, 1991, chron. 265–69
Dworkin, R, *A Bill of Rights for Britain* (London: Chatto & Windus, 1990)
—— *Freedom's Law: The Moral Reading of the American Constitution* (Oxford: OUP, 1996) (1999 reprint)
—— *Law's Empire* (Oxford: Hart's Publishing, 1998) re-edition
—— *Life's Dominion* (NY: Haper Collins, 1993)
—— 'No Right Answers?' in PMS Hacker and J Raz (eds), *Law, Morality, and Society* (Oxford: OUP, 1978)
—— 'Objectivity and Truth: You'd Better Believe It', Philosophy and Public Affairs 25 (1996) 87
—— 'Rawls and the Law' in *Justice in Robes* (Cambridge, Mass: HUP, 2006)
—— 'Rights as Trumps' in J Waldron, *Theories of Rights* (Oxford: OUP, 1984)
—— *Sovereign Virtue* (Cambridge, Mass: HUP, 2001)
—— *Taking Rights Seriously* (London: Duckworth, 1977) (1991 reprint)
—— 'Terror & Attack on civil liberties', *New York Review of Books*, 6 November 2003

Edelman, PB, 'Free Press v. Privacy: Haunted by the ghost of Justice Black', 68 Tex L Rev 1195 (1989–90)
Edmundson, WA, *An Introduction to Rights* (Cambridge: CUP, 2004)
Ely, JH, *Democracy and Distrust: A theory of judicial review* (Cambridge, Mass: HUP, 1980)
Emerson, TI, 'The Right of Privacy and Freedom of the Press', 14 Harv CR-C-L Rev 329 (1979)
Engelhardt, HT Jr, 'Privacy and Limited Democracy: The Moral Centrality of Persons' in E Frankel, D Miller, Jr, and J Paul (eds), *The Right to Privacy* (Cambridge: CUP, 2000)
Enoch, D, 'A Right to violate one's Duty', Law and Philosophy 21 (2002) 355–84
Eskridge, WN Jr, 'United States: *Lawrence v. Texas* and the imperative of comparative constitutionalism', International Journal of Constitutional Law 555 (2004)
Eskridge, WN, and S Levinson (ed), *Constitutional Tragedies and Constitutional Stupidities* (New York: NYU Press, 1998)
Fallon Jr, RH, *Implementing the Constitution* (Cambridge, Mass: HUP, 2001)
—— 'As-Applied and Facial Challenges and Third-Party Standing', 113 Harv L Rev, 1321 (2000)
Feinberg, J, *Rights, Justice, and the Bounds of Liberty* (Princeton, NJ: PUP, 1980)
—— 'Voluntary Euthanasia and the inalienable right to Life', Philosophy and Public Affairs 7 (1978) 102
Feldman, D, *Civil Liberties and Human Rights in England and Wales* (Oxford: OUP, 2002)
—— 'The Human Rights Act 1998 and Constitutional Principles', Legal Studies 19 (1999) 165–206
Fenwick, H, 'Clashing Rights, the Welfare of the Child and Human Rights Act' (2004) 67(6) MLR 889
Finkelstein, CO, 'Introduction to the symposium on Conflicts of Rights', Legal Theory 7 (2001) 235–38
—— 'Two men on a Plank', Legal Theory 7 (2001) 279–306
Fleming, JE, 'Constitutional Tragedy in Dying: Or Whose Tragedy Is It, Anyway?' in W Eskridge, Jr and S Levinson (eds), *Constitutional Stupidities Constitutional Tragedies* (New York: NYUP, 1998)
—— 'Securing Deliberative Democracy', 72 Fordham L Rev 1435 (2004)
Frederick, MD, 'Physician Assisted Suicide: A Personal Right?', 21 Southern University L Rev 59
Fried, C, 'Privacy', 77 Yale LJ 421 (1968)
Friedelbaum, SH, 'Private Property, Public Property: Shopping Centers and Expressive Freedom in the States', 62 Albany L Rev 1229
Gavison, R, 'Too Early for a Requiem: Warren and Brandeis Were Right on Privacy versus Free Speech', 43 Southern Calif L Rev 437 (1992)
Genevois, B, *La Jurisprudence du Conseil Constitutionnel* (Paris: STH, 1998)
Gerber, SD, 'Privacy and Constitutional Theory' in EF Paul, FD Miller, Jr, and J Paul (eds), *The Right to Privacy* (Cambridge: CUP, 2000)
Gewirth, A, 'Are All Rights Positive?', Philosophy and Public Affairs 30 (1993) 321
—— 'Are there any absolute rights?' in J Waldron (ed), *Theories of Rights*, (Oxford: OUP, 1984)
Gostin, LO, *Public Health: Power, Duty Restraint* (Berkeley: University of California Press, 2000)
—— (ed), *Civil Liberties in Conflict* (London: Routledge, 1988)

Habermas, J, *Between Facts and Norms* (trans W Rehg) (Cambridge, Mass: HUP, 1996)
Halpin, A, *Rights and Law—Analysis and Theory* (Oxford: Hart Publishing, rep. 2001)
Hart, HLA, 'Are There any Natural Rights?' in J Waldron (ed), *Theories of Rights*, (Oxford: OUP, 1984)
—— *Essays in jurisprudence and Philosophy* (Oxford: Clarendon Press, 1983)
—— *Essays on Bentham* (Oxford: Clarendon Press, 1982)
—— 'Kelsen's doctrine of the unity of law' in Paulson and Paulson, *Normativity and Norms* (Oxford: Clarendon Press, 1998)
—— *The Concept of Law* (2nd edn, Oxford: OUP, 1994)
Hasnas, J, 'From Cannibalism to Caesareans: Two Conceptions of Fundamental Rights', 89 Northwestern University L Rev 900 (1995)
Haunch, JM, 'Protecting private facts in France: The Warren & Brandeis Tort is alive and well and flourishing in Paris', 68 Tul L Rev 1219
Henkin, L, *The Age of Rights* (New York: Columbia UP, 1990)
Hohfeld, WN, *Fundamental Legal Conceptions as applied in Judicial Reasoning*, new edition by D Campbell and P Thomas (Aldershot: Ashgate/Dartmouth, 2001)
Holmes, S and C Sunstein, *The Cost of Rights: Why Liberty Depends on Taxes* (New York: WW Norton & Co, 2000)
Hunt, M, *Using Human Rights Law in English Courts* (Oxford: Hart Publishing, 1998)
Kamm, FM, 'A Right to Choose Death? A moral argument for the permissibility of euthanasia and physician assisted suicide', on the web: <http://bostonreview.mit.edu/BR22.3/Kamm.html>
—— 'Conflicts of Rights: Typology, Methodology, and Nonconsequentialism', Legal Theory 7 (2001) 239–54
—— *Creation and Abortion* (Oxford: OUP, 1992)
—— 'Harming Some to Save Others', Philosophical Studies 57 (1989) 251
—— *Morality, Mortality: Death and whom to Save from it* (Oxford: OUP, Volume I, 1993)
—— *Morality, Mortality: Rights, Duties and Status* (Oxford: OUP, Volume II 1993)
—— 'Non-consequentialism, the Person as an End-in-Itself, and the Significance of Status', Philosophy and Public Affairs 21 (1992) 354
—— 'Rights' in Coleman and Shapiro, *The Oxford Handbook of Jurisprudence and Philosophy of Law* (Oxford: OUP, 2002)
Kant, I, *The Metaphysics of Morals* (Cambridge, Mass: CUP, 1991)
Kavanagh, A, 'Interpretation under the Human Rights Act 1998' (2004) 24 OJLS 259–85
Kay, RS, 'American Constitutionalism' in L Alexander (ed), *Contitutionalism: Philisophical Foundations* (Cambridge: CUP, 2001)
Kelsen, H, *General Theory of Norms* (Oxford: Clarendon Press, 1991)
—— *Pure Theory of Law* (Gloucester, Mass: Peter Smith, 1989)
Keown, J, 'European Court of Human Rights: Death in Strasbourg—assisted suicide, the *Pretty* case, and the European Convention on Human Rights', International Journal of Constitutional Law (2003) 722
—— *Euthanasia, Ethics and Public policy—An argument against legalization* (Cambridge: CUP, 2002)
Kleinberg, RD and I Mochizuki, 'The Final Freedom: Maintaining Autonomy and Valuing Life in Physician-assisted suicide cases', 32 Harv CR-CL L Rev 197
Kramer, MH, NE Simmonds, and H Steiner, *A Debate over Rights* (Oxford; OUP, 2000) (paperback)

Levy, RE, 'Dueling Values: Balancing Competing Constitutional Interests in Pinette', 5 Kan JL and Pub Policy 43
Lilla, M, Ronald Dworkin and Rogers Silvers, *The legacy of Isaiah Berlin* (New York: New York Review Books, 2001)
Loeb, H, and D Rosenberg, 'Fundamental Rights in Conflict: The Price of a Maturing Democracy', 77 North Dakota L Rev 27
Loveland, I, *Importing the First Amendment—Freedom of Speech and Expression in Britain, Europe and the USA* (Oxford: Hart Publishing, 1998)
MacCormick, N, 'Children's Rights: A Test Case for Theories of Rights' (1976) *Archiv für Rechts und Sozialphilosophie* 62
—— *Enlightment, Rights and Revolution* (Aberdeen: AUP, 1989)
—— 'Rights, Claims and Remedies', Law and Philosophy 1 (1982) 337–57
—— 'Rights in Legislation', in PMS Hacker and J Raz, *Law, Morality, and Society; Essays in honour of H.L.A. Hart* (Oxford: Clarendon Press, 1977)
—— 'Taking the "Rights Thesis" Seriously' in *Legal Right and Social Democracy—Essays in Legal and Poltical Philosophy* (Oxford: Clarendon Press, 1982)
Markesinis, B, *The Impact of the Human Rights Bill on English Law* (Oxford: OUP, 1998)
Marmor, A, 'On the Limits of Rights', Law and Philosophy 16 (1997) 1–18
—— *Positive Law and Objective Values* (Oxford: OUP, 2001)
Marshall, G, 'Interpreting Interpretation in the Human Rights Bill', Public Law (1998) 167
Mathieu, B, and M Verpeaux, *Contentieux Constitutionnel des Droits Fondamentaux* (Paris: LGDJ, 2001)
—— and M Verpeaux, *Contentieux des Droits Fondamentaux* (Paris: Montchretein, 2001)
Meyer, LR, 'Are Constitutional Rights Personal?', Legal Theory 6 (2000) 405–22
Molfessis, N, *Le Conseil Constitutionnel et le Droit Privé* (Paris: LGDJ, 1997)
Montague, P, 'When Rights Conflict', Legal Theory 7 (2001) 257–77
Moreso, JJ, 'Conflitti tra Principi costituzionali', *Ragion Pratica* 18/2002, 207–227
Nagel, T, *Concealment and Exposure & Other Essays* (Oxford: OUP, 2002)
—— *Exposure and Concealment* (Oxford: OUP, 2001)
—— 'Personal Rights and Public Space' in T Nagel, *Concealment and Exposure & Other Essays* (Oxford: OUP, 2002)
Neill, Sir B, 'Privacy: A challenge for the next century' in B Markesinis, *Protecting Privacy* (Oxford: Clarendon Press, 1999)
Paulson, S, 'Material and Formal Authorisation in Kelsen's Pure Theory' CLJ (1980) 39 172–93
Perry, MJ, *Toward a Theory of Human Rights* (Cambridge, Mass: CUP, 2007)
—— *We the People—The Fourteenth Amendment and the Supreme Court* (Oxford: OUP, 1999)
—— 'What is the Constitution (and Other Fundamental Questions)' in L Alexander (ed), *Constitutionalism: Philisophical Foundations* (Cambridge: CUP, 2001)
Pfersmann, O, 'Esquisse d'une théorie des droits fondamentaux' in L Favoreu et al., *Droits des libertés fondamentales* (Paris: Dalloz, 2000)
Philipson, G, 'Transforming Breach of Confidence? Towards a common law right of privacy under the Human Rights Act' (2003) 66 MLR 726
Picard, E, 'The Right to Privacy in French Law' in B Markesinis (ed), *Protecting Privacy* (Oxford: Clarendon Press, 1999)
Post, R, 'Three Concepts of Privacy', 89 Georgetown LJ 2087 (2001)
Prosser, D, 'Privacy', 48 Calif L Rev 383 (1960)

Putnam, H, 'Are Moral Values made or discovered?', Legal Theory 1 (1995) 1–15
Rachels, J, 'Why privacy is important', Philosophy and Public Affairs 4 (1975) 323
Rakowski E, 'Book Review—The Sanctity of Human Life', 103 Yale LJ 2049
Rawls, J, *A Theory of Justice* (Oxford: OUP, 2000) (revised edition)
—— *Political Liberalism* (New York: Columbia UP, 1993)
Raz, J, 'Freedom of expression and personal identification' (1995) 11 OJLS 303
—— 'Legal Principles and the Limits of the Law', 81 Yale LJ 823 (1972)
—— 'Legal Rights' (1984) 4 OJLS 1
—— 'Rights and Individual Well-Being', Ratio Juris 5 (1992) 127–42
—— 'Rights in Politics' in J Tasioulas (ed), *Law, Values and Social Practices* (Aldershot: Dartmouth, 1997)
—— *The Morality of Freedom* (Oxford: OUP, 1986)
—— *Value, Respect and Attachment* (Cambridge: CUP, 2001)
Rials, S, *La déclaration des droits de l'homme et du citoyen* (Paris: Hachette, 1988)
Richards, DAJ, *Sex, Drugs, Death, and the Law—An essay on Human Rights and Overcriminalization* (Totowa, NJ: Rowman and Littlefield, 1982)
Rosen, J *The Naked Crowd: Reclaiming Security and Freedom in an Anxious Age* (Random House, 2004)
—— *The Unwanted Gaze—The destruction of privacy in America* (New York: Vintage Books, 2000)
——, 'The purposes of privacy: A response' 89 Georgetown L J 2117 (2001)
Ross, A, *On Law and Justice* (London: Stevens, 1958)
Rousseau, D, *Droit du contentieux constitutionnel* (Paris: Montchrestien, 1999)
Rowan, JR, *Conflicts of Rights* (Oxford: Westview Press, 1999)
Rozenberg, J, *Privacy and the Press* (Oxford: OUP, 2004)
Ruiz, B, 'The Right to Privacy: A discourse—Theoretical Approach', *Ratio Juris* 11 (1998) 155–67
Ryan, A, *The Idea of Freedom—Essays in honour of Isaiah Berlin* (Oxford: OUP, 1979)
Sadurski, W, 'Judicial Review and the Protection of Constitutional Rights', (2002) 22 OJLS 275–99
Saint-James, V, *La conciliation des droits de l'homme et des libertés en droit public français* (Paris: PUF, 1995)
Scalia, A, *A matter of interpretation: Federal Courts and the Law*, The University Center for Human Values Series (Princeton, NJ: PUP, 1997)
Scanlon, T, 'A Theory of Freedom of Expression', Philosophy and Public Affairs 1 (1972) 204
Scanlon, TM, 'Adjusting Rights and Balancing Values', 72 Fordham L Rev 1477 (2004)
Schauer, F, 'A Comment on the Structure of Rights', 27 Ga L Rev 415 (1992–1993)
—— 'Can Public Figures Have Private Lives?' in EF Paul, FD Miller, Jr, and J Paul (eds), *The Right to Privacy* (Cambridge: CUP, 2000)
—— *Free Speech: A Philosophical Enquiry* (Cambridge; CUP, 1982)
—— 'On the supposed defeasability of Legal Rules' (1998) CLP 223–40
—— 'Rights as Rules', Law and Philosophy 6 (1987) 115–19
—— 'The Generality of Rights', Legal Theory 6 (2000) 323–36
Scoglio, S, *Transforming Privacy: A Transpersonal Philosophy of Rights* (Westport, CT: Praeger, 1998)
Sebok, A, *Legal Positivisim in American Jurisprudence* (Cambridge: CUP, 1998)
Steiner, H, *A Debate Over Rights* (Oxford: OUP, 2000)

—— 'Working Rights' in M Kramer, N Simmonds, and H Steiner, *A Debate Over Rights* (Oxford: OUP, 2000)
Sullivan, K, *Constitutional Law* (New York: Foundation Press, 2001)
Sunstein, C, 'Proptem Honoris Respectum: Rights and their Critics', 70 Notre Dame L Rev 727
Sunstein, CR, 'Constitutional Agreements without Constitutional Theories', Ratio Juris 10
—— *Legal Reasoning and Political Conflict* (Oxford; OUP, 1996)
Thompson, JJ, *The Realm of Rights* (Cambridge, Mass: HUP, 1990)
—— *Rights, Restitution, and Risks* (Cambridge, Mass: HUP, 1986)
—— 'Self-Defense and Rights', reprinted in *Rights, Restitution, and Risks* (Cambridge, Mass: HUP, 1986)
Tribe, LH, *Abortion—The Clashes of Absolutes* (New York: WW Norton, 1992)
—— *American Constitutional Law* (3rd edn, New York: Foundation Press, 2000) Vol 1 and 2
—— 'Lawrence v. Texas: The "Fundamental Right" that Dare Not Speak its Name', 117 Harv L Rev 1893 (2004)
Tur, R, 'The leaves on the trees' (1976) Juridical Review
Turpin, *Contentieux constitutionnel* (Paris: PUF, 1994)
Tushnet, M, 'Legal Conventionalism in the U.S.—Constitutional Law of Privacy' in EF Paul, FD Miller, Jr, and J Paul (eds), *The Right to Privacy* (Cambridge: CUP, 2000)
—— *Taking the Constitution Away from the Courts* (Princeton NJ: PUP, 1999)
Veitch, S, *Moral Conflict and Legal Reasoning* (Oxford: Hart Publishing, 1999)
Viala, A, *les réserves d'interprétation dans la jurisprudence du Conseil Constitutionnel* (Paris: LGDJ, 1999)
von Wright, G, *The Logic of Preference* (Edinburgh: EUP, 1963)
Wadham, J, and H Mountfield, *Blackstone's guide to the Human Rights Act 1998* (London: Blackstone Press Limited, 1999)
Waldron, J, 'Fake Incommensurability: A respone to Professor Schauer' (1994) 45 Hastings LJ 813
—— *Law and Disagreement* (Oxford: OUP, 1999) (2001 Paperback)
—— *Liberal Rights* (Cambridge: CUP, 1993)
—— 'Rights in Conflict in J Waldron *Liberal Rights* (Cambridge: CUP, 1993)
—— (ed), *Theories of Rights* (Oxford: OUP, 1984)
Warren and Brandeis, 'The right to privacy', 4 Harv LR 193 (1890)
Wellman, C, *An Approach to Rights* (Dordrecht: Kluwer Academic Press, 1997)
Wellman, CH, 'On Conflict Between Rights' in Law and Philosophy 14 (1995) 271
—— 'The Concept of Fetal Rights', Law and Philosophy 21 (2002) 65–93
—— *Real Rights* (New York: OUP, 1995)
Wenar, L, 'The Nature of Rights', Philosophy and Public Affairs 33 (2005) 223–52
Weyland, I, 'Idealism and Realism in Kelsen's treatment of Norm Conflicts' in R Tur and W Twining, *Essays on Kelsen* (Oxford: OUP, 1986)
Whitman, JQ, 'The Two Western Cultures of Privacy: Dignity versus Liberty', 113 Yale LJ 1151 (2004)
Williams, B, 'Conflict of values' in A Ryan, *The Idea of Freedom—Essays in honour of Isaiah Berlin* (Oxford: OUP, 1979)
Zimmerman, DL, 'Requiem for a Heavyweight: A farewell to Warren and Brandeis' privacy tort', 68 Cornell L Rev 291 (1983)
Zagrebelski, G, *Il diritto mite. Leggi, Diritti e Giustizia* (Torino: Einaudi, 1992)

Index

FLRs = fundamental legal rights

abortion 4, 152–3
absence of obligations, rights grounded in 32
absolute FLRs 60–4
    attribution of rights 63–4
    conflict of 60–1
    constitutional status 61
    prima facie rights 60–1, 63
    relative, rights as 61
    'two men on a plank' case 61–2
    United States 91
accommodating conflicts 131–2, 137–41
affirmative action 51
Alexy, Robert 5, 6, 8–12, 19–25, 93
amicus curiae, **moral philosophers as** 156–60
assisted suicide 143–6
attribution of rights 63–4
autonomy 58, 139–40, 157–8, 160

balancing FLRs 9–10, 12, 88–90, 169
    constitutional framework 84–90, 134
    constitutional rights, procedural theory of 19–22
    France 88–9
    freedom of the press 132–7
    incommensurability 85–6, 90
    language of 86–7
    life, right to 88, 164–5
    physician-assisted suicide 164–6
    priority of FLRs 90
    privacy 88, 132–7, 139, 164–5
    qualified and unqualified rights 81
    ranking of values 22
    solving conflicts between FLRs 132
    subsumptive theory of reasoning 19–20
    trumps 85, 91, 134
    United Kingdom 87–8, 136–7
    United States 89–90, 132–4, 139
benefit theory of rights 33–4
Bentham, Jeremy 32–4, 61
Berlin, Isaiah 15–16
bills of rights *see also* **constitutions**
    choice or will theory of rights 35
    constitutional reading of 26
    constitutional status 41–2, 65
    constitutions 68–9
    guidance 24–5, 169
    statements of rules in 47–8
    United Kingdom 71–2
    United States 70
bodily integrity 44–5, 106, 151
breach of confidence 111–12, 121–3

categorising interests 132–7
charters 68–9
choice or will theory of rights 32–6, 49
    autonomy 58
    bill of rights 35
    children 37
    claims, rights as 35
    discretionary domains 57–8
    external theories 58
    Hart, HLA 32–7, 55
    interest theory of right 37–8, 55–6, 59–60
    privacy, right to 102
    waiver of rights 58
claims 29, 35–6, 47
common good 39, 40
competences
    judges 142–3, 162–3
    powers and, distribution between 169
competition of principles and conflict of rules 9–23
    application of other rules 10, 11–12
    invalidity of rules 11–12
    policies 10–11
    pluralist values 23
    rules 9–12
    weight of principles 10, 12
coherentism 17–18
concept of fundamental legal rights 27–48
    content or scope of FLRs 27, 42–5
    definition 47–8
    function or external dimension of FLRs 27, 45–7
    reductionism 27–9
    structure and point of FLRs 27–42
conflict of values 14–17, 21–3
    fusion thesis 14–15
    monism of values 15–16, 18
    poverty, liberty and 16–17
    preferences 22–3
    sovereign virtue 18–19
    value pluralism 15–17
conjoined twins, right to life and 151
constitutional constructivism 91–2, 138
constitutional dilemmas 26

constitutional framework to deal with conflicts
    of FLRs 67–94
  balancing 84–90, 134
  coherence 92–3
  constitution, conflicts with the 68–74
  deference 79–84
  interpretation 74–9, 92–3, 134
  moral and political philosophy, superiority
    over 92
  priority 93
  values from rights, distinguishing 134
constitutional-perfecting theory 92, 137–40,
    161
constitutional rights 19–23
  balancing or proportionality 19–21
  coherentist assumptions 14–19
  conflict of values 14–19
  fusion thesis 14–15
  interest theory of rights 38–9
  moral theory 14–15
  objectivity 13–14
  principles 20–1
  procedural theory of 19–23
  right answer thesis 12, 13–14
  sovereign virtue 18–19
  substantive theory of 13–19
  subsumptive theory of reasoning 19–20
  weighing principles 13–23
constitutional status as ground of FLRs 41–2,
    55, 64–5
  absolute or prima facie rights 61
  bills of rights 41–2, 65
  court, need for special 42
  freedom of expression 42
  immunity 41
  inalienability of constitutional status 64
  institutional mechanisms in enforcing FLRs
    60
  inviolability, notion of 45, 48
  life, waiver of right to 66
  normative inconsistencies 59
  passive or active status 42
  permissions 48
  privacy, right to 102, 107
  social practices 41–2
  trade-offs 59
  typology of conflicts 64–5
  waiver 64
constitutional tragedies 4–5, 160–2
constitutions *see also* bills of rights
  bills of rights 68–9
  charters 68–9
  conflicts with 68–74
  declarations 68–9
  documents 68–9
  France 69–73
  guidance 68, 69, 94

  implementation 77–8
  interpretation 70–1, 77–8
  intepretativists 70–1
  judicial power 79
  norms 68–71, 73
  originalists 70–1
  rules 69
  symbols 68–71, 73
  United Kingdom 69–70, 73–4
  United States 69–71, 77–8, 83–4, 89–90
content or scope of FLRs 27, 42–5
  defining the scope of 5–6
  inviolability, notion of 42–4, 48
  negative rights 43–4, 48
  positive rights 43–4, 48
contraception 103

decisional privacy and right to life, conflicts
    between 141, 142–67
  abortion 152–3
  anatomy of conflict between FLRs 148–56
  assisted suicide 143–5
  autonomy 157–8, 161
  balancing 164–6
  blood transfusion, refusal of 155
  bodily integrity 151
  comparative examination 145–8
  conjoined twins 151
  constitutional tragedy 160–2
  deference 162–4
  definition of life 149
  dignity 152–3, 155–6
  ethical committees, referral to 163
  European Convention on Human Rights
    148–50, 153–5, 166
  euthanasia 143–4
    non-voluntary 144
    slippery slope argument 144
    voluntary assisted 157–9
  France 148, 152–3, 155
  Human Rights Act 1998 147–8
  intentional killing 143–52, 162–3, 166–7
  judges, competence of 142–3, 162–3
  letting someone die, killing and 156,
    159–60
  moral and legal conflicts 156–60
  necessity 150, 151
  Netherlands 145–6
  omissions, acts and 156, 159
  persistent vegetative state 160
  physician-assisted suicide 143–56
  priority 166–7
  private life, right to respect for 147–8, 149,
    153–5, 166
  quality of life 151
  reasoning with law 159–60
  refusal of treatment 156–7

religion 143, 151, 152
sanctity of life 143, 148, 152
self-determination 144, 153–4
simple interest 144
slavery and forced labour, prohibition against 150
slippery slope argument 144, 157–8, 159, 165, 167
solving the conflict 162–6
state interests 144
statutory interpretation 162–3
substituted judgment 158
suffering, duty to relieve 145–6, 156–7, 159–60
technical knowledge 163
United Kingdom 147–51
United States 146–9, 152, 154–60
value of life 143, 158, 160
vertical conflicts 168–9
waiver of right to life 144, 150
defamation 129–30
deference 79–84, 169
  constitutional framework 79–84
  democratic grounds for 80–1
  democratic powers, subject-matter within the responsibility of 81
  expertise in institutions, level of 81
  France 79, 82–3
  institutions 79–84
  judicial power 79–80
  legislature 79–83
  life, right to 163–4
  privacy 163–4
  rationales for 80–1
  right at stake, dependent on the 81
  types of 79
  United Kingdom 79–81
  United States 79, 82–4
definition of FLRs 27, 47–8
deliberative autonomy 139–40
democracy 79–81, 139–40
dignity
  abortion 152–3
  France 89, 104–5, 110, 152–3
  life, right to 152–3
  physician-assisted suicide 155–6
  privacy 104–5, 110, 152–3
directional duties 46, 48
disagreement, phenomenon of 49–50
discretion
  discretionary domains 57–8
  enforcing FLRs, institutional mechanisms for 60
  interpretation 8–9
duties, rights correlative to 29, 31–3, 38
Dworkin, Ronald 5, 6, 9–12, 94
  balancing 9–10

coherentist assumptions 14–19
constitutional rights
  procedural theory of 20, 21
  substantive theory of 13–14
Freedom's Law 17
fusion thesis 14–15
interpretation 8–9
lato sensu conflicts 50–1
legal positivism 8–9
life, right to 143
Model of Rules 14
monism of values 15–16, 18
moral reading of constitutions 23–4
moral theory 14–15, 18–19, 23–4
principles 8–23, 92
privacy 143
right answer theory 9, 12–14, 25
rules 9–12
sanctity of life 143, 152
source thesis 10
Taking Rights Seriously 8, 10
utilitarianism 28
value, conflict of 14–17

England *see* **United Kingdom**
entrenchment 170
equality 18–19, 51
European Convention on Human Rights
  France 119–21, 130
  freedom of expression 121
  freedom of the press 119–23, 126, 130
  life, right to 148–50
  margin of appreciation 80
  physician-assisted suicide 153–5, 166
  privacy 98, 103, 111–12, 119–23, 126, 130, 148–50
  sexual orientation 98
  United Kingdom 73–4, 80–1, 111–12, 121–3, 126
  United States 103
euthanasia 143–4, 157–9
expression, freedom of *see* **freedom of speech**
external dimension of FLRs *see* **function or external dimension of FLRs**

Fallon, Richard 77–8, 89–90
false light, tort of 118
Feinberg, Joel 35–6
Fleming, James 161
framework to deal with conflicts of FLRs *see* **constitutional framework to deal with conflicts of FLRs**
France *see also* **France, right to privacy in**
  balancing 82–3, 88–9
  conciliation 83, 88
  Constitutional Council 71–3, 78–9, 82–3, 88–91

France (cont.)
  constitutions 69–73
  Declaration of Rights 1789 71–3, 78
  defence 79, 82–3
  dignity 89
  hierarchy of texts 72–3
  institutions 82–3
  interpretation 78–9, 90–1
  judicial power 79
  judicial review 71–2
  Laws of the Republic 78
  legislature 79, 82–3
  parliamentary sovereignty 88
  Preamble of Constitution 1946 71–3, 78
  primacy of rights 73
  proportionality 88–9
France, right to privacy in
  abortion 152–3
  Cassation Court 135–6
  Civil Code 109, 119, 121
  commercial and non-commercial privacy 110
  Constitution of 1791 119
  Constitutional Council 104–5, 135–6
  death of person 130–1
  Declaration of Rights 105, 119–20
  defamation 129–30
  dignity 104–5, 110, 152–3
  European Convention on Human Rights 119–21, 130
  freedom of speech, conflict with 108–9, 119–21, 135–6
  freedom of the press 108–9, 135–6
  general interest 135–6
  historical overview 108–9
  honour 119–21
  image, right to one's own 108
  intellectual property 135
  honour 108
  life, right to 148, 152–3
  physician-assisted suicide 155
  private information 130
  social norms 101
  solving conflicts 135–6
  truth 129–31
  United States 108, 110
freedom of assembly 53–4
freedom of expression *see* freedom of speech
freedom of speech *see also* privacy and freedom of expression, conflict between
  censorship 44
  constitutional status 42
  European Convention on Human Rights 121
  France 119–21, 135–6
  freedom of assembly 53–4
  freedom of the press 116, 118–21, 123, 129–34
  government 44
  interest theory of rights 56–7
  interpretation 75
  inviolability, notion of 44–5
  state, role of the 44–5
  United States 91
freedom of the press *see* informational privacy, freedom of the press and
function or external dimension of FLRs 27, 45–7, 58
  definition 27
  directional duties 46, 48
  government and individual, general duties between 46
  institutional duties 46, 48
  inviolability, sphere of 47
  public/private divide 46
  separation of powers 45–6
  vertical distribution of freedom 46
fundamental legal rights (FLRs) *see also* **fundamental legal rights (FLRs), conflicts of**
  characterization of 25
  concept of FLRs 27–48
  definition 47–8
  duties, existence of correlative 29
  firmness of rights 25
  main features of 47–8
  statements, contained in 47–8
fundamental legal rights (FLRs), conflicts of 3–4
  absolute or prima facie FLRs 60–4
  competition of principles 9–12
  constitutional dilemmas 26
  constitutional tragedies 4–5
  core of conflicts 52–5
  external conflicts 65–6
  external solutions 58
  genuine conflicts 4, 51–2, 79, 91, 168
  hierarchy 4
  incommensurability 54–60
  instantiation 65–6, 170
  internal conflicts 65
  internal solutions 58
  lato sensu conflicts 50–2
  legal positivism 7–8
  medical ethics 24
  moral reading 24
  normative inconsistencies 53–60
  principles 9–10
  reality of rights 7
  rules 9–10, 25, 29
  scope of FLRs, defining the 5–6
  solving conflicts between FLRs 123–4, 131–41
  spurious conflicts 4, 49–52
  strength of FLRs 6
  typology 64–6, 140
  weight 11

Index

generality of rights 7, 63
genuine conflicts of FLRs 4, 51–2, 79, 91, 168
goods, rights as 37–8
government
   freedom of speech 44
   individual and, general duties between 46
   power, boundaries of 102
   privacy, right to 102
   public/private divide 46
   separation of powers 46
   vertical distribution of freedom 46

Hart, HLA
   absolute duties, criminal law and 34
   analytical theory of rights 30
   benefit theory of rights 33–4
   Bentham, Jeremy 32–3
   choice or will theory of rights 32–7, 55
   discretion 8–9
   immunity 35, 36
   interest theory of rights 37–8, 59
   lato sensu conflicts 50
   liberty-right 32–3
   normative inconsistencies 53
   normative justifications for rights 36–7
   permissions 32
   redundancy theory 38
   relative duties, criminal law and 34
   rights correlative to duties 32–3, 38
   structure of rights theory 29, 32–6
hierarchy of FLRs 4
Hohfeld, WN 7
   analytical theory of rights 30, 36–7
   claims 29, 35–6, 47
   Fundamental Legal Concepts 29
   immunity 29, 31–2, 34–5, 41, 47
   immunity/disability 31, 41
   jural correlatives 30–1
   jural opposites 30–1
   power 29, 31, 34, 47
   power/liability 31, 41
   privilege 29, 31, 47
   privilege/no rights 31
   rights/duties 31–2
   structure and point of rights 29–32, 36–7
   table of jural relations 30–2
Holmes, Stephen and Sunstein, Cass R *Cost of Rights* 43–4
honour 108, 119–21
Human Rights Act 1998 73–7, 80–1
   balancing 87–8
   constitutions 69–70
   Convention rights, interpretation of 76–7, 80–1
   freedom of the press 121–2
   interpretation 76–7
   life, right to 147–8

margin of appreciation 76
privacy 105–6, 112, 121–2, 147–8
reading in and reading down 76
specification, exercise of 77
stricto sensu interpretation 77

immunity 29, 31–2, 34–5, 41, 47
incommensurability 54–60
   balancing 85–6, 90
   conflict of FLRs 93–4
   constitutional tragedies 85
   interest theory of rights 57
   priority 85
   strong and weak, distinction between 85–6, 90
   trumps 85
   United States 90
informational privacy, freedom of the press and 114–41
   accommodating conflicts 137–41
   accurate constitutional theories 137
   balancing interests 132–7
   categorising interests 132–7
   constitutional-perfecting theories 137–40
   death of person 130–1
   defamation 129–30
   European Convention on Human Rights 119–21, 126, 130
   false light, tort of 118
   France 108–9, 119–21, 123, 129–31, 135–6
   freedom of expression 116, 118, 119–21, 131–4
   horizontal conflict 115, 168
   intrusion, tort of 118
   lionized privacy 117–19
   misappropriation of one's name or identity, tort of 118
   permissions 116
   politicians, private lives of 140
   practice of rights, learning the 124–6
   priority 141
   private information 116–17, 118, 124–30
   procedural rules 141
   public/private distinction 116–17, 125–6
   social norms 117
   solving conflicts 123–4, 131–41
   truth 116, 118, 124–5, 127–9, 131, 138
   United Kingdom 121–6, 136–7
   United States 117–19, 123, 126–8, 133–4, 138–40
   vertical conflict 115
institutions
   deference 79–84
   expertise in, level of 81
   France 82–3
   function or external dimension of FLRs 46

Index

institutions (*cont.*)
  qualified and unqualified rights, balance between 81
  rules 69
  separation of powers 46
  United Kingdom 122
integrity 18, 24, 44–5, 106, 151
intentional killing 143–52, 162–3, 166–7
interest theory of rights
  absolute rights 61
  associated duties 56
  attribution of rights, reasons for 38
  children 37
  choice or will theory of rights 37–8, 55–6, 59–60
  common good 39, 40
  constitutional rights 38–9
  freedom of speech 56–7
  goods, rights as 37–8
  incommensurability, problem of 57
  normative inconsistencies 58–9
  priority of duties 56–7
  privacy, right to 102
  quantitative commensurability, doctrine of 56
  simple rights 59
  structure of FLRs 37–9
  trade-offs 56–60
  utilitarianism 38, 55–6
interpretation 74–8, 169
  comprehensive interpretations 74–5, 78–9
  consistency 75
  constitutional framework 74–9, 92–3, 134
  discretion 8–9
  France 78–9, 90–1
  freedom of expression 75
  Human Rights Act 1998 76–8
  implementation of constitutions 77–8
  legal positivists 8–9
  life, right to 162–3
  modest interpretations 74–5, 78
  norms 74–5
  plurality of perspectives 75
  public interest 90–1
  specification 75, 76–8
  stricto sensu 75, 76–7, 79
  United States Constitution 77–8
interpretavists 70–1, 90
intrusion, tort of 118
inviolability, notion of 40–6, 48

judges
  competence 142–3, 162–3
  constitutions 79
  defence 79–80
  France 79
  integrity 18

  life, right to 142–3, 162–3
  physician-assisted suicide 163
  privacy 142–3, 162–3
  United Kingdom 79–80
  United States 79, 83–4, 90

Kamm, Frances M 40–1
Kant, Immanuel 52, 61–2
Kelsen, Hans 8–9
Keown, John 157–9

language 28
lato sensu conflicts 50–2
  collective goals 50
  equality, conflicts involving 51
  limit of rights 50
  norms 50
  scarce resources 51–2
  spurious conflicts 50–2
  technological developments 52
  trumps, conflict of 50–1
legal positivists 7–9
legislature 79–83
liberalism 138
liberty
  equality 18–19
  liberty-right 32–3, 36
  mutual adjustment of basic liberties 91
  perimeter of obligations 33, 36
  positive and negative 15
  poverty 16–17
life, right to *see also* decisional privacy and right to life, conflicts between
  abortion 4, 152–3
  privacy 65–6, 88
  property, right to 62–3
  waiver 66

MacCormick, Neil 37–8, 55
media *see* informational privacy, freedom of the press and medical ethics 24
misappropriation of one's name or identity, tort of 118
moral reading of bills of rights and constitutions 23–4
moral theory 14–15, 18–19, 40–1, 106

Nagel, Thomas 40–1
negative rights 43–4, 48
Netherlands, physician-assisted suicide in 157
normative inconsistencies
  constitutional status of rights 59
  empirical proof 54–5
  implications of 62–3
  interest theory of rights 58–9
  meaning 52

permissions and conflict 53–4
rules 54–5
supreme courts, legitimacy of 54–5
unity of legal systems, threat to 54
norms
conflicting 49–50
constitutions 68–71, 73
entrenchment 170
France, privacy in 101
Hart, HLA 36–7
inconsistencies 49, 53–60
interpretation 74–5
lato sensu conflicts 50
legal positivism 8–9
open texture 8
privacy, right to 103–7
social 101, 117
structure of FLRs 36–7

obligations imposed by law, rights grounded in 32
originalists 70–1, 90, 161

parliamentary sovereignty 81, 88, 105–6
permissions 32, 47–8, 53–4, 116
physician-assisted suicide 143–56
amicus curiae, moral philosophers as 156–60
autonomy 157–8, 161
balancing 164–6
blood transfusion, refusal of 155
comparative look at 145–8
constitutional tragedy 160–2
defence 162–3
dignity 155–6
European Convention on Human Rights 153–5, 166
letting someone die, killing and 156, 159–60
France 155
judges 163
Netherlands 145–6
omissions, acts and 156, 159
persistent vegetative state 160
private life, right to respect for 153–5, 166
reasoning with law 159–60
refusal of treatment 156–7
self-determination 153–4
slippery slope argument 157–8, 159, 165
substituted judgment 158
suffering, duty to relieve 145–6, 156–7, 159–60
United States 146–7, 154–60
value of life 158, 160
voluntary assisted euthanasia 157–9
point of fundamental legal rights (FLRs) *see* structure and point of fundamental legal rights (FLRs)

policies and principles, competition of 10–11
politicians, private lives of 140
positive rights 43–4, 48
power/liability 31, 41
practice of rights, learning the 124–6
preferences 22–3
press *see* informational privacy, freedom of the press and presumption of priority
prima facie rights 60–4
principles
competition of 9–23
constitutional rights, procedural theory of 20–1
definition 21
fundamental legal rights (FLRs) 9–10, 25
irreconcilable 12
optimization requirements, as 9, 21, 25
proportionality 9
rules 7–12, 23, 47
values 21–2
weight 10–23, 25, 92
priority
balancing 90, 93
duties 56–7
freedom of the press 141
interest theory of rights 56–7
internal relations 60
life, right to 166–7
privacy 141, 166–7
qualified 141, 170
rules 141
state interests 141
privacy 97–113 *see also* decisional privacy and right to life, conflicts between; France, right to privacy in; informational privacy, freedom of the press and; privacy and freedom of expression, conflict between; United Kingdom, privacy in; United States, right to privacy in
abortion 4
bodily integrity 106
choice or will theory 102
consent 102
constitutional status 102, 107
delusional privacy 100
enforcement 102
European Convention on Human Rights 98, 103
freedom of speech 6, 52
government power, boundaries of 102
horizontal distribution 102
individuals, misunderstandings or misrepresentation of 100–1
interest theory 102
legal protection 107–12
life, right to 65–6, 88
moral right to privacy 106

privacy (cont.)
  norms 103–7
  object to functions 107
  physical property 100
  public interest 100
  public/private sphere 99–100
  self-definition 100–1
  sexual orientation 98, 104
  social norms 101
  strength of 97
  structure of right 101–7
  technological developments 52
  theories of rights 101–2
  vertical distribution 102
  waiver 66, 102
  weakness of 97
privacy and freedom of expression, conflict between 4, 6, 52–3, 112–15
  absolutism 136–7
  advantages 117
  balancing 136–7
  France 108–9, 135–6
  freedom of the press 116, 118, 119–21, 131–4
  horizontal protection 115
  political speech 117
  presumptions 168
  proportionality 137
  public interest 137
  truth 117
  United Kingdom 112, 114, 136–7
  United States 97–8, 114, 117–18, 132–4
privilege 29, 31, 47
procedural rules 169–70
property rights 62–3
proportionality 8, 19–22, 87–9, 137
public interest 90–1, 100, 132–3, 137
public/private divide 46, 99–100, 116–17, 125–6

qualified and unqualified rights, balance between 81
quantitative commensurability, doctrine of 56

ranking of values 22
Rawls, John 91–3, 138–9
Raz, Joseph 38–9, 40, 55
reductionism 27–9
  analytical reductionism 28–9
  explanations 131–7
  language 28
  philosophical reductionism 28
  utilitarianism 28
redundancy theory 38
relative duties, criminal law and 34
right answer theory 9, 12–14, 25
right to life *see* life, right to

rules 9–12, 25, 29
  application of other rules 10–12
  constitutions 69
  formal 69
  institutional arrangements 69
  internal 141
  material 69
  normative inconsistencies 54–5
  permissions 47–8
  principles 7–12, 23, 47
  priority 141
  procedure 69
  qualified 141
  statements in bills of rights 47–8
  substantive 141, 170
  validity 11–12
  weight 12

sanctity of life 143, 148, 152
scarce resources 51–2
separation of powers 45–6, 48
sexual orientation 98, 104
simple rights 59
slavery and forced labour 150
slippery slope argument 144, 157–8, 159, 165, 167
social practices 41–2
solving conflicts between FLRs
  accommodation 131–2
  balancing 132
  categorizing interests 132
  explaining away conflicts 131–7
  France 135–6
  freedom of the press 123–4, 134–41
  privacy 123–4, 134–41
  reductive explanations 131–7
source thesis 10
specification, exercise of 75, 76–8
spurious conflicts 4, 49–52
state
  freedom of expression 44–5
  interests 141, 144
  life, right to 144
status theory of rights 40–1
Steiner, Hillel 57–8
structure and point of fundamental legal rights (FLRs) 7–12, 27–42
  analytical theory of rights 30, 36–7
  choice or will theory 32–7
  constitutional status as ground of FLRs 41–2
  definition 27
  general, FLRs as 7
  interest theory of rights 37–9
  legal positivists 7–8
  normative justifications for rights 36–7
  particular, FLRs as 7

Index

principles, rules and 7, 8, 9
privacy, right to 101–7
reductionism 27–8
rules, principles and 7, 8, 9
status theory of rights 40–1
substantive theory of constitutional rights *see* **constitutional rights, substantive theory of**
suicide 143–56 *see also* **physician-assisted suicide**
supreme courts, legitimacy of 54–5
symbols 68–71, 73

taxes, redistribution of 51
technological developments 52
terrorism 50
trade-offs 59–61
Tribe, Laurence 103–4
trumps
  balancing 85, 91, 134
  incommensurability 85
  lato sensu conflicts 50–1
truth 116–18, 124–31, 138–9
typology of conflicts of FLRs 140
  constitutional status 64–5
  external conflicts 65–6
  instantiations of FLRs 65–6, 170
  internal conflicts 65–6, 170

United Kingdom *see also* **Human Rights Act 1998, United Kingdom, privacy in**
  balancing 87–8
  Bill of Rights 71–2
  constitutions 69–70, 73–4
  deference 79–81
  democracy 79–81
  European Convention on Human Rights 80–1
  European Court of Human Rights 73–4
  judicial power 79
  legislature 79, 80–1, 83
  limitation of rights 87
  parliamentary sovereignty 81, 87–8
  proportionality test 87
  qualified and unqualified rights 81, 87
  unwritten constitution 73
United Kingdom, privacy in
  breach of confidence 111–12, 121–3
  European Convention on Human Rights 111–12, 121–3, 126
  freedom of expression 112, 114, 136–7
    absolutism 136–7
    balancing 136–7
    freedom of the press 121, 136–7
    proportionality 137
    public interest 137
  freedom of the press 121–6, 136–7

Human Rights Act 1998 105–6, 112, 121–2
institutions 122
judicial power 79
life, right to 147–51
parliamentary sovereignty 105–6
United States 108, 111, 112
values and FLRs 137
United States *see also* **United States, right to privacy in**
  absolute FLRs 91
  application, exercise of 77
  balancing 89–90
  best lights device 71
  Bill of Rights 70
  Constitution 23–5, 69–71, 77–8, 83–4, 89–90
    amendments to text 69
    intepretativists 70–1, 90
    originalists 70–1, 90
    philosophical reading 24–5
  deference 79, 82–4
  freedom of speech 91
  historical reading 24–5, 70
  incommensurability 90
  interpretation 70–1, 77–8, 90
  intepretativists 70–1, 90
  judicial supremacism 83–4
  judicial tests, shaping 90
  meaning 70
  moral reading 23
  originalists 70–1, 90
  Supreme Court 83–4
United States, right to privacy in
  abortion 152
  amicus curiae, moral philosophers as 156–60
  balancing interests 132–4, 139
  breach of confidence 111
  categorization of interests 132
  Constitution 103–4, 117–19, 132–4
  constitutional constructivism 138
  constitutional essentials 138–9
  constitution-perfecting theories 138–40
  contraception 103
  deliberative autonomy and democracy 139–40
  equality interest 146
  European Court of Human Rights 103
  First Amendment 103–4, 117–18, 132–4
  Fourteenth Amendment, due process clause in 103–4
  France 108, 110
  freedom of expression 97–8, 114, 117–18, 132–4
  freedom of the press 117–19, 123, 126–8, 133–4, 138–40
  liberalism 138

United States, right to privacy in (*cont.*)
  liberty interest 146–7, 164–5
  life, right to 148–9, 152
  penumbra theory 103–4
  physician-assisted suicide 146–7, 154–60
  private information 126–8
  public interest 132–3
  Rawls, John 138–9
  regulation 138–9
  sexual orientation 98, 104
  slippery slope 146–7
  state interest 146–7
  terrorism 50
  truth 127–9, 139
  United Kingdom 108, 111, 12
  values 134
unity of legal systems, threat to 54
utilitarianism 28, 38, 55–6

values
  balancing 22
  conflict of 14–19, 21–3
  distinguishing rights 134
  life, right to 143, 158, 160
  monism 15–16, 18, 23
  physician-assisted suicide 158, 160
  pluralism 13–17, 23
  principles 21–2
  privacy 134, 136
  ranking 22

waiver
  choice or will theory of rights 58
  constitutional status 64
  enforcing FLRs, institutional mechanisms for 60
  life, right to 66, 144, 150
  privacy, right to 66, 102
Waldron, Jeremy 55–7, 59–60, 85–6
weighing principles 12–23, 25
Wellman, Carl 7, 63
  An Approach to Rights 35–6, 55
  choice or will theory of rights 35–6, 55
  dominion 36, 47
  generality of rights 63
  recognition of right by court 63
will theory of rights *see* **choice or will theory of rights**